This Is So Awkward

Modern Puberty Explained

Cara Natterson, MD,
and Vanessa Kroll Bennett

RODALE

NEW YORK

Published in the United States by Rodale Books, an imprint of Random House, a division of Penguin Random House LLC, New York.
RodaleBooks.com
RandomHouseBooks.com

RODALE and the Plant colophon are registered trademarks of Penguin Random House LLC.

Library of Congress Cataloging-in-Publication Data
Names: Natterson, Cara, 1970- author. | Bennett, Vanessa, author.
Title: This is so awkward : modern puberty explained / Cara Natterson, MD, and Vanessa Kroll Bennett.
Description: First edition. | New York : Rodale, [2023] |
   Includes bibliographical references and index.
Identifiers: LCCN 2023017696 | ISBN 9780593580950 (hardcover) |
   ISBN 9780593580967 (ebook)
Subjects: LCSH: Puberty. | Adolescence.
Classification: LCC QP84.4 .N38 2023 | DDC 612.6/61—dc23/eng/20230706
LC record available at https://lccn.loc.gov/2023017696

ISBN 978-0-593-58095-0
Ebook ISBN 978-0-593-58096-7

Printed in the United States of America

Illustrations by Isabella Huang
Book design by Andrea Lau
Jacket design by Pete Garceau
Jacket photograph by Jupiterimages/PHOTOS.com>>/Getty Images Plus

10 9 8 7 6 5 4 3 2 1

First Edition

To our kids, the best teachers we've ever had. Without you, we wouldn't laugh nearly as much about puberty . . . or anything else in life.

And to our invaluable interns,
congratulations on being published authors!
Samson Bennett
Ber Bennett
Amanda Bortner
Teddy Cavanaugh
Peggy Helman
Isabella Huang
Talia Natterson
Ry Natterson
Cadence Sommers
Rebecca Sugerman

CONTENTS

TEN SLIGHTLY SHOCKING
FACTS ABOUT MODERN PUBERTY

1. The average kid starts puberty more than two years earlier than they did a generation ago, and puberty takes much longer—it now lasts almost a decade.

2. The brain doesn't finish maturing until early adulthood, leaving a huge gap between body maturation (starting at around age 8 or 9) and smart decision-making (fully in place between 25 to 30 years old).

3. Body image issues, fueled by social media, have skyrocketed: well over half of all tweens and teens report having them, with guys affected just as much as girls.

4. Twenty percent of all people in the United States who identify as transgender are between 13 and 17 years old.

5. Rates of vaginal intercourse in high school are down, but anal sex is up.

6. Fifty percent of all males will develop breast buds during puberty, but most of those buds disappear after a while.

7. Bye-bye pads and tampons—today's period products of choice include menstrual cups and period underwear.

8. Millennials and Gen Zers of all genders are much more likely than Boomers and Gen Xers to perform major landscaping to their pubic hair by shaving, waxing, or permanently lasering it—sometimes all off.

9. The average age of first exposure to porn is 12 years old for boys, and not much later for girls.

10. Data from 2021 shows that 40 percent of all high school students reported feeling persistently sad or hopeless; it's even higher among females (60 percent) and LBGTQ+ kids (70 percent).

INTRODUCTION

All adults are survivors of puberty, but for most of us the scabs of our memories feel bizarrely fresh even decades later: Vanessa's stomach still turns at the thought of getting her first period in borrowed blush ballet tights (no, they were not returned to their rightful owner), and Cara still winces when she flashes back to her brothers' repeated taunts, *You're so flat, the walls are jealous!* For those of us who traveled through puberty before 1990 or so, it started sometime around age 11 for most and lasted three or four years tops, even though it felt like a lifetime.

The puberty of the past bears little resemblance to what kids live through today. Now this transformation starts younger, takes longer, and unfurls with social media and cell phones in the mix. What used to be a sometimes painful and sometimes laughable but mostly cringey middle school dash has become a slog lasting many years. *Many*. Like, twice as many.

That's especially true when puberty is defined in its broadest sense. Strictly speaking, puberty is the path to sexual maturity, ultimately enabling a person to reproduce. In genetic females, this covers everything from breast growth to getting the menstrual cycle up and running; in genetic males, the penis and testicles convert into sperm production and delivery machines. But in reality, puberty extends far beyond groins and breasts, partially because the hormones in charge also affect distant organs like the skin and bones, and partially because those same hormones circulate around the brain, profoundly impacting one's emotional and social existence. This explains why puberty is credited (or blamed) for everything from hair sprouting up across the body, to pungent odors making their debut, to reckless decision-making, to eye rolls so deep it's not entirely clear the pupils will come back into view. Moodiness does not make a person reproductively capable, nor do zits or growth spurts or any of the rest of it. But they result from hormonal shifts and turn out to be humongous players in the life experience of kids this age.

This is why we define puberty broadly, including sexual maturation for sure, but also all of the other shifts that happen in and around the body on account of the hormonal surges that lend themselves to sexual maturation. In this more expansive definition of modern puberty, we have essentially equated it with adolescence, which is precisely what the entire world seems to do anyway. It's this whole kettle of fish that's taking longer—body changes, emotional shifts, and friend dramas too.

It's also why we wrote a book offering information and guidance to help make sense of this seemingly endless awkward roller coaster ride. Puberty gets a bad rap for many reasons, but one of the biggest is that a pubescent child is not a sweet baby anymore. When they start to stink and whine and make choices that baffle us, they are also moving away from being cuddly and dependent. Don't be fooled! Tweens and teens still need their adults to love and support them, maybe more than they ever did. Living through puberty can be confusing, uncomfortable, and scary. Kids need information and reassurance, love and affection. Even the silent ones want an open space to ask questions. The purpose of this book is to define the new normal and offer language for some of the hundreds of tiny conversations that have replaced The Talk of yore.

Starting with chapter 3, there are four parts to each chapter in this book: the science of puberty and what's happening in the body; how things have changed over the past few generations; how to talk about all of this stuff; and what older kids have to say. These youth voices of wisdom are a peek into how today's kids think, what they experience, and what they need—storytelling from kids recently out the other side to help avoid painfully awkward moments.

Lest you think that we've got this caring-for-kids-through-puberty thing in the bag, we've got news for you: yes, Cara is a pediatrician and Vanessa a puberty educator, but we are also parents who have blown it more times than we can count. Our hard-earned knowledge comes not just from two decades of working with kids and their caregivers, but also from being in the trenches with our own families. It's living both sides of the coin that has evolved us into true "experts." The most important lesson is this: Guiding kids is easier when we give ourselves permission to not know everything, to screw up occasionally, and to get a grip on this new world order. It works better when we separate what they're going through from our own feelings and personal histories.

Forget (almost) everything you thought you knew about puberty, because modern puberty is more complex, more fascinating, and more demanding of our understanding than the version that we lived through.

CHAPTER 1

The Big Picture: Starting Sooner, Lasting Longer

The most jaw-dropping fact about modern-day growing up is how much earlier it begins. Today's kids enter puberty an average of two years younger than their parents did. In fact, it's not uncommon to hear about kids riding their first wave of hormonal surges three, four, or even five years sooner than the people raising them.

The second most stunning fact is how much longer this whole process lasts. Thanks to its mood swings and painfully awkward physical shifts, puberty as a stage of life tends to be equal parts feared and dreaded by parents. At least, reason would dictate, by starting *earlier* it must progress *faster*, expediting everyone through this phase. Right? Actually, no. Rather than speeding up, the time line of puberty has stretched like taffy. One simple example can be found in the average age of a first period: while puberty itself is starting a couple of years sooner than it used to, since the 1940s the age of a first period has barely budged.

So today, it is simultaneously true that many kids begin to develop physically well before they ever hit double digits and also that most kids experience hormonally driven changes—from acne to eye rolling—years longer than prior generations. From start to finish, the process can take nearly a full decade. As a result, even though the puberty of the past may not have been kinder or gentler, it was most certainly later and a heck of a lot shorter.

The measuring of the pubertal time line is relatively new science. Research looking at "normal" puberty began in earnest in the 1940s, when Dr. James Tanner, a pediatric endocrinologist (aka hormone doctor for kids), launched a study that would span three decades. Starting in 1948, Tanner documented the physical changes of kids living in a postwar orphanage in Harpenden, outside of London. There are several reasons why this study could never be done today, not the least of which is that Tanner didn't do any hands-on physical exams but rather studied photographs of each child taken several times per year to examine their pubertal development over time. The growth he tracked was limited to breast or penile and testicular size, depending upon gender, and appearance of pubic hair for all. Tanner then created a numeric scale to classify the progress: stage 1 meant prepubescent with no visible sexual maturation; stage 5 meant fully developed, adult; and stages 2, 3, and 4 fell somewhere in between with certain specific hallmarks.

Because Tanner's staging was so simple and visual, it caught on. And it stuck! This explains why today, 75 years after his study first began, doctors across the world still use Tanner staging to describe progression along the path through physical maturation.

Tanner's scale became particularly helpful as a sort of yardstick for shifting hormones inside the body. Moving from Tanner stage 1—entirely prepubescent—to Tanner stage 2 confirmed that the sex hormones governing these particular body changes were actually present. This, in turn, meant that in the days before certain hormones could be measured in a laboratory, and decades before others had even been discovered, doctors had a way to confirm that sexual maturation was in process.

In addition to staging *how* kids go through it, Tanner wrote the norms for *when* they go through it too. His data documenting the adolescence of Baby Boomers showed that the average girl entered puberty just after she turned 11, while the average boy was 11.5 years old. It's thanks to Tanner's stages that people are so startled by how early puberty begins these days: if there wasn't a time expectation, we wouldn't label it as "early" or "late."

Of course, there's always been a range of pubertal timing—none of us expects to set a clock to these changes. That said, there's an average age for the onset of puberty and an expected swing on either side, with anything much earlier or later getting noticed. It doesn't take much to recall the kid in your fifth-grade class who looked like a full-on adult, and another kid in junior year of high school lagging way behind. In puberty parlance, the kids who develop first are called early bloomers and the ones visibly late to the party, late bloomers. For a long time—certainly before and even long after Tanner's data was published—there was no agreed-upon definition of what made someone early or late, at least not outside of medical circles. Instead, this was the kind of thing labeled by kids and parents alike, generally not kindly.

Tanner examined images of naked kids, but in real, day-to-day life, puberty's most visible landmarks can even be observed while kids are clothed because the earliest sign for girls is typically a pair of breast buds that seem to poke out of every T-shirt, sweater, and certainly leotard. For boys, though, puberty's shifts are only publicly obvious a little later on, when some combination of a growth spurt, voice drop, and wispy mustache come into play. Tanner knew that penile and testicular growth were far more accurate measures here, but in a clothed society these go unnoticed and they're even more subtle because kids tend to move toward privacy just about the same time that their hormones start to surge. So when boys close the door and otherwise keep their clothes on, parents often miss the fact that they're developing. All of this is why even with robust studies documenting the path through puberty, there has always been lots of room for confusion about who is actually in it, especially among the guys.

One potentially misleading indicator: hair. Ask just about anyone, and they'll consider pubic hair part of the sexual maturation of puberty. But ask an endocrinologist or a scientist studying this stage of life, and they'll say something very different: hair might make someone *look* sexually mature, but it doesn't make them capable of reproducing. Pubic hair growth is largely governed by hormones released from the adrenal glands sitting on top of the kidneys. These hormones, called adrenal androgens, start to circulate around the same time that estrogen and testosterone are producing the changes of puberty, but don't be fooled, adrenal androgens are on their own independent path. They might appear at the same time as the hormones ruling puberty, or they might show up much earlier or later.

The adrenal androgens stimulate more than just hair follicles—they also tell pores in the skin to secrete sweat and oil, explaining why crops of pubic hair tend to appear along with acne or waves of newly pungent body odor. But none of these downstream impacts signify sexual maturation. Even Tanner didn't really appreciate the distinction here, which explains why he measured pubic hair as one of his hallmarks of puberty. It's confusing that the hormonal pathways through the body don't always work together, even if things look that way from the outside.

Following Tanner's groundbreaking research, the pipeline of studies of "normal" puberty ran dry. This makes sense, because once a phenomenon has been defined as "normal," it isn't scientifically sexy to redocument. But in the early 1990s, a nurse practitioner named Marcia Herman-Giddens felt compelled to reexamine Tanner's assumptions when the patients walking into her office repeatedly defied the expectations he had set: girl after girl appeared to be in Tanner stage 2 well before age 11. Herman-Giddens was quite aware of normal variation, early bloomers and late bloomers, but the trend flowing through her office motivated her to apply for funding to run a fairly large study, ultimately including 17,000 girls. In 1997, she published the results showing that puberty was indeed beginning sooner for genetic females—depending upon ethnicity, anywhere from a year to a year and a half earlier than expected. Herman-Giddens documented a massive shift in puberty and made headlines everywhere.

PRECOCIOUS PUBERTY

Many people wonder about the difference between earlier puberty and *precocious puberty*. Precocious puberty is a diagnosis for kids whose bodies begin developing before what is considered "normal."

The age at which we call puberty precocious has shifted as the average age of the onset of puberty has gotten younger. Most medical texts currently define it as sexual development in a genetic female before age eight and sexual development in a genetic male before age nine. However, because there are racial and ethnic differences in the age of onset of puberty, those parameters are changing, pushing many experts to lower the age limits in some of these subpopulations down to seven in females and eight in males.

In 2005, a group of researchers, including pediatric endocrinologist Louise Greenspan, set out to replicate Herman-Giddens's findings. Why? Because Tanner had defined "normal" and Herman-Giddens had thrown that definition into question. Scientists routinely set out to confirm (or deny) novel findings. It took only five years for Greenspan and her colleagues to endorse Herman-Giddens's results and add a twist of their own: puberty was starting *even earlier* than she had noted. According to Greenspan's data, by age nine more than half of all girls had begun to develop breasts. Greenspan also confirmed Herman-Giddens's conclusions about racial differences: in Greenspan's study, not only did Black girls enter puberty youngest, but nearly a quarter of them showed signs by age seven, and half of them by age eight.

While the data is surprising—and maybe even new to you—this science is not hot-off-the-presses. Greenspan published it in 2010.

Until 2012, earlier puberty was posited as a girl phenomenon. This was fueled by the fact that early-stage estrogen-dependent changes (breast growth, curves, and turbulent wear-them-on-your-sleeve moods) are more obvious than early testosterone-driven ones (namely penile and testicular growth). But at last, someone—Marcia Herman-Giddens, to be precise—decided to look at boys. Herman-Giddens pulled herself out of retirement and, in a study published in 2012, proved that earlier puberty was not limited to genetic females. Guys, too, were entering the path to sexual maturity up to two years earlier than Tanner predicted, somewhere between 9 and 10 years old. And as in all of the other recent studies, a clear racial skew emerged, with Black boys developing the youngest: a stunning 72 percent had evidence of puberty by 9 years old.

So when we say that puberty has changed, one of the first and most profound ways is in its timing: puberty begins much earlier than ever before. Of course, not for everyone, but Tanner's "normal" age range has clearly trended down since today's parents and grandparents lived it. These days, doctors don't bat an eye if they see seven-year-old girls or eight-and-a-half-year-old boys showing signs of circulating estrogen or testosterone. To put this into perspective, this is three to four years earlier than what Tanner predicted. Said another way, most kids turn seven in first grade. Normal pubertal onset is earlier these days, and early is *really* early.

The obvious next question is: Why?! The deeply disappointing answer is: no one really knows. Theories abound about all of the chemicals (namely the ones called endocrine disruptors) that we put into and onto our bodies, from the foods we eat, to the liquids we drink, to the cosmetics we slather on, to the air we breathe. There's good emerging data that antibiotic overuse, especially in livestock, and chronic stress contribute as well. And the extra weight carried by so many people across the globe—the phenomenon the medical community calls the obesity epidemic—plays a role when fat cells convert certain hormones, including sex hormones, from one form to another. We don't get deep into the *why* of it all in this book because we don't have a definitive answer. Several scientists are looking to answer that question through ongoing research, though, and some of them have written phenomenal books on the topic (we're looking at you, Louise Greenspan and Julianna Deardorff, and your book *The New Puberty*).

We are as frustrated as you that we cannot explain the underlying phenomenon. But just because there's no clear answer to *Why?* doesn't mean there's less urgency about *How the hell to deal with this?* How can we all care for kids in modern puberty, especially now that they're in it at such young ages?

———

With kids starting puberty years earlier than they did a few decades ago, it means there is a deepening disconnect between what an 8-, 10-, or 12-year-old *actually* looks like versus what the adults in their lives *expect* them to look like. This incongruity between external characteristics and chronologic age can create discomfort and confusion, both for the child and for the adult. It's hard to treat them like they're 10 when they look more like 14.

To this end, here's the single most important thing to remember, a piece of advice we will harp on throughout this book: treat them how old they *are*, not how old they *look*. Most kids think according to their chronological age, not their apparent age—a 10-year-old might very well still play with dolls or snuggle on a parent's lap or build Legos. When kids look older and like they're capable of acting in more grown-up ways, the presumption sets everyone up for failure. No matter how maddening it is to watch a kid's social impulsivity around peers because he *seems* old enough to control himself, remember his true age; no matter how exasperating it is to have a kid constantly forget her cleats or shin guards, remember her age. Just because they look mature—and even if they sometimes act mature—their executive functioning skills haven't ripened, nor has their ability to make smart, consequential, long-term choices.

Another critical thing to remember here: just because kids look more sexually mature doesn't mean they want to have sex. Our society has long conflated the onset of puberty with becoming a sexual being. Which is fair, because the path to sexual maturity does, indeed, include the emergence of sexual urges and desires. But with the earlier start to puberty, for many kids beginning around fourth grade, the onset of puberty and the onset of sexual activity are no longer in sync. They never were, really—sexualization has a range just like everything else that occurs during adolescence, and it evolves not just because the body parts develop but also because the maturing brain, soaked in the hormones controlling puberty, guides it to. Yes, the physical changes of puberty are starting earlier, but brain maturation isn't happening any faster.

And so adults shouldn't assume that just because a kid in sixth or seventh grade looks like a high schooler, that kid has the same urges as an older teen. An 11-year-old girl who has breasts, widened hips, and pubic hair may appear to adult eyes ready to be sexually active, but she is still 11. With the hope that kids will have sex when they're ready to handle the emotional and physical responsibilities, all adults—parents, along with relatives, teachers, coaches, and mentors—need to model what it looks like to treat a child their age because this will minimize the pressure those kids feel to act as old as they look.

This said, there's a darker side to the story: research clearly shows that girls who develop at a younger age are at risk for earlier sexual activity. Let's be super clear here about causality. This is not because their earlier puberty means they are seeking sexual experiences sooner but rather because kids who develop at a younger age are treated older and expected to act older. This can leave them at risk for sexual predation. Younger girls with more physically developed bodies face a significantly higher risk of sexual assault. They're also at a higher risk for anxiety, depression, eating disorders, and risk-taking such as premature experimentation with drugs and alcohol. All of which makes raising an earlier-developing girl feel really scary. But it bears saying again: earlier development does not *cause* this. There are several middling steps along the path.

Then there are the kids who are late to the puberty party, the ones with the opposite issue. Later bloomers will always exist because *late blooming* is a relative term: it simply refers to the last 2.5 percent of kids to jump onto this hormonal roller coaster. Being a "late bloomer" can mean showing no external signs of puberty until age 13 or 14 or later. By then, most kids have been in puberty for years, some for half their life! The dreaded signs of physical maturation in grammar school are badges of privilege by middle school. If a kid doesn't have any by high school, social and emotional hurdles can begin to appear. So in the same way that the stretching of puberty like taffy has made life increasingly tricky for younger kids who look older, it has also made it very challenging for older kids who look younger.

It's incredibly important that adults talk with candor about *not* heading into puberty. Having conversations about what isn't happening can release the pressure valve, reassuring kids. Speaking to a pediatrician can help tremendously, especially for those who don't feel equipped to reassure. Either way, talking is always the best strategy, even when nothing is going on—or, in the case of late bloomers, particularly when nothing is going on.

Right, talking! That is often the part that trips people up. Adults need to know the science, the *what* of caring for kids through puberty, and also the *how* of the intimidating task of being in conversation. With the backdrop of puberty's expanding time line, before we get to the specifics, we need to lay out honest and realistic guidance for the many (many!) talks we will have with kids we love.

CHAPTER 2

The Other Big Picture: How to Talk About All of It

The first time Vanessa talked to her oldest child about sex, it went some-thing like this: She was frantically trying to feed her four kids breakfast on a Sunday morning before running out the door to one kid's soccer game. Splashing milk into cereal bowls and pulling bagels from the toaster, she was running through the litany of chores for the day when her 10-year-old son looked up from the sports section of the newspaper and shouted, "Hey, Mom, what's rape?"

Without skipping a beat, Vanessa hollered back, "It's when a man forces a woman to have sex with him," and went back to putting break-fast on the table.

Several hours later, while she was driving in the car with said 10-year-old, it dawned on Vanessa all the ways she had gone wrong with her answer. For starters, she had completely bungled the definition of rape. That's when it also occurred to her that her kid probably didn't even know what the word *sex* meant and that she hadn't defined it *at all*. She had also failed to ask if he had any more questions about a deeply com-plicated and scary topic. So Vanessa took a deep breath, looked in the rearview mirror, and asked, "Hey, buddy, do you know what the word *sex* means? I realize I used it this morning, but I never really asked you if you knew."

"Um, no, not really," he replied.

There are so many ways conversations can go wrong, and Vanessa had hit a perfect storm. That Sunday morning, running around like a chicken with her head cut off, she was scattered instead of present; she answered a question without wondering why it was being asked; she forgot who knew what and didn't define the terms; and she gendered an issue that didn't warrant gendering.

But her second attempt at the conversation turned into a talk that stretched the entire car ride home, covering definitions of terms and then traveling into deeper corners like whether a women can rape a man (for clarity's sake: yes, of course). That one failed conversation was the first of many, many successful talks about sex with her son over the years. It also became her touchstone for what it means to talk to kids this age—and more importantly, to always define the terms you use. Never assume they know.

All this talk about talking can feel overwhelming, especially at the outset of a book that's going to point out the zillions of small conversations demanded by puberty. It's like having the world's longest to-do list and almost every single item on the list is one you'd rather avoid. Pornography, periods, masturbation, wet dreams, vaping, drinking, body image, sex, consent, heartbreak, and on and on—these are the twenty-first-century basics before even getting to the seriously dumb stuff kids do like cheating, lying, shoplifting, sending nudes, crashing cars. Given the tsunami of adolescent possibilities, it's a wonder any of us get out of bed in the morning.

Some of these conversations can be outsourced to other people, like teachers, coaches, counselors, or relatives, and some can be covered in a strategically placed article or book. But ultimately, it's our job to keep kids safe and healthy, to transmit our values plus our love to help get them through these years. And here's the kicker: when these conversations go well, there is nothing, *nothing*, more gratifying or meaningful than knowing you've provided them with critical knowledge they will use for the rest of their lives. None of it is easy. Frankly, much of it is scary and stressful and confusing. But you'll be fine if you remember a few fundamental truths: It's not one talk, but many, and you will sometimes screw them up. Small conversations are more effective than long lectures. This means you will have *many* of them over a decade or two. And if you handle one (or a bunch) imperfectly, there's lots of opportunity to try again. Amazingly, it's the moment when we repair our screwups that our relationship with a kid grows stronger.

Every chapter in this book has a section called "How to Talk About It" because the most common question we get from adults is *How the hell do I talk about this stuff?* Topic by topic, we offer very specific suggestions. There are times when you will know precisely what information you want to pass along, but you don't have the script to get from A to B. And there are times that you will be flat-out flabbergasted by kids' behavior itself or the subject in general, with no sense of where to even begin. This chapter is intended as an overlay to everything else in this book, like a piece of tracing paper to put on top of the unique challenges in your home. By learning the tools of the talking trade, you get to write all over that tracing paper and then reuse it, applying the tactics to different scenarios that pop up over time.

There is no one-size-fits-all approach here. But there are some amazing truisms that work for almost everyone, almost all of the time. They are our SparkNotes of How to Talk to Tweens and Teens.

Listen (don't just talk)

The temptation to lecture kids is strong, especially when we're stressed, angry, or out of our depth. There are highly valid reasons for lecturing instead of listening, like when a kid has royally screwed up, when their safety is in jeopardy, or when they urgently need critical information. If you've ever verbally dumped on a kid without stopping to hear what they have to say, you are in excellent company with the *entire* rest of the global adult population. That said, kids tell us that having adults listen instead of lecture makes a world of difference.

It's a little weird to start a chapter on how to talk about stuff by emphasizing the importance of *not* talking, but it turns out to be the key to great conversations. That said, very few people are born with the superpower to shut up and listen—most of us have to develop the skill. If you are exhausted just by the prospect of attempting this, here's why listening is so important.

> **Listening helps kids feel valued:** Listening tells them that their ideas and questions are important; it validates their feelings and reminds them that adults are available resources. This sounds trite, but it's actually huge. Listening turns a one-way monologue into a two-way conversation. It also models for kids what it looks like to pay attention to another person, recognize someone else's feelings, and value their thoughts. Maybe most importantly, it creates a pathway for further conversation when you zip your lips and let them talk.

> **Listening can steer the conversation in the right direction:** Have you ever answered a kid's question only to realize you've answered something they didn't actually ask? An answer is far more effective when you know what someone is *really* wondering before diving in—listening first gets you to a better response. If you're not sure what they need to know, here's a favorite go-to strategy: answer their question with a question like *That's so interesting. What made you ask that?*

> **Listening educates us about a kid's current reality:** Many adults love to be experts, but teenagers have always had their own language and ecosystem meant precisely for

adults *not* to master. Today's kids are on a gazillion social media platforms and have just emerged from a global pandemic—we cannot possibly know what it feels like to be an adolescent. The very kids we aim to help turn out to be our best guides because they are the experts in their unique reality.

Listening buys time to formulate thoughts: While listening, you can take a deep breath, not freak out, and think for a moment, all absolutely necessary when talking about hard stuff. Please do not confuse this with staying silent—kids need us to talk!—but a pause usually makes whatever we say more effective.

Step slowly into tricky conversations

While listening is king, talking is still extremely important. Considering the crazy amount of information kids need to absorb over this complicated decade of growing up, the adults who love them are often their best sources. But *what* is said is as important as *how* it is delivered. The goal is to give kids what they need without having them walk out of the room. FYI, that will happen too. Plenty of times.

In our puberty workshops, we use a well-honed strategy for getting into tricky conversations. Whether these talks are born of a question (*What is rape?*) or the need to impart critical information to a kid unsolicited (*I need to tell you about fentanyl*) or a kid royally screwing up (*You missed curfew by two hours*), the first step is always finding a way in. This approach can feel a little forced, but with practice it becomes second nature and creates a road map to navigate all sorts of complicated topics.

Breathe: No matter the origin of the conversation, start by taking one (or several) deep breaths to calm the nervous system and buy some thinking time.

Gently dig a little deeper: If the conversation starts with a tough or surprising question from a kid, this is the moment for *That's so interesting. What makes you ask that question?* If the conversation is one you raised, you can begin with something like *I'm wondering what you know about . . .*

Don't lie: Don't ever, ever lie. Lying may solve some short-term discomfort, but it will come back to bite you in the ass someday, guaranteed. By the way, you can choose not to answer a question or an accusation—the options here aren't limited to full disclosure or a bold-faced lie—but once one person in a relationship has lied, they've lost all credibility when they expect the other person to be honest and forthright. It doesn't matter if that other person is decades younger.

Own your nervousness: Everyone loves when someone admits to feeling uncomfortable because it's proof that the conversation is important enough to endure difficult feelings. Acknowledging awkwardness also models that people are capable of moving through discomfort. You can literally say: *I'm nervous to talk about this, but it's really important, so let's dive in.* Pro tip: avoid making eye contact if that helps dispel the discomfort—this is why every single parenting expert on the planet recommends having awkward conversations in a car.

Admit when you don't know: *I don't know* are three of the most important words we use! Saying this shows kids how to admit it too. Acknowledging you don't know also spares you from making up a wrong answer on the spot or sending a kid to look something up online (the younger they are, the worse that idea). But you can look it up together, call an expert on the topic, or press pause and circle back when you have an answer. Just don't forget to circle back!

Don't lecture: See above for the millions of reasons why listening, not lecturing, is the best route.

Give them just a few pieces of information: They won't absorb more than that anyhow. And conversations can be short because you're going to have lots of them!

Ask for questions: Do this even if you are thoroughly exhausted and completely relieved to have survived a tough conversation, because it shows that you're always interested and available.

Make space for them to process: Some kids need a couple of days or even longer to process weighty information. They might seem like they weren't listening and might not have any follow-up questions. Don't freak out or get annoyed; everyone handles these topics differently. It's quite possible you have the kid who, a week later while you're walking the dog together, comes out with a zinger of a follow-up question that will knock your socks off.

Leave your baggage at the door

For so many of us, our adolescent memories are burned into our brains, shaping lifelong behaviors that date back to our own formative years. These memories are neurologically hardwired in a uniquely intense way, kind of like a superhero's origin story if the origin story starred acne and erections.

The years of puberty are also the years when the brain is rapidly constructing its superhighway of neural pathways. In that time, it transforms from being linked by the neurological equivalent of bumpy dirt roads into a network of five-lane expressways. It's no coincidence that, decades later, adults hold on to (even relive!) memories from those years with such ferocity.

These adolescent experiences are seared into all of our brains, and yet, in order to do our jobs better, we need to put them aside when guiding kids. While it's incredibly tempting to share the deep scars or thrilling successes of our own adolescence with our kids, much of the time this is the exact opposite of what kids need. Leaving that crap outside the conversation can require Herculean strength, but the goal is to prepare kids to go on their *own* journeys, not to rehash ours in excruciating detail. Kids have the painfully wonderful privilege of writing their own stories. The need to leave your baggage at the door will come up repeatedly as you engage in conversations throughout puberty, so here's how to practice doing that.

Literally, leave it at the door: Cast your mind back to a seminal puberty memory—doesn't matter if it's something funny or difficult—and write it down in a few words on a piece of paper. Share that "baggage" with another adult, someone you trust, and then take the note and symbolically remove it from your day-to-day life by folding it up and tucking it away or even scrunching it up and throwing it in the garbage. The goal is not to eliminate that formative memory from your own narrative but to keep it out of your conversations with kids.

When in doubt, cut it out: When adults see their kids hurting or struggling with an issue, the urge is to unload their own painful story, starting with *I know just how you feel.* This attempt at empathy only moves the focus from them to us. Often kids just want adults to listen and support, something like *That really sucks. I can imagine it feels pretty painful right now.*

Find another adult to talk to: Sometimes there's a specific issue—like body image or acne—that's particularly hard for an adult to deal with, even 30 or 40 years down the road. This is the moment to stop, seek out a fellow adult, and acknowledge your struggle. Unload on them, don't project onto a kid.

Share sparingly, mostly with humor: There are moments when it makes sense for adults to share their puberty memories with kids, especially when it humanizes you and allows them to be in the driver's seat. Humor is everything here, like this story that might or might not have become an instant classic in one of our families: *I know you're nervous about your trip. When I was your age, I was so nervous I didn't speak for the first 24 hours of my program, to the point where people thought I spoke another language. When I finally opened my mouth they were so excited to hear me talk!*

Take do-overs

When we mess up, and we all will, it's critical to recognize and admit it. Taking the do-over lets us get past that and make it right. It's the rewrite of the sex conversation Vanessa had with her son. It's the simplest piece of follow-through that we often forget to take advantage of.

When you have made a mistake, go back and repair it: This models that it's okay to fail—a mantra everyone uses these days but kids don't necessarily buy (and who can blame them?). Show them that a person can make an error, acknowledge it, and get past it. This will be highly applicable to many of the tricky conversations through puberty because some are guaranteed to go south and will need a do-over.

Remember that nothing is written in cement: Do-overs are not always about royal screw-ups or failures. Sometimes they are simply rethinking a parenting choice. When we give our kids things—devices or privileges or gifts—it's easy to think of those things as *theirs*. But all of us overindulge from time to time or make choices that quickly feel regrettable. Take the do-over and take it back. Just let your kid know why and promise to reconsider in the future.

Make sure to explain why: If you're taking a do-over and you don't share the rationale, you've wasted an opportunity. This is especially true when you are taking something back, be it a promise or a cell phone. If you want them to understand why, you have to explain but you don't have to apologize.

The do-over has no expiration date: It doesn't have to happen in the moment—it can happen days, weeks, even years after the original event. But whenever you realize that you owe someone a do-over, it's never too late to say, *I was a jerk and I'm sorry* or *I got that fact totally wrong and I want to clarify.*

Let them mock you for being fallible: It's brutal, for sure, to be reminded of *that time when* . . . But there's nothing more powerful than stepping off a pedestal, getting eye-

to-eye with a kid. Anticipate that when you take do-
overs, occasionally they will lord that over you . . . just
laugh.

It's a long list, but each of these talking tips shows up throughout the
book in the context of specific topics. Some will work for some of you;
none will work for all. The bottom line is that it's one thing to understand how and why puberty has changed so radically over the past few
decades, but it's just as important to have the skills to talk to the kids
going through it.

CHAPTER 3

Breasts, Boobs, and Buds

Breasts—known to everyone under a certain age as boobs—seem to pop up from out of nowhere. Starting out as a bud and morphing into a fully grown breast, this sensitive process (literally and figuratively) happens over several years.

 LET'S START WITH SCIENCE

It turns out, breast tissue is present from birth, but it remains mostly dormant until the ovaries begin to produce and release estrogen and progesterone, the hormonal rising tides marking the start of female puberty. We say "mostly" because many babies have swollen or puffy nipples for the first few weeks of life, a side effect of the maternal estrogen that floods a pregnant body and crosses into the baby's bloodstream via a shared placenta. After birth, those maternal hormones slowly decrease over time. Fun fact: as maternal hormones regress, many babies also break out with baby acne, literally an infantile version of the zits kids will face when hormones shift again a decade or so later.

Back to puberty: when tween ovaries begin churning out estrogen and progesterone, these hormones travel up to the dormant breast tissue, stimulating it to grow. In genetic females, developing breasts slowly collect fat and establish an intricate system of ducts and glands that will eventually carry milk to the nipple should the body become pregnant. This milk production and distribution system is not fully formed until after the onset of periods—in fact, it's not completely finished until there is a birth followed by lactation, which is a nice reminder that periods aren't any sort of end point for physical maturation but rather very much a middle-marker. And as anyone with breasts knows, boobs continue to shift and change all the time, even after they are "done growing."

That moment when breast tissue first appears is what doctors call *thelarche* but everyone who's not a doctor refers to it as breast budding: a small, firm, highly sensitive mound about the size of a short stack of dimes pops up underneath the nipple. Budding almost always happens on one side before the other, a fact that makes many kids and their parents panic, given our cultural hyperawareness of breast cancer. Don't freak out! One bud appearing before the other is entirely normal and par for the course.

For some, the time from breast budding to fits-in-a-bra breast growth is a matter of months; for others, this process can take years. Like everything else along the pubertal time line, breast growth progresses differently for each person. That said, there are some common denominators experienced by most, and at the top of that list is tenderness: boobs can ache or feel sore; the skin on top can be itchy or supersensitive to clothing rubbing against it; and if an errant elbow or backpack flies into the path of a growing boob, forget about it!

Size asymmetry is also par for the course. For starters, in the same way that one bud often appears before the other, more developed breasts are not always the same size, a fact well known but little discussed by people with boobs. As Cara likes to say, "They don't talk to each other." Add to that the fact that once someone begins having a period, breast size shifts throughout the month—the size discrepancy between two boobs in a pair can increase dramatically during the days when the breasts are their most swollen. Usually, the two sides are balanced enough not to cause logistical issues (like bra fit) or self-esteem issues, but there are certainly kids—and adults—who have to manage significantly uneven breasts some or all of the time.

A moment on breast growth across the genders: At some point during puberty, a large number of genetic males—some studies suggest up to 50 percent—will have noticeable breast development, ranging from buds to more fully formed boobs. Most of the time, the breast tissue grows and then reverses its own growth, a phenomenon called involution; but sometimes the tissue grows and remains. This can happen on one side or both, in kids of all shapes and sizes. The medical term for this is gynecomastia, a word that should be known widely given how common it is. But many adults have never heard of it (even if they lived it), and as is so often the case, leaving something unnamed can confer shame.

How is it possible that guys develop breasts when they don't have ovaries making the estrogen and progesterone required in the process? The answer lies in the fact that everyone, regardless of sex, has a little bit of both dominant puberty hormones, estrogen and testosterone, because the testicles actually produce estrogen and likewise, the ovaries produce testosterone too. There's also a phenomenon called peripheral fat conversion, where fat cells in the body convert one hormone into another—for instance, androstenedione into testosterone—which explains why bodies have different amounts of various hormones depending upon how much fat they carry. But remember that gynecomastia can affect people of all weights—it's the *balance* of the hormones, not just the absolute amounts, that affect distant parts of the body like breasts.

WHAT'S CHANGED OVER THE PAST 20, 30, 40 YEARS

The big headline here: breast budding starts sooner. Two generations ago, the average age for a genetic female to start budding breasts was 11; now it's somewhere around 8 or 9, depending upon race or ethnicity.

The natural follow-up question is why, and unfortunately, there's no great answer yet. As we touched on in chapter 1, what we know for sure is that our world is increasingly crowded with chemicals that disrupt the way hormones work inside the body. These chemicals are essentially everywhere, which is how they get into and onto us. What we don't know is precisely which of these chemicals or which family of chemicals is to blame; if there were a common denominator (or two or three), the advice would follow that we should all avoid that ingredient, but the science isn't there yet.

Another big change impacting breast development is the mass marketing of sports bras. On the upside, wide access to sports bras increases the likelihood that more women, especially big-busted women, will engage in athletics. The benefits of increased exercise are known to everyone (another change in the past few decades), so increasing comfort increases accessibility to working out, in turn improving health. But the downside of sports bra popularization is that younger and younger kids are wearing them all day long. This is especially true during the early years of breast growth, because breast buds can feel less tender or sensitive when they are tightly bound in a sports bra. There's very little data about the impact of restricting growing tissue all day every day. Will this cause wearers to develop increasingly dense or cystic breasts because their new boobs have to try to grow through resistance? Unclear. What is clear is that the synthetic, athletic-style material used for most sports bras can irritate skin and trap smells. So there's that.

The shift in obesity rates has also impacted breast growth, but there's conflicting data about how. Researchers have well documented the rise in body weight among kids and adults across the United States. In the last 20 years alone, this country has seen obesity skyrocket in all age groups, increasing from an average prevalence of 30.5 percent in 2000 to 41.9 percent in 2020. Kids are less affected, but rates still hover around 20 percent, representing about 15 million children across the United States. When broken down by age group, obesity prevalence increases from 12.7 percent among toddlers to 20.7 percent among school-aged kids to 22.2 percent in middle and high schoolers, with numbers further skewed when considering race and socioeconomic status. We dive deeper into this data in chapter 9.

Thanks to peripheral fat conversion of hormones, the more fat a person accumulates, the higher their baseline level of certain hormones. This biochemistry is thought to be partially responsible for tipping kids into puberty. But researchers have recently asked whether the extra hormones generated in fat tissue translates specifically into breast growth and development. The most current thinking—based upon studies looking at kids going through puberty; measuring their body weight, hormone levels, Tanner staging, and ovarian size; and using ultrasound to document the actual progression of breast development—is that the appearance of accelerated breast growth in heavier kids is likely just that: appearance. Extra fat tissue collects in and around the breast, fooling people into thinking that there's breast development, but it's not genuine breast tissue growth and development. What a child's chest looks like and even their Tanner stage can be out of whack with how the breast tissue is actually developing under the surface. You can bet that more research is on the horizon, and, who knows, future data may very well land at an opposite conclusion.

Still, though, to the outside world—and to the child—fat accumulation around the nipple and breast tissue growth looks like boobs. And all of the same emotional and social implications exist, regardless of where this curviness comes from. These kids often want to wear bras or other undergarments that minimize the prominence of their chests.

One major sidenote here that will certainly come up in future studies: Some scientists have used the findings of increased breast fat over breast tissue to argue that kids aren't really going into puberty that much earlier after all. Instead, they say, these kids are being inaccurately Tanner staged and called "pubescent" when really what they have is breast fat deposition. But this doesn't explain the other hallmarks of puberty that are happening earlier and earlier, everything from mood swings to penile and testicular growth to, yes, breast budding. As Louise Greenspan says, the very first sign of puberty in most kids is a slamming door. These days, many doctors, teachers, coaches, and parents report seeing earlier-onset mood swings. Moodiness is not a function of fat deposition in the breasts but rather a downstream consequence of hormones surging through the brain. Penile and testicular growth often fly under the radar because of new-onset privacy, a topic we get into in detail in chapter 4. All of which is to say that if breast growth were the only sign that kids are tipping into puberty earlier, we'd give the naysayers more credence. But since it's not, we strongly disagree with their conclusions. Stay tuned for more public debate and conflicting research on this front.

HOW TO TALK ABOUT IT

It's no surprise that boobs have become a lightning rod for parental concerns, especially with how early they appear these days. Shock sets in when an eight-year-old walks into a room with breast buds poking out of her T-shirt—ultimately inevitable but expected two or three years down the road. This might feel surprising, but it's not freak-out-worthy. In fact, it is completely possible—and downright important—for the adults in the room to manage their own reactions about changing bodies, which keeps kids more comfortable too.

Let's start with our own reactions and expectations. Parents often assume that their kids will be the same age they were when they developed breasts, grew pubic hair, got their periods, broke out with acne, all of it. While genetics certainly play a role, clearly things have changed, particularly when it comes to the new determinants of pubertal timing. So if a kid has breasts years before you did, you might feel surprised or worried, but you are most definitely not alone.

Younger and younger breast development makes some adults acutely uncomfortable because of what breasts represent. Sexual maturity. Reproductive capability. Objectification. These are huge looming issues. The puffy, raised nipple of a breast bud might be small, but it carries tremendous baggage for some people. Adults who were early bloomers often hope their kids will develop breasts later than they did; adults who were late bloomers can feel the opposite. Some adults describe embarrassment that their child is well on the way to physical maturation, as if the only explanation is that they did something wrong, like feed them unhealthy foods or lather them with chemical-laden products. Others worry that with growing breasts, their kid will be on the receiving end of unwanted looks or comments. And then there are the adults downright confused by the emerging breast buds on their sons.

All of these reactions are legitimate and valid internal monologues in response to kids' puberty, with an emphasis on *internal* here, because self-reflection can backfire when it gets blurted out uncensored in conversations with kids.

Let's say the internal monologue starts something like this: *Ugh, I'm so depressed that my daughter has started growing breast buds.* The first thing to do is clock that internal reaction. *What am I feeling?* It could be sadness that she is growing up or worry that her life experience as a woman will be harder than her experience as a girl. Maybe your own transition into adolescence was really challenging and you don't want her to have the same negative experiences you had.

The next step is to find support from other adults. This provides an alternative to dumping on our kids. Tap into a network of other adults or even just one with whom you can share some of your hardest, darkest thoughts—a spouse, a trusted friend, a therapist.

All the while, remember that kids are kids and it works best to treat them according to their chronological age, not the age they appear to be. It is perfectly normal to feel a sense of loss as they develop physically and feel nostalgia for when they were little. But that said, breast buds do not mean childhood is over. In fact, this is one of the first opportunities to practice helping a kid feel comfortable about their slowly evolving body, which is no small task.

What are the tactics? How can we talk to different types of kids without layering on any shame or any of our own baggage? Here is some specific advice.

For the kid who "needs" a bra but doesn't want one

A classic puberty dilemma: a kid's body has changed, but they either don't notice or don't want to notice. The same conundrum exists around when a kid should start wearing deodorant, shaving, using acne medicine—there's a long list they aren't asking for or about, and in some cases they're resisting altogether. We can't force our kids to do anything they don't want to do, nor does that approach help teach underlying lessons about the importance. We can, though, make available the items or skills needed. Bras are never an absolute necessity—there are cultures across the globe that don't embrace them and plenty of people locally who make the same choice. But some kids will sit out activities if they're uncomfortable without a bra, or they might begin to wear loose-fitting clothing to hide their emerging curves. Do your best to ask how they feel—physically and emotionally—in their changing body. Or try this: *Here are a couple of comfortable bras I got for you if you're into wearing one. Let me know if any of them feel good on your body.*

For the kid who wants a bra but doesn't "need" one

Need is a very subjective term here. When there's no physical necessity, still consider the social or emotional circumstances, like a sense of belonging with their peers. The good news is that there is a continuum of bras beginning with an unstructured top which provides no function, really, beyond wearing an undergarment, basically a cut-off camisole. Many younger, flatter-chested kids love these. They also work wonders for late bloomers, surrounded by friends who all wear bras out of necessity—older kids who often just want to fit in. Stock up on a couple of inexpensive bras or camis if it will help ease social difficulties.

For the kid whose clothing is not always breast bud–friendly

Lots of clothing made for kids turns out to show everything underneath, from moisture-wicking shirts that seem to accentuate breast buds (kids call them "nipply") to sheer white uniform shirts and jerseys. Without shaming kids about their growing bodies, we have an obligation to help them keep their bodies private if kids don't always notice what's visible to other people. This flips from being an issue about appearance to one about safety or self-esteem, sometimes requiring more directness: *If you want (or need) to wear that top, you'll need to wear a layer underneath—I got this bra for you.*

For the kid who has no intention of wearing a bra

Opting to go braless is super common among Gen Z, so get used to it. The cultural shift away from wearing bras, whether as a fashion or a political statement, can be a big shock for people who grew up on Victoria's Secret catalogs. Every generation makes different choices about how they present themselves, a tale as old as time. The bottom line is that if they're not hurting themselves or anyone else, we need to let it go, even if bralessness makes us uncomfortable.

 FROM PEOPLE JUST OUT THE OTHER SIDE

J.S., she/her, age 20

On first bras

The summer I was nine years old, when I was at sleep-away camp, my mom bought me a training bra on visiting day. I was irate. There was no freaking way that I was going to add another layer of fabric under my already heavy and hot camp-issued top. And besides, I barely had boobs to begin with! Though I don't totally remember, I'm sure what happened next was me telling my mom I would wear it and then proceeding to stuff it under my bed for the rest of the summer. I'm sure the summer heat played a role in my original bra aversion, but I had also really wanted to be able to pick out my own bras and try everything on, especially the first time. When I came home, I told my mom I wanted to go bra shopping, and the two of us went to a local store and picked out a few bras together.

My advice: Don't force your child to wear a bra if they don't want to, and help them feel in control of a body that is changing out of their control!

On fears of breast cancer

I remember getting a text from a friend once in middle school that read, "my right tit is killing me i think i have breast cancer." Needless to say, I was shocked. How could my friend, my 13-year-old friend, possibly have suddenly developed breast cancer? The next day, I got a message that the pain was gone, so she was probably fine, and I breathed a sigh of relief, but only until the same thing happened again a month later. After a quick phone call with her doctor, my friend (and I) came to realize that she did not, in fact, have breast cancer. She just had her period, and she was experiencing swelling leading up to her cycle.

My advice: Explain about how periods may affect boobs and that this is normal!

CHAPTER 4

Penises and Testicles

Every conversation between adults and kids—frankly, between two people of any age—is better when there's clarity. This is true even for the most external (and joked-about) body parts, like the penis. Just because everyone seems to talk about it though, doesn't mean they actually understand how it works and changes.

 ## LET'S START WITH SCIENCE

The penis is the male genital organ found in all higher vertebrates. Its job is to carry both sperm and urine (at different times) out of the body. The longest part of the penis, stretching from the pelvis almost to its tip, is called the shaft. Inside the shaft is erectile tissue that can fill with blood, making the penis stiff. Also inside the shaft is a tube called the urethra, which carries the sperm and the urine (again, at different times!) from the inside of the body out. The tip of the penis has a rounder and fuller segment called the head, covered by a piece of skin called the foreskin.

A circumcised penis is one with this foreskin removed, revealing the head. Circumcision usually takes place in the first few days of life, though there are reasons why it can happen later, a list including relatively uncommon medical issues like recurrent balanitis (inflammation of the head of the penis), phimosis (when the foreskin is too tight to pull itself back over the penile head), paraphimosis (a medical emergency in which the foreskin gets stuck in the retracted position, causing the head of the penis to swell), penile cancers (sometimes caused by the human papillomavirus, also known as HPV), and plain old personal choice (some guys who are not circumcised early on want to do it later in life).

Now on to the testicles! These are the pair of round balls—yep, that's where they get their catchy nickname—sitting in a sack of skin called the scrotum, next to and slightly behind the penis. The two testicles are approximately the same size and usually hang at about the same level, but not always. The testicles are responsible for making both testosterone and, in a reproductively mature genetic male, sperm. Testosterone is microscopic and, when it's secreted from the testicles, absorbs into the bloodstream. Sperm, by comparison, are huge. They leave the testicles through a small coiled structure called the epididymis; then they travel through a tube called the vas deferens; next they pass by the fluid-secreting seminal vesicle; and eventually this liquidy concoction reaches the prostate, which adds even more fluid to the mix, making a liquid called semen. During ejaculation, semen flows through the urethra and out the tip of the penis.

The first physical sign of puberty in a genetic male is the growth of the penis and testicles. In fact, in the first couple of years after testosterone starts to surge, this is often the *only* sign of puberty for some guys. Given that many kids get quite private right around the same age they begin to experience hormonal shifts, these changes may be basically invisible to everyone except the kid himself—and that assumes he's the noticing type.

The penis will eventually double in stretched length, growing from two to three inches long up to five to six inches. Yes, that's a stretched length, which is exactly what it sounds like: the penis is stretched gently, then measured from the base of the pubic bone all the way to its tip. Very relevant sidenote here: this is not an erect length. Unlike a standard height and weight, stretched penile length is almost never measured in a pediatrician's office, largely because it isn't predictive of anything—it doesn't correlate with health or even where a kid is in puberty. (Also, from Cara's years in practice, attempting this measurement wouldn't land well with about 99 percent of tweens and teens.)

Testicle size, on the other hand, is a pretty good proxy for determining pubertal stage. To measure testicles accurately, doctors use a tool called an orchidometer, which looks like a necklace with a dozen sequentially larger beads. The smallest beads represent prepubescent testes, typically ranging in size from one to three milliliters or about one-quarter to one-half teaspoon—yes, testicles are measured by volume. The biggest bead on the orchidometer is the "fully adult" 15- to 25-milliliter piece (3 to 5 teaspoons). However, just like penises, testicles also vary from person to person in both size and shape. While it may seem obvious, we're going to note this for anyone who is wondering: no, you should *not* measure your kid's testicular volume to see where he is along the path of puberty. Even Cara didn't do that, and she's a pediatrician!

Penises and testicles fundamentally change their function during puberty more than almost any other organs in the body, which is why we cannot talk about penises and testicles without talking about erections and wet dreams. While these topics are awkward for many of the kids living them, evidenced by the number of absurd punch lines they invoke, adults seem to be even more uncomfortable discussing them.

Erections aren't a new phenomenon in puberty—infants get them all the time—they just happen far more than ever before. They are caused when blood fills up the spongy erectile tissue in the shaft of the penis; by the way, that blood must drain out in order for the penis return to its flaccid, and usually smaller, baseline. Sometimes erections are prompted by certain types of thoughts (some sex ed teachers call these "sexy thoughts," a cringey but fair description). It turns out, though, that as puberty peaks, erections often happen for no clear reason at all. In fact, there are studies showing that they even occur on their own version of a circadian rhythm, as frequently as every 60 to 90 minutes.

Wet dreams (aka nocturnal emissions) describe the phenomena of semen leaving the penis during sleep. Because they happen when unconscious and without a rush of pleasure, they are not orgasms. If puberty had a catchphrase, it would be "range of normal," which applies perfectly here because not all guys have these, and some have them far more often than others. The classic teaching about wet dreams is that they will make themselves known by a moist spot on the bed in the morning. That said, some people sleep wearing a tight-fitting bottom layer—not necessarily ideal in terms of airing out the groin at night, but one way to catch the semen before it hits the sheets. It's also not uncommon for guys to think they have peed in their sleep when they wake up after a wet dream, but here's how to tell the difference: urine usually leaves a much bigger mark, plus it has a distinctive smell. And if you are wondering whether wet dreams are associated with sexual dreams, the answer is a big fat maybe. Nobody really knows.

 ## WHAT'S CHANGED OVER THE PAST 20, 30, 40 YEARS

According to many—including pediatric endocrinologist Louise Greenspan and lots of parents out there too—the earliest behavioral sign of puberty in any kid, regardless of gender, is often a slamming door. But the earliest physical sign of puberty in a genetic male is actually enlargement of the penis and testicles. And because puberty now begins at younger ages for most kids, this means that penile and testicular growth starts sooner too. According to Marcia Herman-Giddens's study published in 2012, the average onset is somewhere between ages 9 and 10. Bear in mind that data is more than a decade old, leaving some to wonder if puberty starts even younger now.

Before you flip out, a few comments: First, just because penises and testicles are starting to enlarge at younger ages doesn't mean that this growth happens quickly. In fact, it's typically so slow and gradual that even the kids who are living it don't notice. The path through genital maturation can take years. Second, most adults living in homes with kids experiencing these changes have absolutely no clue they're happening. That's because this is about the same age when many kids—especially boys—become exceptionally private. Haven't seen your kid naked in a few months (or years)? You're not alone. Finally, while the penis and testicles slowly enlarge, often nothing else is happening. *Nothing*. Nada. Zilch. Zippo. No bulging muscles, no cracking voice, no growth spurt. Which is why, when we give talks and tell parents that odds are their 10-year-old boy is in puberty, many think we have no clue what we're talking about.

But it's true that by age 10, at least half of all boys are experiencing surges in testosterone and shifts in their physiology. And that's different from how it was when you were growing up—close to two years different. Some people think it's unnecessary to know what exactly is going on and when: they say that once the more obvious changes appear, like growth spurts and dropping voices, they'll start talking to their kid. But here's an important counterargument: hormones don't just circulate below the neck—they also surround and infiltrate the brain, affecting the way kids make decisions and respond emotionally. We have a whole chapter on mood swings (chapter 12), but it's worth saying here that slamming doors and monosyllabic responses might show up in tandem with growing penises and testicles. Knowing that hormones are rising and falling inside of fourth and fifth graders can help adults support, love, guide, and understand them. The fact that the hormonal surges of puberty start earlier *is* important in this context.

It's equally important to recognize that some kids do not have any puberty hormones on board at 9 or 10 or even 12 or 13. The oldest among them are called "late bloomers," kids who head through all of these transformations far later than most of their friends. Knowing when your kid *isn't* in puberty can be as significant as knowing when he is. Why?

Because being late to puberty can present physical, emotional, or social difficulties. If everyone is going through it earlier but your kid is "on time" according to your family history, then relatively speaking, he's late.

WHAT COUNTS AS A LATE BLOOMER?

In the same way that early bloomers fall outside of the statistically expected age range for the onset of puberty, so too do late bloomers, just on the other end. Two key differences here: First, while early puberty has shifted earlier, the timing of late-onset puberty has hardly budged at all. Second, because the earliest signs of male puberty are penile and testicular growth, many kids who appear late to develop don't realize that they're actually already in process. And for lots of good reasons, neither do their adults.

The definition of a late-blooming genetic male is someone with no measurable testicular growth by age 14. But remember, it can take a couple of years between the start of testicular growth and other external signs of puberty, so figuring out whether a kid is a true late bloomer often requires a physical exam by a healthcare provider. Anyone who is concerned shouldn't hesitate to reach out for a professional opinion, even if the child has not yet hit 14.

 HOW TO TALK ABOUT IT

Our culture has created an unfair mythology around tween and teen boys: a kind of comic shorthand for them as hormone-crazed, acne-ridden maniacs sporting raging erections, furiously masturbating at every given opportunity. And yes, there is some truth to this caricature, which we explore in excruciating detail throughout this book. However, these broad generalizations miss the nuances of male puberty, the biggest being that kids with penises have lots of questions, concerns, and feelings about their changing bodies. The image of a silent 12-year-old boy watching TV with his hands down his pants is a classic trope (and a fair one too), but we do a disservice when we assume that they don't also have confusion or worries.

Consider this: in any given group of guys, some will have growing penises and testicles beginning in grade school, most by middle school and through high school, and a few, even stretching into college. The path is not unlike breast development with measurable stages (thanks, Dr. Tanner), but no one really talks about guy stuff this way. As a result, kids are conditioned not to ask about penile and testicular growth, only to joke about it or to act like it's no big deal.

This makes it seem as if guys don't have questions, which couldn't be further from the truth. That's the theme of this chapter: appearances can be deceiving. Most kids really want to understand how they will grow and change. Okay, some want to know exactly how big their penis will be, and the answer there is never anything except *I don't know*. But the vast majority are generally looking for normalization of a long, drawn-out, mystifying process. If we don't talk about it, some of them will develop the impression that one morning they will simply wake up with an adult-sized penis and testicles encircled by a shock of hair. Conversation helps ease worry, reduce self-consciousness, and manage expectations.

Even though genetic males often go quiet in puberty, we can—and should—still talk to them about what's happening. Their reticence does not give us an excuse for avoiding discussion ourselves; rather, it requires us to be more creative and, yes, persistent on the topic. Here's how.

Talk about timing

While kids constantly compare themselves to each other in every way, penis comparisons are infamous. Which is why it's important to state the obvious, something not always obvious to them: everyone's penis will get bigger, but not necessarily at the same time, and when all is said and done they'll wind up slightly different sizes . . . and shapes. Early bloomers develop adult-size genitals years before late bloomers, timing that can feel tricky for all, even the ones smack in the middle.

Don't forget the testicles

People often assume that testicles are perfectly round and exactly the same size, but no and no. All testicles have a small lump at the top, where the epididymis sits—and it's not uncommon to mistake that for a worrisome mass when discovered. Also, most testicles aren't exactly a matched pair: one is almost always slightly smaller than the other, and one sits slightly higher in the scrotum. All of this is normal, but if there's a worry, encourage a conversation with your healthcare provider. Just like breasts and vulvas, testicles are not necessarily symmetrical—this knowledge can bring serious relief.

Lean into their lingo a little

We're big believers in using anatomical names to minimize conversational confusion and encourage personal safety, so talk about a penis as a penis. That said, somehow the word *testicle* feels very formal, and many adults use the nickname *balls* instead. Just make sure you're all clear on what you're actually talking about from the get-go, and then use language that opens up dialogue without shutting it down. If you're willing to try this, it will likely lead to an amazing conversation: ask your kids to share the nicknames and slang terms they know for different body parts. You're guaranteed to laugh, you'll have an opportunity to point out the absolute no-go words, and you'll learn a new term or two for sure. If you haven't heard the term *junk,* get ready to start there—it refers to the whole kit and caboodle.

Size doesn't matter

This has always been an important thing to talk about with kids, but especially today, when the average age of a kid's first exposure to porn is around 12 years old. In this context, penis size—always a big topic (sorry about the pun)—takes on outsized proportions (sorry, not sorry). It must be said in many ways and at many different times that penises come in all sizes and even shapes: some are curved and some are straight; some are circumcised and some have foreskins; and most of the time, they look nothing like the penises that belong to porn stars. Adult film actors tend to have much bigger penises than average, sometimes naturally and other times via cosmetic surgery. You have many years to cover all of this territory!

Erections happen all the time

Compared to when they were younger, most tweens and teens have lots more erections, some spontaneous and some thanks to imaginative thoughts or hands down the pants. Normalize it all! Help them come up with strategies to handle spontaneous erections, especially the ones that pop up at the most unfortunate moments (presentation in class, anyone?) to avoid waves of shame and humiliation. Come up with techniques for handling inconvenient erections, like the most popular one we hear: tucking it in at twelve o'clock. Talk about how an underwear style shift can make a big difference, since tighter briefs hide more than loose boxers. And try to avoid the common embarrassing erection moment that happens when you walk into their room to wake them up in the morning and there it is. Here's an easy solution: an alarm clock! Or, knock and then actually wait for permission to open the door before barging in.

Keep the touching private

Kids deserve to know what parts of their bodies feel good so that as they grow and mature they can appreciate the pleasure their bodies offer. But on the couch in the den while the whole family is watching a movie? No thanks. So talk about self-pleasure, but also talk about self-pleasuring in private, ideally in a bedroom or bathroom with the door closed.

There's no shame in any of this . . . including wet dreams

Older guys often describe to us in great detail the shame and embarrassment they feel around having wet dreams—not just teens, but grown men reflecting back on their adolescence. This is a perfect example of the pitfalls of assumptions: when boys don't openly talk about stuff or ask questions, they don't feel things deeply. Very few kids want to raise this particular subject, but they're all relieved to learn that wet dreams are completely normal, not to mention that it's easy to spot-clean sheets or run a load of laundry. An awkward conversation suddenly turns into a double teachable moment!

 FROM PEOPLE JUST OUT THE OTHER SIDE

S.H., he/him, age 19

In middle school, I was often confused because my penis became erect randomly. Luckily, many of my friends experienced a similar phenomenon. We discussed ways to combat the issue in class. We eventually discovered the term *NARB*, which stands for No Apparent Reason Boner. When someone would get a NARB, you would simply waistband your boner in your underwear to hide it. Any underwear worked with this method. I would wear athletic underwear, which masked my erection well. However, you would have to waistband your boner discreetly. If a girl saw, she would often reveal that you had a boner, and it was shameful. When someone was caught waistbanding, it was difficult. Everyone in our grade would find out. I remember one of my friends was crying in the bathroom after a girl spread rumors about his erection during a class. My worst nightmare was a girl seeing my boner through my pants.

The worst aspect of someone else seeing your bulge was the fact that girls would tell their friends about how small it is. The size of your penis often correlates to your masculinity. If a girl said your penis was small, it was one of the most demeaning insults. When guys and girls began hooking up, I would often waistband my penis to ensure the girl could not comment on the size of my penis.

The most difficult part of erections in middle school was when a girl gave you a hug. My friends and I all experienced hugs from developed girls, which made us go crazy. I remember the first time I got an erection from a girl, I freaked out after. Luckily, she was mature and understood that it was a natural reaction. At the time, I did not understand why I would get erections. I think the fact that I did not understand parts of my body was confusing to deal with.

CHAPTER 5

Periods

Oh, the menstrual cycle! For those who haven't pondered the mechanics of periods—recently or ever—get ready to be transported back to high school biology, because the basics haven't changed.

 ## LET'S START WITH SCIENCE

First, some vocabulary: *Menstruation* is the periodic flow of blood mixed with water, mucus, and tissue from the uterus. It's also called "menses" by some people, "the menstrual cycle" by others, and "having a period" by pretty much everyone. The words make sense: *mensis* is Greek for month; *period* is short for periodic; and *cycle* refers to recurring at regular intervals, which is precisely what menstrual cycles do about every three to five weeks. We can all be happy that the Old English word for the process—*monadblot*—"month blood," didn't stick.

Menarche is the medical term for a first period. Makes sense, as *-arche* means "original" or "from the beginning." While menarche does mark the first menstrual cycle, it helps to know that the cycle usually has no particular rhythm or regularity at first. This means that calling out the inaugural period is simply that: putting a name to the first blood down there without a promise of when the next one will come. Most new menstruators report periods happening more frequently than anticipated (sometimes every couple of weeks), less frequently than anticipated (they can be spread out for months), or the most common pattern, which is no pattern at all. Periods usually become regular—with a predictable cycle—within a year or two of menarche.

That first period, by the way, does not necessarily resemble bleeding. Most people find thick dark brown goop in their underpants or when wiping with toilet paper. The color and texture are so far afield from what they are expecting that it's not uncommon for a new menstruator to think she has pooped in her pants before realizing she has gotten a period. The semiliquid goop looks brown because it has been sitting around the uterus for a while and has been exposed to oxygen, which oxidizes it, turning its color to rust. For every cycle that follows—or at least most of them—while the initial bloody tissue looks red, over the next few days, oxygen makes its way up to the shedding lining, turning it brown.

Now for the body parts involved. The *uterus*, also called the womb, is a pear-shaped muscular organ about the size of a closed fist that sits in the abdomen, halfway between the belly button and the vaginal opening. The lowest and narrowest part of the uterus is called the *cervix*. During pregnancy, the cervix functions as a sort of cap, remaining narrow and tight to help hold the growing fetus in the womb. Beneath the cervix sits the vagina, a long (about six or seven inches in most adults) cylindrical muscular tube that stretches to the outside of the body. People often mistakenly think the word *vagina* refers only to the external portion visible from the outside, but that's just the vaginal opening. The organ itself occupies much more space inside. Flanking either side of the vaginal opening are the *labia*—literally "lips." The smaller, thinner pair closest to the vaginal opening are called the *labia minora;* the ones that are fuller and farther out are the *labia majora*. Put it all together and the constellation of both sets of labia plus the vaginal opening, the clitoris, and the opening to the urethra are collectively called the *vulva*.

Traveling the other direction from the uterus, deeper inside the body, the *fallopian tubes* stretch out from the top of the uterus like long antennae on either side. Beyond each fallopian tube sits an *ovary*, a gland about the size and shape of an almond. The ovaries are hormone production machines, churning out estrogen and progesterone (and even a little testosterone). They also hold immature eggs (medical name: *ova*). Each cycle, the ovaries take turns maturing and releasing an egg (ova), which explains where the term *ovulation* came from. That ovulated egg travels from the ovary through the corresponding fallopian tube and into the uterus. If it remains unfertilized, it will pass out of the uterus and continue on its journey through the cervix, then the vagina, and then out the vaginal opening. With the egg gone, hormone levels shift and the uterine lining sheds—a period! A fertilized egg, on the other hand, will remain in the uterus, attempting to implant itself into the uterine lining. If it does so successfully, the lining will not shed, and instead the fertilized egg will begin to grow. Voilà! Pregnancy.

Now on to the most complicated piece of the puzzle: hormonal cycling. Even people trained in medicine lose track of which hormones go up and down at different points in time during the menstrual cycle. The simplest way to think about it is to remember that three different parts of the body communicate: the brain, the ovaries, and the uterus. Inside the brain—fairly deep inside, as if you drew a line from the space between the eyebrows straight back—sits the hypothalamus. It's a gland, which means it secretes hormones, and is a part of the brain at the same time. The hypothalamus plays a massive role in all sorts of bodily functions, from appetite to body temperature regulation to sex drive. In terms of the menstrual cycle, the hypothalamus releases a hormone called GnRH, short for *gonadotropin-releasing hormone*. GnRH then travels to another gland in the brain, this one much closer to the forehead, called the pituitary gland. As GnRH levels go up, the pituitary releases two other hormones, luteinizing hormone (LH) and follicle-stimulating hormone (FSH). These two hormones then leave the brain and travel down to the ovaries.

Once they arrive there, rising levels of LH and FSH tell the ovaries to produce their native hormones, estrogen and progesterone. This is called positive feedback: the presence of one or more hormone(s) triggering the release of another. As estrogen and progesterone levels rise, though, they do the opposite: they signal to both the hypothalamus and the pituitary gland to *stop*. The positive and negative feedback loops work in concert, with LH and FSH telling the ovaries to turn up their volume (positive feedback), while estrogen and progesterone tell the brain to quiet down (negative feedback). When there's plenty of estrogen and progesterone coursing through the body, the hypothalamus doesn't need to pump out GnRH and therefore the pituitary doesn't make more LH or FSH, causing the ovaries to stop producing more estrogen and progesterone. But, once estrogen and progesterone hit low enough lows, the hypothalamus starts cranking out GnRH once again, followed by LH and FSH from the pituitary, and the cycle begins anew. One extra sidenote here, as if your brain can hold even one more piece of hormone information: the eggs actually make a little hormone of their own—progesterone—that helps fine-tune the body's overall hormonal ebbs and flows.

Here's how all of this hormonal seesawing translates into the phases of the menstrual cycle. And then, we promise, your high school biology lesson will end.

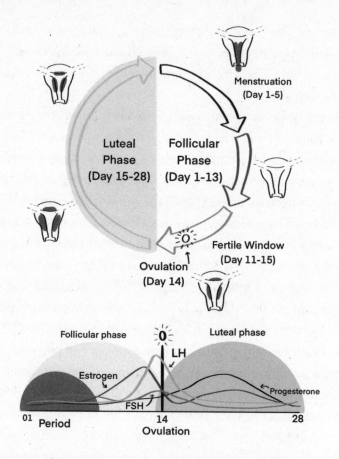

The first part of the cycle is called the follicular phase. It begins just after someone starts a period and lasts until ovulation—typically about two weeks. During this the part of the cycle, a follicle (egg) matures inside one of the ovaries, while simultaneously the uterine lining (medical term: *endometrium*) builds itself up in preparation for a possible fertilized egg. This process coincides with rising estrogen, FSH, and LH levels, followed by a precipitous estrogen drop.

Ovulation is the moment about halfway through a menstrual cycle when the ovary releases its mature egg.

Some people can feel ovulation—a sharp, twingy sensation that lasts only a couple of seconds with an amazingly fun name: *Mittelschmerz.*

The luteal phase occupies the second half of the menstrual cycle. The pituitary gland has turned off LH and FSH production. Estrogen has a second, lesser, rise, then a fall, while progesterone—produced by the ovulated egg (now called a *corpus luteum*)—surges for several more days. The presence of progesterone maintains the blood and tissue lining inside the uterus only until the unfertilized corpus luteum, begins to disintegrate a few days later. No more corpus luteum, no more progesterone. Now both estrogen and progesterone levels head south.

When estrogen and progesterone hit low enough levels, the uterus sheds its lining. This is the menstrual phase, which can last anywhere from three to seven days, sometimes longer.

A fun fact about the menstrual phase: it is considered to be the start of a cycle, not the end. This convention probably began because it's a very obvious physical marker that doesn't require a doctor's exam or a lab test—if you're bleeding, you're likely in the menstrual phase. Okay, as promised, we're done!

 ## WHAT'S CHANGED OVER THE PAST 20, 30, 40 YEARS . . .

Believe it or not, very little has changed about actual physical periods. With so much talk about puberty moving earlier and earlier, many people assume that menarche—the first period—is starting sooner too. It's not. Well, at least not recently.

If we turn the time machine way back, data from skeletal remains dating to the Paleolithic era (between 2.5 million years ago and 10,000 B.C.) suggests menarche began sometime between ages 7 and 13. That's a fairly wide range, but so is the time span: we're talking about anthropological data stretching back more than 2 million years. Flash forward to the medieval era (roughly A.D. 500 to A.D. 1500), when there's evidence that menarche had shifted later, falling sometime between ages 12 and 15. It got even later following the industrial revolution, peaking at age 16 in the pre–Civil War days. The later onset of first periods is attributed not to something positive but rather to poor living conditions and inconsistent access to nutritious food supply, a significant sidenote since many people interpret earlier-onset periods as "bad" and therefore later onset "good." That's a fallacy. Beginning at the start of the twentieth century, in places where standards of living steadily improved, menarche arrived younger and younger. So by 1995, in the United States the average age for a first period was just before the 13th birthday—this was notably younger than for kids born 100 years earlier (the great-grandparent and grandparent generations) but not all that different, actually, from onset for their own moms, who got their periods for the first time in the 1960s and 70s.

In fact, the timing of first periods has remained fairly level over the past five or six decades. It's tricky data to follow because there's variation among the studies, with some noting slightly bigger declines: depending upon the research you're looking at, today's average age of menarche sits anywhere from 12 to 12.5 years old. It's hard to say how significant this variation is or to project where the data will land another 20 years from now. But what is clear is that all of the other physical manifestations of puberty have accelerated far more than period onset: breasts are budding, penises and testicles are growing, and moods are swinging two years before they used to. The timing of a first period is inching back ever so slowly by comparison.

How about cycles? Are they longer these days? Shorter? Less predictable? No, no, and no. Now, this comparison across the generations isn't quite as straightforward, because unlike first-period data, this type of information hasn't been collected with any sort of consistency over long periods of time. For a while there, researchers were thrilled at the prospect of a data deluge thanks to period-tracking apps that can gather all of this information and more. Unfortunately, the bloom quickly faded from that rose when it became clear that these same apps can be mined for data to enforce abortion restriction laws. As a result, millions of people are pulling off the apps—they don't want anyone to have access to their cycle information if it can one day be weaponized against them. (Wise move!)

Meanwhile, cultural conversations about periods have seen a cataclysmic shift: they carry far less shame and much more empowerment than ever before. Even a decade ago, we would help kids strategize how to manage their period products discreetly. Classic advice back then included slipping a pad or tampon up a shirt sleeve to hide it from plain sight. Thinking back, that advice feels cringey. Why did we lean into a social convention that stigmatized periods? Plenty of kids still want to keep their period business to themselves—and we're all for that too—but the prevailing wisdom now looks quite different. Just the other day, one of our own kids opened a delivery box to find the pads she had ordered online. In front of her boyfriend, she unboxed the product, made a passing comment about how relieved she was to be restocked, and handed said boyfriend a box to carry into her bathroom. Her dad almost passed out at the scene unfolding in front of him.

Another big change: period products. The shift in available period products has been so radical, this section could fill a book in and of itself. But we're keeping the descriptions brief. These days, kids can use any and all of the following:

> **Pads** come in all shapes and sizes, but miraculously, even the most heavy-duty overnight pads are now paper-thin compared to what used to be available.

Tampons also come in a variety of sizes, with different types of applicators (or none at all), and many are now made with organic cotton (pads are too).

Period underwear is quite possibly the biggest market game changer of all time when it comes to a menstruator's lifestyle. Gone will be the days when people share their I-bled-into-my-white-pants stories now that period underwear—which in some iterations can hold up to two pads' worth of blood—are widely available. And, wait for it, now there are period bathing suits too!

Menstrual cups aren't for everyone, but these insertable silicon cups collect menstrual blood for 8 to 10 hours at a time; then you remove, rinse, and reinsert. So long as there's access to a clean water supply, one of these environmentally friendly replacements can be used for years.

One more shift—the newest and in some ways most major—deserves a mention: a move to change period language to be inclusive of all genders. For instance, some have suggested replacing gendered nouns like *girl* and *woman* with gender-neutral terms like *people with vaginas* or *people who bleed.* This pivot has not been smooth, especially because conversations about inclusive language tend to get very heated, very quickly. Some don't agree with ungendering terms related to periods; others think they're not ungendered enough. Some find the new terminology confusing, while trans activists are quick to point out inaccuracies in the old language. We're clearly at a point of inflection, when conversations around puberty have changed dramatically, yet not enough. And if clarity is king, then we all need to be extremely mindful of how we choose our words here, because in an effort to be inclusive, someone inevitably gets left out. We learned that lesson from a cis-gender female who was born without a uterus, making her neither a person who bleeds nor someone who would identify as the opposite of that. Words are important, and, on this front, they're still evolving.

HOW TO TALK ABOUT IT

In our culture, first-period stories are often synonymous with shame, humiliation, and mystification. You can't throw a rock without hitting someone who has lived with the burning embarrassment of getting their first period in the most awkward of situations. The cult animated Netflix show *Big Mouth* devoted an entire episode to a character's first-period story; you could probably watch it instead of reading this section and learn just as much.

It's bananas that half the population on Earth menstruates and yet the subject is still considered taboo—even now in many places, periods are meant to be hidden and not talked about. Gen Z has made great strides in destigmatizing menstruation, but there's still a ways to go to exchange shame for informative, empowering, no-nonsense conversation.

Topping that list is talking about the stress of not knowing exactly when blood will flow—what day, what time of day, how many days. The mystery of it all can feel exasperating. This is especially true for a first period: parents and their kids are starving for knowledge about when it will happen. Here's the annoying answer: no one knows, *especially* about the first period. Sure, there are signs. If there's some breast development and maybe a little pubic hair (maybe a lot), and if clear vaginal discharge appears in the underpants pretty much every day over a few weeks or months, well then, all indicators point to *soon*. Beyond that, it's anyone's guess.

For the younger kids who have yet to get a period, the talking tips are pretty specific. For older kids, they're more vague. We've got both, because the conversations don't stop after the first period has arrived.

Normalize!

Even if you've got a famously mortifying period story of your own, let your narrative go and focus on your kid here. Periods are normal. Everyone who gets one gets a first one. Some people feel like their usual selves during their period, while others feel bloated or cranky or tired. Normalize it all and open it all up to conversation. How? Try mentioning it in a casual way: *Hey, I've got to run to the bathroom and change my tampon before it leaks.* Show kids of all genders living in your house how different menstrual care products work—they're pretty fascinating (especially demonstrating science by inserting a tampon into a narrow-neck water bottle). And point out the garbage cans in the bathroom meant for disposable period products to save kids the embarrassment of clogging a toilet with a nonflushable item.

> **Describe what periods can look like:** Especially the first! Let's say it again because it bears repeating: many people mistake their first period for poop in their underwear.

> **Cover the fake finish:** Periods have this way of winding down to almost nothing and then—wham!—the blood is back. Kids who aren't taught learn this the hard way—it's kinder to give them a heads-up.

> **Teach them how to clean blood out of underwear or off of sheets:** Empower them to be part of the cleanup, because it reduces shame. Besides, doing laundry is totally normal! And amazingly, blood often washes out with some bar soap, water, and a little bit of fabric-on-fabric friction.

> **Teach them how to wrap a pad or tampon:** If they're not the one cleaning the bathroom—be it at home, at school,

or anywhere else—they should think for a moment about the person who is. How should they respectfully dispose of their used pad or tampon? It takes two seconds to wrap it up in a little toilet paper and make sure it lands in into the trash can. For those of you with dogs at home, make sure your kid has a garbage can with a lid so that bloody period products don't become Rover's new favorite toys.

Talk about vaginal discharge

Why does the term *vaginal discharge* make people want to crawl under a table or leave the room? It's normal and healthy! Discharge provides an incredible self-cleaning mechanism for the vagina, and it can also operate as an indicator of what's going on inside the body. It should look clear, mucus-y, almost like a raw egg white. It appears every few days or weeks when kids are just starting puberty but usually increases to daily the weeks or months before a first period will start. If it ever looks deep yellow, green, or white and curdled like cottage cheese, check in with a healthcare provider to make sure there's not an infection down there.

Logistics, logistics, logistics

Kids who haven't had a period often want to anticipate every step of their day when they start bleeding, working out the kinks in their sports schedules or after-school routines. These are very fair requests, so work through the logistics together. Create a period kit that includes the following (and make sure they know how to use each product): a clean pair of underwear, pads of different sizes and absorbencies, a couple of tampons (if they're interested), and a spare pair of leggings or shorts.

Handling periods at school

This is a big one, because some schools don't have easily accessible bathrooms, or the bathrooms are accessible but not private, or they're private but gross. Some kids have teachers who won't let them leave class to use the bathroom; others describe being uncomfortable asking a male teacher. Many schools have tampon and pad dispensers in the bathroom, but kids report them empty all the time. There's PE stress (*What if I have it when swimming?*) and leak worries (*Who will tell me?*). This is the start of an endless list of period-at-school worries, and a reminder that opening up this conversation—*Is there anything you're worried about when it comes to getting your period at school?*—will turn into 100 important conversations over time.

 FROM PEOPLE JUST OUT THE OTHER SIDE

J.S., she/her, age 20

When my friend got her first period, she had no idea what was happening to her. In fact, she passed out in the bathroom of a sushi restaurant when she saw her underwear. She described wishing she had better access to information about puberty from a young age so that she didn't have to feel so scared about something so normal. Luckily, I had a mom who told me aaalllllll about periods and what to expect. My desk was piled with puberty books starting in the fifth and sixth grade, and my bathroom was stocked with pads under the sink well before my period came. My mom even had a little necklace ready to give me when I got my first period to make me feel celebrated for reaching this biological and cultural milestone, and I always felt comfortable asking her about anything period related.

My first period came a month or two before I turned 13. I remember going to the bathroom at home and seeing blood in my underwear and calling for my mom, who came running down the hall with a pad in hand. I was off to a strong start—but maybe too strong.

Right off the bat, even within the first six months of menstruating, I noticed that my periods were heavy and lasting longer than seven days. I told my best friend, who had just gotten her first period, about how heavy mine were, and was shocked to hear that her periods lasted only three or four days and were mostly pinkish compared to my deep red and brown periods, and that she didn't have to change her tampons as frequently as I did, even though I was using a larger size. When I told my mom about this discovery, she explained how everyone's periods are different, that she also had heavier, longer periods, and that it must be genetic. I even remember asking my pediatrician about it once, who provided a similar response. At the time, this was no sign for alarm and was totally normal, but because it had been normalized by everyone around me, later it became an issue that I did not even think to address.

Around the time I turned 17, my periods became increasingly heavy and long, even heavier and longer than they already were. I'd often have to change my pad or tampon every two to three hours or run the risk of bleeding through due to my ultra-heavy flow. Additionally, the cramps that I had always alleviated with some Advil and chocolate were now debilitating, and even after taking the maximum recommended dose of ibuprofen, I was still curled up in bed with a heating pad feeling absolutely miserable. Even though I knew none of my friends dealt with this when they were on their periods, I yet again figured that I was just on the heavier end of what I assumed to be a "normal" spectrum for periods. After all, I had been taught from the beginning that there is no true "normal" for periods or any function of puberty, so why should this be any different?

These heavy, long, and painful periods lasted for a year until new symptoms began to set in during the original wave of the COVID-19 pandemic in March 2020. I was lethargic and depressed, my hair was falling out, and my muscles felt like Jell-O, even though I wasn't even exercising and shouldn't have been sore. However, given global circumstances, I blamed each of these symptoms on lockdown. Of course, I was depressed and had low energy—we were in a pandemic! And of course my hair was thinning—I was stressed because of the pandemic!

However, when I went to my pediatrician for my yearly checkup and mentioned these symptoms, she sent me to an endocrinologist, and I was diagnosed with hypothyroidism, or an underactive thyroid. I was prescribed medication to combat my body's inability to produce enough thyroid hormone, which controls and regulates the body's metabolism, or how we use energy. Pretty immediately after starting this medication, my symptoms began to melt away. However, the most magical effect of this medication took place when my next cycle came around. My period, which at this point could last eight or nine days, shortened to a five-day cycle, and my flow was noticeably lighter. For the first time, I could wait longer than two hours to change a pad or tampon without fear of bleeding through, and my cramps became tamable with a little ibuprofen again. I finally realized that *this* was a "normal" period.

I wish I had known earlier that I didn't need to suffer through so many painful, heavy cycles. Although periods aren't always super fun and can cause cramps and mood swings, they shouldn't be getting in the way of your daily life in the way that they got in the way of mine. Normalizing the wide range of what a normal period looks like is important, but so is understanding when you can, and should, get help. Even though I had asked my doctors before, I had to ask again and again, and it took years to address this issue. Through this experience, I learned that if something feels wrong to you, always go back and advocate for yourself.

There are so many modern inventions to ease life with a period. Getting a period-tracking app changed my life. Sure, it was helpful to get a push notification that my period should be arriving in the next three days so I could make sure my pad and tampon supply was stocked. Where it really helped me was with my premenstrual syndrome (PMS) and mood swings.

I am not an overly emotional person. I approach the world through a lens of practicality and optimistic realism. Yet once a month I find myself crying at the drop of a hat. Even after *years* of having my period, the two or three days before I started bleeding, when I would be feeling my most emotional, never ceased to catch me off guard. Only once I actually got my period was I given the perspective to understand why I was feeling so emotionally volatile.

However, with the help of a simple push notification, I was able to tell in advance when I might start feeling out of sorts. Knowing ahead of time that my PMS window was approaching allowed me to name my feelings, which helped me keep them in check. Slowly, my charged emotional state when I was PMS-ing grew less, and I really attribute this to being able to prepare myself for what was coming. Instead of feeling sad or irritated for no reason, I was able to know that it was because my period was about to start, and I could separate myself from these feelings.

CHAPTER 6

Hair

Hair is a fixture on most human bodies from birth and until the end, though it shifts colors and changes textures, growing in and falling out across the life span. It can be thick in some places, wispy in others; a mix of blonds and reds and browns and black for some but certainly not all. Hair grows on the crown of the head, along the brow and lash lines, and as a fine—or sometimes not so fine—coating up and down the arms and legs. Look closely, and you'll see that most people have teeny-tiny hairs covering much of their bare-seeming skin, sprouting basically everywhere except their palms, soles, teeth, eyeballs, lips, and nails.

 LET'S START WITH SCIENCE

New, thicker, usually darker and curlier hair is a hallmark of puberty—sort of. While it tends to crop up around the same time as puberty, it is not technically a part of the process of sexual maturation. We say this over and over throughout the book, repeating ourselves to hammer home its importance. Remember that puberty is, in its narrowest definition, the path to reproductive capability, governed by estrogen made (mostly)

in the ovaries and testosterone produced (mostly, too) by the testicles, with a series of other hormonal actors playing parts as well. Hair growth follows a different hormonal path with a different name: adrenarche. It grows under the guidance of hormones called adrenal androgens, which are made in and released by the adrenal glands sitting atop the kidneys. The adrenal androgens are responsible for much more than just hair, by the way: their hormones cause increased sweat and oil production too, the precursors to greasier, smellier skin, and eventually zits and body odor.

The main reason we beat the adrenarche-is-not-equal-to-puberty fact to a pulp is that some kids will enter adrenarche well before they are anywhere near puberty, causing lots of confusion. Pubic hair on a five-year-old? It's alarming. But if you understand that the hair is growing not because of sexual maturity but rather because the adrenal glands are pumping out a specific hormone telling that pubic hair to grow, the situation feels a little less overwhelming (though it still doesn't feel great—just ask the parents of the five-year-old).

Now, all of this said, even though the hormones of puberty don't directly trigger adrenarche, there are some studies looking at the reverse: whether adrenarche can lead to puberty. This is a confusing concept—quite frankly, the adrenal glands can be as complex as they are small—but we'll try to simplify it. The adrenal glands have multiple layers called zones, and each zone makes lots of different hormones with very long names, so abbreviations are often used. The adrenal androgens most responsible for hair are DHEA and its sulfated version, DHEAS. These are produced in the layer of the gland called the zona reticularis. The reason puberty and adrenarche are considered separate processes is that DHEA production is turned on by a hormone called ACTH, *not* by any of the primary puberty pathway hormones (GnRH, LSH, FSH, estrogen, or testosterone).

However, it turns out that DHEA has the potential to directly affect the puberty feedback loop, particularly estrogen and testosterone, because DHEA can actually transform into those hormones. Estrogen, testosterone, and DHEA are basically cousins: very similarly structured hormones that can convert from one form into the other if the right enzyme is hanging around.

Stick with us here! This is why puberty doesn't cause adrenarche but adrenarche can raise estrogen and testosterone levels, which might start the puberty wheels churning. Now add to this the fact that the adrenal glands make a small amount of estrogen and progesterone too, not enough to trip kids into sexual maturation but enough to explain one reason why genetic females have testosterone even though they don't have testicles and genetic males have estrogen even without ovaries. (Important reminder: testicles also make a little bit of estrogen and ovaries also make some testosterone.)

It turns out that when DHEA leaves the adrenals and circulates throughout the body, it can be converted into an active hormone, or start a chain reaction where other hormones flip as well. This is called peripheral conversion: a process in which hormones change molecular structure ever so slightly in a part of the body far away from the place where they're usually produced. When peripheral conversion turns a hormone from a weaker form into a more active or higher-impact one, that's when most people take notice. One place peripheral conversion tends to happen is in the fat cells at the periphery of the body, like in the fat tucked under the skin. This explains why people with higher body weight can have higher concentrations of potent androgens (like testosterone) and estrogen. It also turns out to be one of the leading theories as to why kids with early adrenarche—specifically kids labeled with "premature adrenarche," like a six-year-old with noticeable body odor and a shock of underarm hair—often have extra estrogen or testosterone as well as DHEA floating around their bloodstream, even with no other signs of puberty.

A second theory about early DHEA surges implicates a totally different path through the body. This idea is that DHEA (or more likely, the DHEAS variant) acts on the brain, functioning as a neurosteroid. Inside the brain, DHEA can directly affect the way GnRH is released. Since there are way too many abbreviations flying around this chapter, here's a GnRH reminder: it comes from a gland in the brain called the hypothalamus, and it tells another gland in the brain, the pituitary, to release LH and FSH, which in turn tell the ovaries or testicles to produce estrogen and progesterone or testosterone, respectively. So GnRH is the first neurochemical trigger of puberty, the first domino to fall. What if DHEA were responsible for getting this feedback loop rolling instead? Well, then, DHEA, not GnRH, would become the trigger turning on puberty. Some scientists believe this might be the case for some kids.

We're done with hormonal shorthand and biofeedback loops, hurrah! So now let's pull the focus way back to the physical manifestation of all that biochemistry: How much hair will grow, in what order, and to what extent? Frustratingly, there's no predicting, even once DHEA begins to flow. Some kids will get pubic hair before hair grows in their armpits; others experience the exact opposite. Some will notice leg hair thickening dramatically in grammar or middle school, while others see it in high school, and some are still waiting for it to sprout in college. Some kids will grow thick, curly dark hair; others lighter or straighter hair. Sometimes hair is visible up and down the arms, sometimes only up to the elbows. The ones with the bushiest eyebrows also tend to have hairier legs—but not always! Perhaps the worst part of the entire hair journey is that no one can predict how hairy—or bare—they will wind up, and it's this unpredictability of the end point that's probably the biggest stressor of all.

One more note about the biology of all this new hair: because it's generally thicker than its predecessor, it can get stuck. Ingrown hairs are hairs that have lost their way as they try to emerge out onto the skin, instead coiling in on themselves. They continue to grow, though, and eventually, as the pore holding the hair follicle becomes more and more crowded with an elongating hair spiral, the immune system activates, sending inflammatory cells to the site. Now the pore swells with a coil of hair (like a miniature ball of yarn) and a collection of white blood cells, all stuffed into one compact space. This can eventually pop out onto the surface in the form of a whitehead, or it can remain underneath the surface, visible only as a mound of swelling, a cystic (and un-poppable) zit. Sometimes, the follicle becomes infected, causing the skin on top of and around the congested follicle to turn itchy or red or tender or, you guessed it, all three. This usually warrants a call to the doctor, a smarter move than popping it yourself, as tempting as it might be!

 ## WHAT'S CHANGED OVER THE PAST 20, 30, 40 YEARS

Adrenarche has held fairly stable across the generations—or at least there hasn't been much research declaring otherwise. Unlike puberty, which has clearly accelerated its starting point, adrenarche seems to be happening at about the same time it always has. And on a related note, the total amount of hair growth, its distribution, and its general appearance haven't budged much either.

What *has* shifted are the social mores of grooming and hair removal, particularly for Gen Z on down. The collision of changing cultural norms and science has resulted in dramatic advances in hair removal technology, namely electrolysis and laser hair removal. Both provide long-term or even permanent hairlessness by damaging hair follicles enough to interfere with hair growth—electrolysis uses shortwave radio frequencies for more permanent effect, while laser uses concentrated high heat that damages but doesn't entirely disrupt the follicle (this is why, in order for it to be permanent, laser even more than electrolysis needs to be repeated for several rounds). These processes can be expensive, time-consuming, and seriously painful. But for many people body hair provokes so much self-consciousness or embarrassment, the investment feels worthwhile.

The technological advances and wide availability of hair removal have driven Gen Z's approach to the hair on their bodies, including the increasing popularity of removing *all* of their pubic hair regardless of gender. While Brazilian waxes on women were definitely on the menu in the 1990s, you know what wasn't? The Manscaper. Today, though, many people with penises and testicles tend to their pubic hair as assiduously as people with vulvas, using specially designed electric razors to keep their hair tidy and trim.

Another reason for these shifts: pornography, where bald-down-there is standard fare. If teens are watching porn actors flaunt hairless genitals, this may inform choices about their own bodies. Responsibility (or blame) for this trend falls on the pornography industry, the ubiquity of the internet, and the presence of age-old rituals. Grooming is nothing new, but styles come and go. Undoubtedly, in another 30 years, there will be new social norms about body hair, not to mention products and tech designed to achieve them. Who knows? Maybe thick hair sprouting everywhere will be de rigueur, leaving those who permanently wiped their slates out of fashion. Regardless of where trends land in another couple of decades, today's teens are nearly guaranteed to utter the evergreen line: *In my day, no one would ever . . .*

HOW TO TALK ABOUT IT

In the hierarchy of difficult puberty issues, body hair seems to sit relatively low on the list. But while hair might not be the sexiest topic, it grows in *so many* places and can suddenly become so much more visible. All that hair may present a series of emotional and logistical challenges if it's unwanted, requiring significant time, money, and pain. This is especially true when hairlessness is a body ideal.

Here's a major challenge for many adults: hair can represent a big part of self-expression for adolescents aggressively working to individuate. From their heads to their pits to their legs, each patch of hair can become a vehicle of distinction, an announcement of a burgeoning identity. And when layered on top of cultural norms that vary by ethnicity, race, and religion, suddenly hair can evolve into a multifront battleground. Some kids wage the battle with the hair on their head, dyeing it wild colors, growing it superlong, buzzing it all off, or ironing it straight. Others focus on the hair on their face: sporting a wispy mustache on the upper lip, growing sideburns down to their chin, or plucking their eye-brows into nonexistence. And then there's the hair on the rest of the body: some opt to wax it *all* off, others to grow it *all* out, and many mix and match with bushy armpits and hairless genitals or vice versa.

You get the gist, which is why, when adults ask us, *How do I deal with my kid's hair?* it's impossible to offer one right answer. There are so many factors at play, from your cultural background, to your own relationship with hair, to your comfort with a kid's self-expression. Still, general guidelines exist for engaging in conversation about grooming.

Body hair and self-esteem

Start with body hair and self-esteem. It's not uncommon to hear kids—especially ones in the early days of puberty—complaining, *I hate my hair! I wish it was straight (or curly or blond or red or brown). The hair on my legs (or arms or face) makes me so self-conscious.* While most parents would do almost anything to save their kid from a sinking feeling, we're well aware (from our own prickly lived experiences!) that everyone has things they don't like about their appearance, some of which are not fixable . . . at least not yet. So when it comes to hair, should we help them get more comfortable with the discomfort? The best answer lies in finding out where their comments are coming from. Did someone at school make fun of them? Are they on social media accounts or watching content that presents hairless bodily ideals? What about the banter concerning hair at home? Does it involve words like *gross* or *ugly*?

In the scramble to figure out what to do or say—a puzzle that can take a good chunk of time to solve—it helps to normalize body-hair changes through puberty and beyond.

Hair hygiene

In the meantime, don't forget the link between hygiene and hair. Some kids couldn't care less about the changing hair on their bodies, to the point that their indifference butts up against cleanliness. The oily hair on their head? No need to wash it. Those whiskers over their lips? Happy to leave those. The underarm hair steeped in body odor? Just fine. The pubic hair poking out of a bathing suit? A nonconversation.

Our own cultural indoctrination tells us (screams at us!) that these things must be addressed. Sometimes hair opinions are just that, opinions; but sometimes they cross over into hygiene territory. Regardless, it's always better to talk this stuff through, starting conversations from a place of curiosity to figure out what they're thinking and why. Long hair can look amazing, but it can also trap oils or dandruff or both. Experimenting with different colors may be the safest form of rebellion at the moment, but have they considered what they are putting onto their scalp? Opening the door to talk about hair gives you a new window into a kid's evolving sense of style and self; it also gives you cred in case they find themselves on the receiving end of judgment. How do you walk this fine line? Try one of these approaches:

> **For the kid who avoids showers:** *I don't think we've ever talked about this* (even if you have 100 times!), *but one thing that changes for kids around your age is that their hair and skin start to get oilier, so your showering and hair-washing routines probably need to change.*

> **For the kid who isn't sure what products they want:** *Want to go to the store and pick out some new stuff to try? Or we can jump online to check out some options?*

> **For the kid who needs more specific guidance:** *We never went over how to wash your hair, and especially your scalp, to keep everything looking and smelling fresh. I'd love to walk you through it.*

Hair removal

Hair removal can be a highly personal, supersensitive topic, literally and figuratively. Sometimes kids want to remove hair and we aren't ready for it; other times we're desperate to help them get it off and they have no plan whatsoever to give up a single strand. When third or fourth graders sprout mustaches, pubic hair, or underarm hair, adults need to tread especially lightly. This situation is fraught—hairy in the truest sense of the word—for everyone, but it doesn't have to be a source of shame. One way around this is to err on the side of curiosity and open-mindedness by taking these steps:

> **Start a conversation about hair removal,** including the option *not* to remove it at all. Recognize that our society offers a bodily ideal that is largely hairless below the neck, and then they will get to decide what to do with the hair on their bodies.

> **Lay out the variety of ways people groom the hair** on their bodies. Maybe even ask kids what their friends do or what options they've seen online. There may be new methods that you haven't even heard of yet!

> **Get granular, explaining how it's done,** whether or not it hurts, what it looks and feels like when it grows back, or whether it's permanent—going deep is a great way to build trust with them (particularly if removal is going to hurt like hell).

Remember there is no "right" age to remove body hair, a fact as important for you as it is for them. That said, permanent hair removal is usually not available to kids under 18 without an adult's consent. We love these laws because younger teens change their minds as often as they change their clothes, and permanent hair removal is a big decision. Not to mention that when hormones are flooding the body during adolescence, permanent hair removal methods might not be fully effective— so save yourself some time and money and wait.

FROM PEOPLE JUST OUT THE OTHER SIDE

A.C., she/her, age 20

When I came out of the womb, my head was already covered in hair.

Over the years, the wispy baby hairs grew into locks that framed my face and became a part of my identity. My father dedicated hours to meticulously detangling my hair after every shower, literally pulling individual strands apart so as not to break any. It pained him when I ran the brush through my hair in a rush, breaking strands in the process. He also had his "favorite curl" that he would always point out, a curl that tended to fall on the right side of my face and was usually more defined and tighter than the rest. My cousin would say, "Can I bring you to the hair salon to show them that this is what I want?" However, despite these compliments and affirmations of the beauty and delicacy of natural hair, I never respected my hair. In fact, I despised it.

I told my parents all the time that I would rather be bald than have my naturally curly hair. I chewed on the edges of my hair consistently, leaving my dad's "favorite curl" in my mouth so often that it would dry straight and hard from the saliva on it. My parents made the decision to cut my hair above my shoulders before I entered kindergarten to stop this bad habit, but as soon as it got long enough I continued. By fourth grade, I took every slightly special event as an opportunity to try to convince my mom to let me straighten my hair, and when she did I would keep it for days, reveling in the sleekness and comfort despite the greasiness of not washing it for so long.

Somewhere along the journey from lower school to now—at 20 years old—I realized that I actually love my hair, even the dark hairs that are very visible on my pale arms. A full 180-turn from how I felt 15 years ago, but I cannot imagine going back to that state of mind now. I realized that the natural uniqueness of each person's hair sets them apart from others. I have tried different products to tame the frizziness and style my hair in a way that honors its natural form rather than erase it. These days when I scroll through hairstyling videos on TikTok or try out the most recent trends, sometimes they don't work for my hair.

My advice to parents when helping children deal with this challenge is to be supportive and know that one day your child might change their mind—or they might not. When your child expresses interest in changing their hair, be willing to listen and help think of ways to test things or compromises that show that you care about what they want, even if you don't agree. Also, one reason I ended up loving my natural hair was due to the constant affirmations from my parents that made me feel beautiful in my own skin. More than that, my parents modeled the behavior of being happy with their natural hair, which was extremely important to how I viewed myself.

CHAPTER 7

Acne, Backne, Chestne, and Buttne

Zits are the result of a perfect storm: adolescent skin secretes more sweat and oil than ever before; bacteria grow and flourish in this shifting climate; and obstacles—like newly sprouting hair and shedding skin cells, multiplying bacteria, mixed with the immune system's white blood cells aiming to kill those bacteria—plug the skin's pores. This storm, it turns out, rages on almost every single tween or teen body. Literally, 85 to 90 percent of all young people worldwide experience some degree of acne.

 ## LET'S START WITH SCIENCE

Acne's universality is a combination of biology and physics. Pilosebaceous units (PSUs)—the medical name for *pores*—appear as tiny holes scattered across the skin. Each of us has millions of them. But every PSU stretches vertically beneath the surface, shaped like an old-style chemistry flask with a bulbous bottom and a long, narrow neck. The bottom sits deep in the skin while the opening at the top of the neck lines up flush with the skin's surface.

From birth, each PSU has an oil gland, a hair follicle, and a tiny muscle. This combination is where PSU gets its name: *pilo* means hair and *sebum* is human-produced oil. (Why the tiny muscle? It helps hair stand up!) When kids are young, their pores produce watery sebum in very small volumes, which is why most little kids are not particularly sweaty. But around the time they hit puberty, the adrenal androgens—hormones like DHEA and DHEAS released from the adrenal glands—start to surge, causing sebum to become much more oily and also voluminous. In other words, tweens and teens sweat more and they sweat differently. For detailed information about the adrenal glands and their hormones, flip back to chapter 6.

Bacteria grow on our skin normally, part of a healthy microbiome, an icky symbiotic state to think about (microorganisms teeming on the skin), but one that's critical to human health. When the local environment shifts, the balance of bacteria often follows suit. So when adrenal androgens tell PSUs to pump out extra oil and sweat, excess fluid can collect at the bottom of a pore. And when certain bacteria from the skin make their way down into the pore, they thrive in this greasy, low-oxygen environment, multiplying rapidly. One species in particular, *C. acnes*, tends to go hog wild.

There's good news and bad news: the body's immune system is designed to identify invaders and, when necessary, ramp up in order to wipe them out. This is why *C. acnes* can inhabit the skin in small numbers and not cause any problems, but once the population crosses a threshold level, the immune system kicks into high gear. At the tipping point, white blood cells are mobilized and sent to the pore to destroy the growing army of *C. acnes*.

What happens next would probably be less noticeable if pores were wide-open semicircles, but remember they look like flasks with long, narrow tubes at one end. Those tubes can be easily blocked, covered, or congested, making it increasingly difficult for the sebum to get out from the bottom of the pore. When white blood cells arrive on the scene, they clog the pore; when skin cells shed, as they do all the time, they can block the narrow opening; or when a hair grows inside a pore, especially the newer, thicker version of hair that appears during puberty, it can get curled up inside the pore and block it too. If skin doesn't get washed regularly, and if it's coated with makeup or sunscreen or any other products, that pile-on can plug the pore as well. Regardless of what's obstructing the top, a small puddle of greasy fluid begins to fill the bottom of the miniflask, followed by a congested combination of sebum, bacteria, and white blood cells too. Nauseous yet?

Like a balloon filling with air, the base of the pore expands and expands in an attempt to accommodate all its new inhabitants. But eventually two things happen: first, the immune system kicks into even higher gear, now attacking from outside of the pore, recruiting inflammatory cells from deep underneath the skin's surface—this explains the red rings spreading from the bases of lumpy pimples. And then, eventually, the balloon pops. Most of the time it ruptures beneath the skin, its contents heading farther down and triggering even more immune cells and inflammation and irritation in the area—that's the red, splotchy look that goes along with more significant acne. Some of the time it releases its pressure outward, a classic popped whitehead.

During the tween and teen years, acne crops up wherever sebum is greasiest and pores clog the most easily. This typically includes the face (where it's called acne, zits, or pimples), the upper chest (chestne), and the back (backne), though plenty have reported the condition across their butts (buttne, decidedly *not* a medical term) and scattered elsewhere. We've all had a random pimple on a thigh or the back of a hand.

A note about the connection between diet and zits, because there's a lot of urban mythology here: During the tween and teen years, kids often consume junky, high-sugar foods at much higher rates than ever before. They're making lunch choices at school or grabbing snacks at friends' houses, and, left to their own devices, they tend to eat the things that aren't exactly the most nutritious. While it's a complete myth that eating a piece of pizza causes pimples to emerge, here's what *is* true: consuming sugary foods or other foods that cause blood sugar to spike results in an inflammatory response in the body. So if one of the main culprits of acne is inflammation, and if the food that's being consumed (hello, pizza) adds to this baseline inflammation—even just a little bit— then it can exacerbate breakouts. In other words, diet matters, but it's not the whole game.

The same reasoning, by the way, applies to other triggers of acne. Stress is associated with an inflammatory response. Surges in particular hormones are too. In fact, most of the culprits you've ever heard about when it comes to breaking out—from not enough sleep to slathering on a new set of products—share the common denominator of inflammation. Since we get asked about it all the time, a moment on the connection between stress and acne: Regardless of age, when the body feels stress it releases cortisol, a hormone originally designed to help us flee a pursuing wild animal. This system was not meant to be tapped hourly or even daily, but rather every once in a while. It turns out these surges in cortisol cause acne a few different ways: first, cortisol directly stimulates oil production within individual pores, increasing the oiliness of sebum even more; second, cortisol disrupts other hormones affecting sebum, thickening it further and adding to the likelihood of pore clogging; and third, cortisol can be proinflammatory, recruiting white blood cells to the scene. So, that zit—or the entire crop of pimples—that popped up the last time you got super stressed now makes more sense.

One more thing that moves the acne needle is hygiene. Most people can wrap their heads around why poor hygiene makes the skin break out. If pores are clogged with dirt or thick makeup or leftover sunscreen, it's easy to see how they might get blocked. But it turns out that overly aggressive hygiene might be just as bad as no hygiene at all. If we over- cleanse our skin, stripping it dry by removing all of its natural oils repeatedly, then the body tells the PSUs to produce more oil. If cleansers are irritating because they contain harsh chemicals or perfumes, the ir- ritation can kick off its own inflammatory response. Either way, faces washed too enthusiastically can wind up just as red, irritated, or broken out as faces in need of a good wash. So here's a case where the old advice is really the best advice: wash your face with a gentle fragrance-free soap or cleanser every morning and every night. More than that won't do any good . . . and it could backfire.

And one last snippet from the olden days that really does work: moisturize! Even with a gentle cleanser, a washed face has less oil; moisturizers replenish the supply so that the PSUs under the skin's surface don't have to kick into overdrive. So apply a thin layer after each washing, and in the daytime make sure it's got SPF in it to protect the skin from the sun's rays.

 ## WHAT'S CHANGED OVER THE PAST 20, 30, 40 YEARS

Acne itself hasn't shifted much—zits are zits, and they look pretty darn similar to the way they did a generation or two ago. But there are some notable differences in when, how, and why acne appears, starting with the fact that acne shows up a little bit earlier than it used to and more kids seem to have more of it.

Let's start with the timing, because people tend to look at a kid with zits and instantly think, *They're in puberty!* On this point, we cannot be clear (or repetitive) enough: Acne isn't an early sign of puberty or even a sign of puberty at all. The hormonal underpinnings of acne are explained in great detail in chapter 6. Quick recap: It turns out that heavier, darker body hair and acne and body odor all derive from adrenal androgen stimulation. So none of them are technically signs of puberty because none are by-products of the hormones that make a person reproductively mature. That said, acne is definitely exacerbated by the sex hormones, with surges of estrogen or testosterone literally making their mark. This is why earlier-onset puberty and its earlier hormone surges can contribute to earlier breakouts. (Translation: third and fourth graders with zits.) Acne also gets worse with stress, which is at an all-time high. And poor nutrition fuels the acne fire when inflammatory foods become a staple of the daily diet. These days, many of our most accessible sources of nutrition come in the form of calorie-dense, highly processed foods, which are known major triggers of inflammation.

Even when acne makes an early entrance, it doesn't pass any more quickly (which feels profoundly unjust!) for two reasons. First, puberty isn't moving any faster, it's just starting sooner. Acne follows that same exact trend line, stretching like the most forgiving elastic band. Second, external factors like stress and low-nutrient diet are more common than ever and they aren't going away anytime soon. Which means that even when puberty is done, zits remain.

Let's spend a moment on the dietary component, since it's both a massive contributor and more controllable than other pimple provokers. When adults think back to the foods of their childhood, most don't flash back to endless supplies of highly processed grab-and-go snack foods but instead remember plates piled with homemade meals or cookies from the cookie jar. Likewise, the ingredient list looked dramatically different: we ate foods containing far less sugar (or alternative sweeteners called something else, but they're really just sugar), without any partially hydrogenated vegetable oils and other modern-day mass production ingredients that rev up inflammation inside individual bodies. Even foods going by the same name a generation or two later, packaged the same way they were packaged in the past—Wonder Bread! Cheerios! Peanut butter!—often contain vastly different ingredients today compared with decades past. All of these nutritional shifts have unquestionably altered the acne landscape because the consequences of dietary choices start when eating begins.

Another notable change over the years: stress. Mental health has never been so fragile, especially among adolescents. Their list of stressors is long and varied—school, home, COVID, social media, climate change, war, guns, and economic instability to start. Because stressors now come around the clock in the form of news alerts and text dings and social media posts, so does the stress response. There's a ton of data here. Some of the most impactful studies have looked at adverse childhood experiences (ACEs), documenting that nearly 50 percent of all kids in the

United States live with at least one ACE. Everything in this broad category—like experiencing violence, abuse, or neglect; witnessing violence in the home or community; and having a family member attempt or die by suicide—increases stress.

A third shift is environmental. In the case of acne, this boils down to the microbiome on the skin. One of our favorite microbiologists, Yug Varma, describes it this way: "The microbiome is like a rainforest: When it's healthy you're healthy. When you get sick it's out of balance. To get healthy you go from imbalance back to balance, and in this case imbalance is caused by *C. acnes*. There's a tiny, teeming metropolis on your skin, and on any given day, a tiny war can break out."

So, the setup for acne—both the hormonal fluctuations underlying it and the sources of inflammation exacerbating it—has clearly shifted. Perhaps that's why once acne arrives, these days it shows up with a vengeance. Not always and not for everyone, but more kids seem to have raging acne than ever before. Unfortunately, there is not a great body of research on this front, even though every pediatrician, family practice doctor, and dermatologist we've talked to (and yes, most parents too!) have all noticed significant increases in acne intensity over time. But it makes good sense that if the factors necessary to cause massive breakouts in the skin have multiplied, then so too will the intensity of those breakouts.

Acne treatments haven't evolved tremendously since we were wiping our skin with 1970s Noxema. Yes, the packaging has changed, but the core ingredient list of the vast majority of products on the market remains the same: benzoyl peroxide, salicylic acid, and straight-up rubbing alcohol. There's been great research into clean and alternative skin products, but the types that work best ultimately rely upon one or more of these key three ingredients thrown in there as well. Generally speaking, after cleansers and toners and topically applied products, acne treatment moves to include antibiotics, sometimes applied on top of the skin (topicals), other times taken by mouth (orals). These, too, haven't evolved much over the decades, down to the same handful of prescription pills or cylinders of liquid clindamycin solution topped with an (instantly grimy) sponge-tip applicator. Acne's last-ditch prescription option, Accutane, is also fairly old-school. The drug has been around since 1982—happy 40th birthday, Accutane!—but it's definitely used more widely and dosed differently these days.

We're particularly intrigued by companies looking at novel acne therapeutics. Some cleanse without stripping surface oils, while others target the skin's microbiome, adding to it instead of wiping out the good organisms with the bad. These innovations, remarkable as they may turn out to be, don't have a ton of data supporting their use quite yet. Still, at last the ball might be moving down the field.

ACNE PREVENTION AND CARE

Acne affects almost every teenager at some point across the span of puberty. Most cases can be managed with some simple strategies that keep the skin clean, pores open, and oil secretion in check. Dermatologists almost always recommend the following strategies to prevent acne or handle mild cases at home:

1. Wash the face with a gentle cleanser twice daily—in the morning after waking up and in the evening, usually before bed. Choose a cleanser without colors or fragrances, and try to avoid products that contain alcohol, which strips the skin of its natural oils. More washing is *not* more helpful! In fact, washing the face more than a couple of times per day can make matters worse because the skin will dry out and the oil glands beneath the surface will kick into gear, secreting extra oil.

2. The first step in treating breakouts is adding a topical cream or ointment. Most doctors recommend starting with a retinoid, which dissolves dead skin cells sitting on the surface of the skin—the same cells that can block pores. Retinoids literally unclog pores, but they should be used only at night, both because they make the skin especially sun-sensitive and because the sun reduces the effectiveness of the medicine. Even if you use a retinoid at night though, it's important to put sunscreen on the face during the day.

3. Some doctors suggest using benzoyl peroxide instead of a retinoid, because benzoyl peroxide is toxic to the bacteria that cause pimples (*C. acnes*). It also helps promote the shedding of dead skin cells, which unblocks pores (are you seeing a theme here?). Most people use benzoyl peroxide once a day to start—doesn't matter if it's morning or night.

4. If you started with a retinoid and saw no improvement after a couple of weeks, switch to benzoyl peroxide. If you started with benzoyl peroxide and saw no improvement after a couple of weeks, switch to a retinoid. Don't be impatient! These treatments take several days—and sometimes weeks—to kick in.

5. If you have tried these topical treatments one at a time and the acne persists, it's time to use both. In this case, use the benzoyl peroxide after washing and drying the face in the morning; use the retinoid after washing and drying the face at night.

6. Don't forget to moisturize! These topical treatments can be drying. In the mornings, moisturize with a product that has sun protection (SPF); in the evenings you can use a product without SPF. And because pimply skin can be particularly sensitive, try to choose moisturizers without colors or fragrances added.

7. For cases of acne that don't get better, or actually get worse, despite these steps, it's time to see a healthcare provider. Some cases of acne require additional treatment with antibiotics or medications like Accutane.

HOW TO TALK ABOUT IT

Acne management is a perfect example of how our desire to get kids through adolescence unscathed—or at least less scathed—can lead to desperate attempts to change their behavior, which nearly guarantee turning an issue into a battleground. Basic face washing twice a day is an important part of making the skin a clean, less inviting breeding ground for acne. Almost all adults know this, but it doesn't mean kids understand (or follow through). Why don't they just wash their faces?!

After some persistent negotiating on our part—or a lot of zits on theirs—and once this routine begins, the skin generally clears for a bit until, out of nowhere, a massive breakout emerges. If acne management were as simple as face washing twice daily, we wouldn't have written this chapter.

Whether you've tried to help a kid by buying any number of over-the-counter or doctor-recommended products, or you've gotten to the next step of taking the time and spending the money on the path to prescription medications, then you know where this is going: the bone-deep frustration that they don't use what you've bought. Why do so many treatments just sit by the sink or in a bedside drawer, never making it into or onto their bodies? Yes, these words tap a nerve in all of us.

Let's pull the lens back a bit, though, to make sense of how (predict-ably) we got here. Adult worries about acne stem from the concern that zit-covered kids will feel terrible about their appearance, which will, in turn, decimate their self-esteem, a fragile adolescent microbiome of its own. Some of us worry that the acne will scar, creating lifelong remind-ers. Others of us had raging acne as teenagers and will do almost any-thing to spare our children this fate.

But we cannot save them, we cannot protect their self-image, and Lord knows we cannot actually wash their faces for them. Here are some things we *can* do.

If they say they don't care about acne

Some kids swear they don't care about the pimples covering their faces or chests or backs, and a few speak the truth. But a large number are say-ing whatever they need to say to make the hounding adult go away. Leave room for the possibility that they feel good about themselves and know that other kids—including most of the kids in their daily lives—live with zits too. If it doesn't bother them, it shouldn't bother you.

Two notes here, though. First, all kids need to learn good hygiene—this is not negotiable and goes well beyond their opinions about acne. Second, some untreated acne will scar, leaving marks for life. These tend to be cases of particularly fulminant acne in bloom all over the face or deep cystic acne, both dramatic versions that require medical attention. Even if a kid swears they don't mind what's happening right now, it's still on us to ensure they know how to take care of their skin and understand the potential long-term consequences of untreated acne.

If they seem ashamed of their skin

Shaming kids into doing what adults want is an oft-used but ineffective strategy. If you're staring at a massive crop of acne on your kid's face after a week of sports practices or daily applications of makeup followed by no face washing, it's understandable that you'd want to say: *If you had only washed your face like I'd told you to, none of this would have happened. Why don't you ever listen to me?* But blaming just makes a kid feel crummy, plus it still doesn't get them to do what you want them to. You have just added yourself to the heap of judgment they carry around all day. Instead, here's a great opportunity to ask them how they feel about their skin. But ask without judgment!

If they express big feelings

It's easy, with many decades of distance from the awkwardness of our own puberty, to minimize how kids might feel. Our lived experience reminds us that it will get easier—the agony will dissipate over time. Except, the *last* thing adults should say to kids is *It will get easier, so get over it.* Because telling them to feel differently about something doesn't make them feel differently, it just makes them feel bad about how they are currently feeling. It also sends a message that their parents are not the people with whom to share these feelings. Besides, for some kids—many, actually—having zits all over *is* a big deal. They live in an image-based culture that makes the pressures we felt in our youth seem trivial. So let their feelings flow.

If they cannot hear it from you

Welcome to the club! We work in this field all day, every day, and we have lost count of the number of times our own kids dismissed our "expert" advice. On the topic of acne, like so many other issues around puberty, other people are often better messengers. There is almost nothing more brutal than realizing that the kids we love most in the world prefer to take advice from literally anyone else on the planet. Hello, stranger on the street handing out flyers: What should I do for the summer? Hey there, hairdresser I just met an hour ago: Should I break up with my boyfriend? Their refusal to listen to our advice is completely normal. It helps to repeat this mantra: *It's developmentally appropriate. It's developmentally appropriate.*

When our kids individuate from us, one of their first moves toward establishing independence is to take zero parental advice about certain things. Skin care is often one of those hot topics about which we can say nothing helpful. This is a hard one for parents to swallow, but here's the best next step: find someone who a kid *will* listen to (about all this puberty stuff, actually)—an older cousin, a former babysitter, a camp counselor, a doctor, a family best friend. Don't try to impose the choice, but suggest some options. Here's one way through the conversation: *You may not want to come to me with questions, and clearly you don't always take my advice (ha ha ha)—who would you choose to go to instead of me if that's what you need?*

Ways to give information

So what *can* we say? Addressing kids' skin can feel like an absolute landmine, but there's still lots of room to be supportive and instructive without turning this issue into a knock-down, drag-out fight or, maybe even worse, a cold war.

Giving information doesn't always have to entail some deep and meaningful mind-meld. It can be simply: *Here's the info, any questions?*

Boom. End of story. In the case of skin care and acne, it might sound like this: *During puberty the skin produces a lot more oil and sweat. To help prevent zits, you have to wash your face twice a day and most definitely after sports or wearing makeup. I'm happy to share more information if you want.*

It also helps to remember that just because every adult on earth lived through puberty, it doesn't mean we're experts on what every adolescent is feeling at any given time. Not even close. It often works better to ask and listen: *I noticed that your skin looks different these days—wondering how it feels? Are there any products you need for your bathroom? I realized we haven't gotten anything new in a while.* (Sidenote here: that easy-breezy tone filled with curiosity in place of accusation can take practice, lots of it.) There are moments when sharing a snippet of your own history makes a big difference, especially when a story becomes painfully hilarious.

And finally, if a kid opens up and shares that acne is making them feel really crappy, validate, validate, validate. *I am so sorry you are feeling this way. It sucks.* These are the words of someone they can trust with their hard feelings. Another option (from the wise Dr. Aliza Pressman): *Do you want me to just listen or do you want me to help solve the problem?* And if they want to know when the acne is going to go away, be honest that you don't know and there's no magic bullet: *Let's see a doctor to figure out what's going on. There might not be a quick fix, though—I just need you to know that.*

FROM PEOPLE JUST OUT THE OTHER SIDE

J.S., she/her, age 20

I don't remember how old I was when it happened, but I have a vivid memory of getting, or rather trying to get rid of, my first pimple. I had a large whitehead appear on my nose, and I remember my dad holding a hot compress against my face to draw it out. When the pimple only seemed to get larger, my dad told me I had a "screamer," which I'm pretty sure sent my moody middle school self into tears. This was the start of a years-long struggle against acne and a face that was constantly broken out.

For years, my bathroom sink was absolutely covered in all types of acne products, and I had no idea how to properly use them, in what order to apply them, or what combinations of products I should be using. Because I was likely using these treatments improperly, my skin continued to worsen, and finally, my mom took me to the dermatologist, who prescribed me a low-dose antibiotic for a month that cleared my skin. Though I was thrilled to finally have less acne, I knew I couldn't be on this medication in the long term. I saw my newly clear skin as a reset button to allow me to really figure out what products work for me and to create a working skin care routine. However, I still had no guidance on what I should be doing, so I asked my mom to take me back to the dermatologist for a consultation and finally learned how to take care of my skin.

Around the time I turned 17, my acne finally started to clear up, and my skin was responding well to new products from my dermatologist. Slowly, I was able to move into a more minimal skin care routine consisting of moisturizer, cleanser, and spot treatments as needed. But just as soon as I thought my struggle with acne was done, a new problem emerged: backne. Especially in the warmer months or after I worked out, I would find my upper back totally broken out. As a dancer, I often had to wear low-cut leotards that only made me more self-conscious of the pimples dotting my back. Even though I'd rather have acne on my back than on my face, I was frustrated by the persistence of my pimples and went back to the dermatologist once again. I was given a strong cleanser to wash my chest and back with in the shower, but even after a couple of weeks of using this, I didn't see any real improvement in my skin. In fact, my skin only got better once fall rolled around and I stopped sweating as much.

Now, at age 20, I still have the occasional pimple, and without fail I always get a cystic pimple on my chin right before getting my period. I still struggle with backne in the summer months, but I've learned that the only thing I can do is to stop caring as much. Even though I only ever had acne on my face and back, I know many of my friends also had, and still have, acne on their necks, chests, and butts too. Acne can affect people in so many different ways and in so many different places on their bodies, and it can be helpful to talk to friends to see what skin care products they've found to be helpful.

If there's someone in your life who struggles with acne, no matter how many or how few pimples they have, here's my advice: even if you are trying to help, try not to point out your teen or tween's acne in an insensitive manner. No doubt your child is aware that they have acne, and they probably aren't too psyched about it. Also, offer a trip to the dermatologist! For me, it was really helpful to have a doctor look at my skin, especially when over-the-counter acne treatments weren't working. My dermatologist helped me look at my skin realistically and understand that improvement may take a long time. And finally, remind your child that their skin won't be broken out forever. Even though acne is a lifelong issue, it typically gets better with time and with learning what cleansers work for you.

CHAPTER 8

Body Odor

The amazing thing about body odor (BO) is that even though it smells slightly different on each person, it's universally recognized. BO is one of those things that makes us all wonder what purpose it could possibly serve beyond reeking? While the answer to that question remains elusive, science-based information helps explain where BO comes from, why it can be a hallmark of a growing and changing body, and how to minimize it . . . if you want, because depending upon cultural norms, the natural smells emanating from the body may be a nonissue.

LET'S START WITH SCIENCE

The science of body odor is a straightforward-meets-cool story that, once learned, completely simplifies a very pungent issue.

Sweat is the body's way of cooling itself down. When we overheat, sweat glands release oily water onto our skin's surface, and as that water evaporates, the body's temperature begins to drop. The hotter we get, the more we tend to sweat. There's a fair amount of individual variation here: some people have more productive sweat glands than others, explaining why two people working out side by side and equally hard may not necessarily drip to the same extent. The content of the sweat—most notably its oil concentration and its volume of metabolic waste products like urea, ammonia, lactic acid, and sodium chloride—varies from person to person too.

There's sweat variation within (or more accurately on) an individual too: some parts of the body sweat more than others. That's because those parts—places like the armpits, feet, and groin—are often covered in tight clothing or get extra sweaty thanks to skin-on-skin contact reducing local airflow. Those same parts also contain particularly high concentrations of apocrine sweat glands. Unlike the more typical eccrine sweat glands, which secrete very watery sweat across most of the body, apocrine glands make sweat teeming with fatty acids, proteins, and byproducts like ammonium and urea. Sweat itself doesn't smell, which is a critical piece of this story. But the proteins in apocrine sweat are particularly delicious for bacteria living on the skin, and when bacteria consume these proteins (yes, they literally eat sweat), they break them down into acids that release a specific and pungent odor. And there it is!

The bacteria living on our skin are central to the origin story of body odor. The microbiome is an ecosystem of bacteria and other organisms living throughout the body, most notably in the gut and on the skin. Many of these organisms are key to day-to-day health, keeping us in balance. Others are simply interlopers using us for the free lodging but not causing any problems. There are some bad actors in the microbiome, but they tend to be few and far between, and most of the time they wreak their havoc not on the skin but rather cause issues when they dive into the bloodstream or organs below.

Another big player in the body odor narrative is the adrenal androgens. These hormones, covered in detail in chapter 6, are produced in the adrenal glands, which sit atop the kidneys. They don't cause sexual maturation the way that testosterone and estrogen do, but they do show up around the same general time and are deeply involved with shifts in the skin's landscape, telling pubic hair to grow and apocrine sweat glands to flow. It's the surge of adrenal androgens sometime during the tween years around the time of puberty—a phenomenon called adrenarche—that's largely to blame for all sorts of adolescent features, from acne outbreaks to new wafts of BO.

Apocrine sweat glands secrete oily, protein-rich sweat, and the bacteria on the skin consume this tasty feast. As those same bacteria release more and more acid by-product, they produce a smell all too familiar to middle school teachers and anyone who drives an end-of-the-day carpool or even just walks into a room where shoes have been kicked off.

The fix, it turns out, is actually as simple as the explanation of the cause. Getting rid of body odor requires one of two things: either less apocrine sweat or less bacterial consumption of that sweat. Antiperspirants reduce sweat load (*anti* is a prefix meaning "against" and *perspire* is a verb meaning "sweat") so that their wearers don't have as much for skin bacteria to consume. (In contrast, deodorants simply remove odors.) Meanwhile, the act of showering or bathing with soap is enough to reduce the number of sweat-eating bacteria on the skin. Fewer bacteria, less BO. The key here is the soap, because it's the soap—not the water—that physically removes the organisms. But be forewarned that fixes like showering and applying antiperspirant last only a day or so (maybe less in a heat wave or at the gym) before the sweat glands reactivate and the bacteria repopulate. This explains why daily showers and deodorant every morning came to be a thing in many, but not all, cultures.

 ## WHAT'S CHANGED OVER THE PAST 20, 30, 40 YEARS

Not much. As mentioned in the chapters about acne and hair, unlike puberty itself, adrenarche hasn't moved noticeably earlier. While estrogen and testosterone are surging at younger ages, not so for the adrenal androgens. Or if they are, the world hasn't taken notice. Teachers' pleas to shower regularly and wear deodorant still begin around fourth or fifth grade.

That said, there's certainly lots more conversation about sweat and smells than ever before. And the good news is, most of this talk is open and informational, not judgy and mocking. Today's tweens and teens seem far better at talking about common-denominator issues than generations past. This doesn't mean that teasing has disappeared, but once a topic is out in the open and framed as something that can happen to anyone, kids tend to rally around each other rather than mock one another.

The fixes have improved too. Products to address smells have transformed dramatically over the past few decades. The soap aisle at the local store is undoubtedly massive compared to when you were a kid, with all sorts of perfumed, colored, organic, natural, solid, and liquid options. Likewise, the deodorant choices can feel endless: some are gendered, others invisible, and many claim to be free of any scary chemicals, even when the ingredient list reads like an unpronounceable, multisyllabic stew. The massive variety of options can complicate the simple goal of figuring out what works, doesn't irritate the skin, and feels safe enough to put onto the body, so much so that a parallel industry has evolved to help consumers do research without feeling completely overwhelmed.

A sidenote about covering up one smell with another, more pungent one: The Axe solution to the body odor problem deserves a special callout because this approach—which leans heavily into covering up natural stink with pungent cologne—has boomed over the past couple of decades. It's the rare adult who hasn't been nearly knocked over by a whiff of Axe on a kid nearby. If fragrance is a kid's thing, then great, go for it. But adults, you owe it to the kids in your life to tell them that body odor caused by bacterial consumption of proteins in sweat does not disappear, no matter how much perfume or cologne is dumped on top. So encourage them to go back to the basics and wash with soap and water before dousing with fragrances.

 **HOW TO TALK ABOUT IT**

Maybe the most common question we hear from adults caring for kids entering puberty is *How do I tell my kid they smell?* (Tied for second are *When is my kid getting her period?* and *How do I get my kid to take his hands out of his pants?*) This question tops the list because pretty much everyone gets body odor, and body odor can appear before other physical changes. Most adults these days recognize that using shame to get kids to practice better hygiene (*Ugh, you smell like rotting garbage*) might solve the short-term stink but isn't a recipe for long-term health in any way. But so often because parents are concerned that their kid is going to be made fun of—maybe even bullied—for having BO, they're desperate to address the situation before a classmate taunts them. Many of us have memories of the kid in our grade who was the target of that kind of mockery; those of us who *were* that target are particularly eager to nip body odor in the bud.

The question remains: How can we bring it up with our kids without making them feel bad? Turning to a kid and saying, *You stink. Put on deodorant,* is probably not the best option—although there might be kids for whom that approach works. Generally speaking, explaining the causes of new smells, oils, and flakes is a great way to encourage kids to make changes in their behavior, particularly around hygiene. Here are some tried-and-true principles for addressing a stinky kid without making them want to crawl under their bed in shame.

Try science

You could try a straight-up scientific approach with a touch of humor, something like *As your body grows and changes, it produces more sweat and oil. Bacteria living on your skin make a yummy feast out of that sweat and oil and then fart it out, creating body odor. The way to cut down on the smell from this process is to wash those sweaty, smelly areas with soap (plain water doesn't work) and use deodorant.*

If you have a kid who is interested in science, they might want even more specifics, and you can read the first part of this chapter together. Kids really appreciate understanding the *why* behind instructions: *Wash your body with soap* turns out to be a less compelling instruction than *Wash your body with soap because the soap molecules grab onto the dirt and allow the water molecules to rinse them away.* Giving kids credit for their intelligence goes a long way toward establishing credibility. It also offers a rationale for why they should do something or follow your rules even when you're not badgering them.

Handling opposition

Some kids are resolutely opposed to showering, washing with soap, or using deodorant no matter what. The adults in their lives can feel like they've tried absolutely everything, but the smell just keeps growing, which can cause them to say and do desperate things, not always this extreme but along these lines: *You're disgusting—no one will be friends with you smelling like that.* Not helpful, and frankly damaging. Despite your wanting to spare them cruelty from their peers, sometimes the advice is best heard when it's doled out in an honest and straightforward way directly from another kid: *Dude, you smell. Use deodorant.* This route usually works far better (and faster!) than any adult intervention. Most kids fall somewhere between the curious scientist and the antiwasher.

Normalize the changes

Change is scary, for everyone. When it comes to the smells of puberty, kids go from having breath that smells like warm milk and armpits scented like fresh-cut grass one day to having breath that stinks like a rotting corpse and armpits reminiscent an NHL locker room the next. That's pretty darn confusing and can make kids avoid any discussion because they're so out of their depth! We make the most impact when we normalize change.

For a 9-year-old kid with body odor you could try this: *You're at an age where your body is changing, and that's totally normal, but it means you're going to look and smell different. It's my job to help you navigate those changes while staying healthy and taking good care of yourself. I am here to help.*

For a 12-year-old kid with body odor, it might sound more like this: *Your body is like a stew of oils, sweat, and smells during puberty, and you need to be on top of managing it all. I know it feels like a lot of responsibility with all the other things I am always telling you to do, but caring for your body is a lifelong job. It gets easier over time.*

For a 15-year-old who stinks, the approach might be a little different: *I know you got through most of puberty without BO, but news alert—you now smell. What can we get you that will help with it and feel good on your skin? Have you borrowed any products from friends that you like?*

Give them a choice

In order to get them to eat their veggies, most of us gave our toddlers a choice: peas or carrots, perhaps. Adolescence isn't all that different. If you want your kid to wear deodorant, give them options instead of presenting them with just one product. Go to the pharmacy together and meander down the long deodorant aisle, or sit on the couch and look online together at various options. Maybe even try a couple together. Laugh about the names of the deodorants, the packaging. Show them brands you've tried, to disastrous effect. Make it low-stakes fun. Also, sometimes when they were babies, they had to try a new food a dozen or more times before they stopped spitting it out. Don't forget that.

Don't assume they know how. Be really specific

We adults have been washing our bodies for decades—trying new products, changing habits, getting to know what works and what doesn't. Kids are total novices here, so they need very specific instructions like *Wash your body with soap* or even *Wash your armpits, penis, feet, then tush with soap.* Don't assume they know anything—remember this is still the kid who poops, doesn't wash their hands, then walks into the kitchen and grabs a handful of tortilla chips. They need detailed, step-by-step instructions, and some need it written down and taped to the bathroom wall. Also, they need to see you wash your hands *every* time you use the bathroom. Modeling works better than words.

Stay in conversation with your kid

We're often so eager to cross things off our long to-do list that we can forget the follow-up with our kids. Turns out, the follow-up might be more important than the initial step of getting them what they need. If deodorant is a brand-new thing, they don't know what's normal and what's not. They have no idea if it's supposed to sting, feel wet, get all over their clothes, or cause rashes. They might not even know how to tell whether it's working! Most people (regardless of age) tend to think they smell absolutely fine, good even—have you ever witnessed your kids happily smell their own farts? Often the only way they figure out they smell is to stuff their nose deep in their own armpit, and they might not mind even then. Follow-up can sound something like *Do you like the smell of your new deodorant? How is your skin feeling? Any itching or soreness? Is it making a difference?*

One final note: not every culture or society has the custom—or luxury—of bathing daily, and many people choose not to use deodorant. Make room for that fact in conversations about hygiene, because kids will eventually emerge into the wider world and encounter people who have different ways of living. It's hard for them to be open-minded and accepting of other cultural norms if we give them the impression that there is only one way to care for the body.

FROM PEOPLE JUST OUT THE OTHER SIDE

A.C., she/her, age 20

One time when I was in late middle school, my dad was driving me somewhere on the weekend to run errands. When we got in the car, he said to me, "I think you don't smell so great." I explained that I hadn't showered after I worked out the day before but was planning on working out again that afternoon, so it didn't make sense to me to shower in the morning just for a day of sitting in the car and running errands. He listened and responded in a way that demonstrated understanding and approval without ever using a judgmental tone or facial expressions. He simply notified me of my BO and agreed with my perspective on it, which made me comfortable with my decision rather than feeling like I did the wrong or unhygienic thing. A lot of times BO isn't unhygienic, but it can be perceived as just that.

In high school I had this really cute blue T-shirt with little flowers on it that hugged my arms and chest so tightly that any bit of sweat showed right through the shirt very clearly. I wore this shirt on a night out anyway because I liked the way it looked, but after noticing pit stains on the car ride to my friends' house I immediately regretted wearing it, but it was too late. I panicked and stuffed napkins we had in the car under the shirt to try to absorb the sweat and get rid of the odor. It was not super effective, but I was scared people at the party would notice the smell and think that I'm not clean. I realized once I got there that no one seemed to notice or care. I was self-conscious about it, but I've come to realize that sweat and body odor are normal and not necessarily indicative of hygiene, so I try my best to embrace inevitable sweat stains and body odor even though they make me feel uncomfortable.

How can adults help kids with body odor? First of all, a lot of parents out there want their kids to use the cleanest ingredients, but this doesn't always work with body odor. We know our parents want what's best for us, but sometimes stronger deodorant is needed to help with BO, and it would be great if they could understand that. Also, adults could try to gently tell their kids that they don't smell great but use a positive attitude or laugh it off while at the same time offering kids solutions for BO and explaining ways to help with it. If your kid doesn't care about BO, then at the end of the day it's important to respect what your child wants. If they're showering but just tend to sweat a lot, support them in being confident in themselves no matter what their decision is. What parents say and model will rub off on the kids even if they seem to be rebelling against what you say in the moment. Children do hear you, even if it seems like they don't!

CHAPTER 9

Growth Spurts, Weight Gain, and Curves

Puberty doesn't have many eagerly anticipated moments. Accidentally wonderful ones? Sure. But for the most part, it's hard to muster excitement for a stage of life characterized by dreaded mood hurricanes that draw their strength from a sea of greasy awkwardness. The one big exception—the feature of puberty that so many seem to look forward to, or at least don't want to ditch as fast as humanly possible—is growth.

 LET'S START WITH SCIENCE

There are lots of different kinds of growth during puberty, and this chapter will cover them all: from height gain (the famous adolescent "growth spurt"), to weight gain, to the emergence of curves. Vertical stretch is one that kids are universally psyched about, and weight gain that translates into muscle mass or butt mass or boobs also ranks up there for many. What about weight gain that adds curves elsewhere or height that's not keeping pace with friends? Well, those also rank but decidedly in the opposite direction. We'll get to these too.

Let's start with height because this is one feature most kids and adults start with as well. *How tall will they be?* gets asked in doctors' offices from the early days. Like, at the six-month checkup. Not kidding.

This stems from a combination of the high value our culture places on stature plus the quantifiable nature of height. Adult height turns out to be surprisingly predictable, which is why so many parents of toddlers ask about it. And while no doctor can say for sure how tall any kid will be 15 or 20 years down the road, there are two ways to best-guess, both of which are fairly reliable.

1. **Calculate mid-parental height:** This math counts on genetics to predict where a kid's ultimate height will land, plus or minus two inches. Note that all measurements are entered in inches, not feet and not centimeters. Also note that the calculations are different for genetic females and genetic males.

    For males: [Genetic mom's height + 5] + Genetic dad's height

    $$\frac{[\text{Genetic mom's height} + 5] + \text{Genetic dad's height}}{2}$$

    For females: [Genetic dad's height − 5] + Genetic mom's height

    $$\frac{[\text{Genetic dad's height} - 5] + \text{Genetic mom's height}}{2}$$

    While this math turns out to be fairly accurate for the majority of people, it doesn't account for the random outlier relatives—maybe your family has a five-foot-tall great-grandpa or a six-foot-tall aunt who doesn't fit seamlessly into the family group photo. Their genes can (and sometimes do) trickle down the family tree, appearing unexpectedly when a kid turns out to be far shorter or taller than anticipated.

2. **Double the height at age two:** That's right, another ultimate height predictor is as simple as doubling a child's measured height at age two. A couple of fairly sizable caveats here, though. First, in case you've never taken note of how a

two-year-old gets measured at the doctor's office, it's not exactly precise. Most two-year-olds are squirmy at best, so good luck to the person tasked with doing this accurately enough that its result can be multiplied by twofold and offer any credible promise. Second, there are no studies to back up this strategy! But lots of hospital-based medical centers still promote this technique on their websites, and pediatricians use it all the time in their offices, citing anecdotal data and adding that the margin of error is four inches (meaning a kid could wind up four inches taller *or* shorter than this math suggests, twice the range for the mid–parental height equation). Most also add that for genetic females, the equation might be more accurate if the height is doubled for the 18-month measurement, resulting in a pretty big difference—a much shorter adult—compared with the measurement taken 6 months later.

It must be said that both of these methods assume that the kid faces no obstacles to reaching their potential. But obstacles are plenty. Malnutrition caused by lack of access to food sources or a chronically unbalanced diet can affect ultimate height. So can serious illness, either acute (like cancer treated aggressively with chemotherapy or radiation) or chronic (like heart or lung disease that diminishes oxygen supply to the rest of the body). Sleep affects height, a topic covered in detail in chapter 10, as do skeletal issues (like severely bowed legs or scoliosis curves in the spine) and vitamin, mineral, and hormone deficiencies (vitamin D, zinc, and thyroid top these lists, respectively). The best guess of how tall a kid will ultimately be does not take into account any of these or a long laundry list of other potential hurdles.

Beyond the math for where a kid's height will ultimately land, there's the eternal question of when. *When will they grow?!* In the first year of life, kids can stretch 10 or more inches. After that, the rate slows to about 4 inches per year through the toddler years, and then ramps down to an average of 2 inches per year for the next 8 or 10 or 12, whenever they hit their pubertal growth spurt. Many features of life during puberty mimic toddlerhood, and growth is no exception; during the famous adolescent growth spurt, height gain returns to its preschool rate. Typically, girls grow 2.5 to 4 inches per year during that growth spurt, a stretch usually lasting 2 years, sometimes 3; boys gain 3 to 4 inches per year for 2, 3, sometimes even 4 years straight. After this rapid acceleration, growth slows radically but doesn't simply stop: most kids will eke out at least another 1 to 2 inches over the next couple of years.

The adolescent growth spurt accounts for about 20 percent of a person's final adult height, which explains why the tweens who hit it earlier look so gargantuan compared with the rest. But its timing is notoriously tricky to predict. Most kids start to accelerate sometime between the start of middle school and the end of high school. How's that for vague? Genetic females tend to shoot up earlier than genetic males, which is why in a photo of sixth-grade kids, a handful of guys and the vast majority of girls tower over everyone else. These gender differences are driven by growth hormone, the primary player here, but also by estrogen, testosterone, and other androgens like androstenedione, all of which further increase growth hormone levels.

Taken together, this helps explain why, on average, adult males tend to wind up taller than adult females. The males start their growth spurts later than the females do, but they're still growing before this acceleration, grabbing a few extra inches slowly but surely the year or two (or three or four) while they're patiently waiting to skyrocket. Plus, their growth spurt lasts longer. The net effect is more cumulative height for people with both an X and a Y chromosome.

A sidenote about *how* kids grow, because gangly teenagers have a certain look that's fairly predictable. Puppy-like middle schoolers in particular can seem to have massive hands and feet compared with still-short midsections (truncated trunks, if you will). That's because they grow in the periphery first, farthest from the center of their bodies; then their arms and legs grow next (*She's all legs!* said every grandmother, everywhere); and then, finally, the rib cage and abdomen stretch out.

Remember, though puberty begins earlier for so many of today's youth compared with their parents and grandparents, there's still a range, with some kids starting sooner (the early bloomers), others much later (the late bloomers). Just because the average start time has moved up doesn't mean there won't be kids racing ahead at the front end and kids straggling at the back. In fact, that's the very definition of a range—it includes the ones at the ends. Growth spurts are highly intertwined with puberty, perhaps the most visible sign for some. So an early bloomer who develops before the other kids may very well grow before they do too, and the late-blooming kid, well, you know where this is going. Here's more detail about how puberty-onset outliers tend to experience added challenges when it comes to height:

> **The earliest-blooming girls** enter their growth spurts before most of the other kids around them. They sprout head and shoulders above their friends at first, and then they largely stop growing because the same estrogen surges triggering their pubertal development eventually tell the growth plates sitting at the ends of each bone to close. Girls are done growing two years after a person has "regular" periods cycling every three to five weeks. Meanwhile, their later-blooming friends gain height slowly but steadily, and by the time they go through their spurts and get their periods, many of these typically timed bloomers and almost all of the late bloomers wind up taller than the very first girls to grow. Of course, genetics and underlying health issues can change all of this, but the trend is clear: later estrogen surges → later growth plate closure → taller adults.
>
> **The earliest-blooming boys** can have the exact same trajectory as the early girls—growing quickly before other guys and stopping sooner too—but not always. It turns out that early-blooming boys can and often do keep

growing for a few years *after* their growth spurt ends
because their growth plates haven't completely fused yet:
they don't have as much estrogen and their androgen
loads are greater, a combination that delays growth plate
closure. This explains why the first girl to get her period
in the grade is often on the shorter end when all is said
and done, but the first guy to be able to jump and touch
the ceiling with his upstretched arm is just as likely as the
next guy to wind up among the taller kids.

Later-blooming girls tend to become taller adults than
the rest for the reasons explained above: they gain height
slowly but steadily before their puberty hormones surge,
so that by the time they enter their growth spurt they are
taller than the early bloomers were—sometimes several
inches taller. And that's even before their growth
accelerates, when—*wham!*—suddenly some are being
recruited to play basketball. Of course, this scenario
requires that they are genetically programmed to be
tall—if their birth parents are both close to five feet,
chances are they will land there, too, even if they're the
very last to go through puberty. It also assumes that their
puberty isn't delayed on account of nutritional deficiencies
or health issues, because those kids don't always gain slow,
steady height in the years leading up to a growth spurt.

Finally, the later-blooming guys. This is a tricky one,
because it's easy to think that they're going to end up
among the tallest of the bunch. But here the data shows
that many of them actually slow their prepubertal growth
speed, so much so that they gain almost no height in
those years when all of their friends are imitating weeds.
This can make their late-blooming status feel even more

vulnerable for them because late-blooming tween and even teen guys possess no adult features—no increased muscle mass, no voice drop, no broad shoulders—to match their friends. To add insult to injury, they're also not budging an inch. Literally. By the time many of these boys hit their growth spurt, they've fallen fairly far behind on height, enough so that even picking up three or four inches for three or four years straight, they find themselves in the shorter half of the group.

All right, with height explained, we're moving on to weight. And let's start here: kids gain weight. They *should* gain weight. Even through the teen years—especially through the teen years—weight gain to some degree is healthy. This is a tough one for many, especially when the gain comes before the growth. We'll get to that in a moment.

The typical person gains about five pounds for every inch of height. There's a range of normal, of course, with four to seven pounds per inch considered medically healthy. That said, if a person is significantly underweight, they may need to gain more as they grow; if they're carrying extra weight for their height, perhaps their body won't—or shouldn't—gain quite that much, or they might not gain any at all for a couple of inches. The specifics about what's best for any individual are left to that family and the doctor caring for them.

Now for the order of operations: some kids gain height before they gain weight, while others reverse the order, gaining weight before growing taller. The ones who stretch like long string beans, sprouting well before their bodies add extra pounds, tend to be thin, but some are so skinny they report feeling self-conscious about it. In the 1980s thin was in, but now (and even then) a physique of bony arms and legs extending from a spindly frame sends some kids deep into their closets looking for bigger, baggier clothes to cover up. Then there are the ones whose growth comes in the opposite order, who pack on pounds through the tween and teen years, watching as their waists expand, their thighs fill out, their butts or cheeks or upper arms round, sometimes all three. Many of these kids notice their weight gain, and when we ask them (very gently) how they feel, it's no surprise that many don't like it—though new curvy body ideals have shifted this to some degree.

No matter the order of what comes first, some kids who gain weight will "stretch out" once the growth spurt kicks in. Others won't, instead carrying their new curves along with them as they grow. And for those who grow first, some will "fill out" while others remain long and lean. It can be extremely difficult to predict who is simply gaining before growing and who is taking on a new shape for life, especially when the shift is nascent and the growth spurt is nowhere near done—or maybe hasn't even started. In an attempt to make sense of all of this, these are the indicators that the body is doing what it should be doing:

- If a kid is gaining between four and seven pounds for each inch of growth, even if the weight distribution looks new or different, the total amount of weight gain is expected.

- If a kid is gaining more than seven pounds but was underweight to begin with (per your healthcare provider), the difference will be noticeable and, in this scenario, likely a very good thing.

- If eating habits haven't changed and if the diet is well balanced and well portioned but there's noticeable weight gain over several months, it may very well be that the body is holding on to these pounds in anticipation of significant growth. Only time (and those infamous height and weight growth charts) will tell.

At some points along this road, there may be cause for a conversation with your doctor. Notice, though, that we didn't say concern. Weight is such a charged issue—it sits at the top of the list of things that adults worry about because it carries with it very real health and self-esteem implications. Beyond this, many adults cannot separate their own feelings from their child's experience. While this is fully understandable, it doesn't help to introduce tension around the topic. In fact, everyone knows the slippery slope parents and kids can go down when weight or food suddenly takes center stage. But ignoring these issues also has its risks because the more entrenched a habit, the harder the pivot. Pay attention to the circumstances, looking for these flags—if you see any of these, a conversation with a nutritionist or healthcare provider is a good idea:

- The diet has changed, becoming noticeably less nutritious or packed with lots of non-nutrient-dense foods (some people call it "junk food").

- There seems to be a lot of eating outside of meals, especially in moments of sadness or boredom.

- There's evidence of sneaking food: wrappers found in random drawers, backpacks, or bedroom trash cans; food missing from the pantry, fridge, or freezer.

- Quantities have increased dramatically, maybe with more food being consumed at each meal or more snacks in between meals. (Major note here: growing kids are hungry all the time, so identifying this flag is tricky.)

- Weight gain has outstripped height gain for more than a year or two.

These physical and behavioral shifts suggest that perhaps there are other drivers at play, that maybe the weight is more than just pubescent growth-related gain. Or maybe the kids—perhaps the entire family—could benefit from some good nutrition education.

Some kids actually lose weight during puberty, or they hold their weight steady, which combined with growing taller is the physiological equivalent to losing. We get deep into this topic in chapter 14, but it bears mentioning here as well. Just as with weight gain, weight loss isn't necessarily cause for panic. But you should reach out to your doctor if you notice any of the following:

- The diet has changed, becoming increasingly restrictive— this can include adoption of new eating philosophies (like vegetarianism or veganism) or cutting out of entire categories of foods (like carbohydrates).

- Hydration with water becomes excessive, sometimes in an attempt to fill up before meals.

- Complaints emerge around the foods that are available in the house, sometimes with calls for low-calorie options, other times with requests for no more purchases of tempting treats.

- Consumption quantity decreases, with less food being put on the plate or the food being pushed around but not eaten; full lunch bags might return home at the end of the day.

- Clothes are becoming baggy, either because of visible weight loss or because of a choice to put on bigger clothing in an effort to hide weight loss.

- Energy is noticeably low, and mood is either flat (showing less emotion than usual) or swinging wildly.

The data is quite clear that except in specific situations, weight loss is never the goal for a growing kid. Some growing tweens or teens carrying extra weight benefit from slowing or halting their rate of gain. But it's the rare case when putting a growing child on a weight-loss program is ever appropriate.

Here's where things can get even more charged: patterns of weight change are notorious sources of stress within families, and the kids who are living in these shifting bodies often don't like what's happening to them. Once adults jump into the fray with suggestions, suddenly kids can feel ashamed, unattractive, or downright judged. Much more in the section on how to talk about all of this, but it also belongs here because it's science too. Why kids gain weight, how much they should be gaining when they grow, and how they feel about their bodies when they gain too much or too little all affect their ultimate physical and mental health.

We haven't mentioned gender as it relates to weight gain because kids of all genders can (and do) put on pounds. There is, though, a distinct gendering to the distribution of weight. A pubertal body with more testosterone than estrogen (genetic male) will skew toward lean muscle mass over fat deposition; one with more estrogen than testosterone (genetic female) will do the opposite. This is why genetic females are expected to have higher average body fat composition than genetic males. From an evolutionary perspective, these innate differences make sense: a genetic female growing and carrying a fetus needs to have enough energy to accomplish that, energy that can be accessed from fat stores. Chromosomally XX bodies are also generally programmed to develop wider hips and pelvises in order to one day accommodate a baby passing through the birth canal; likewise, they grow breasts (made largely of fat tissue) to feed that potential future offspring. Meanwhile, the classic hunter-gatherer male benefited from more lean muscle mass to hunt food and to run when the intended source of protein chased him down. These days, females still need these energy sources to sustain pregnancy, but males don't typically face the ire of a bison at the grocery store.

**WHAT'S CHANGED OVER THE PAST
20, 30, 40 YEARS**

Across the world, in every industrialized nation, the average person carries more weight than a generation or two ago. This is true for adults, teens, tweens, even young kids. Meanwhile, average heights have not changed.

The medical community refers to this as the obesity epidemic. The word *obesity* means a person's body mass index (BMI) sits above a certain threshold. The BMI itself has become a controversial index—not everyone agrees that its math should be the basis for a standard of health. And, to make matters more confusing, the absolute numbers on the BMI scale mean different things at different ages. Toddlers, for instance, should have higher BMIs than adults. Organizations supporting the body positive movement take issue with the terminology because research shows that labeling someone as obese can do tremendous psychological and emotional harm, on par with the potential physical repercussions of carrying extra weight. Meanwhile, medical associations like the American Academy of Pediatrics have published recommendations addressing excess weight intended to improve physical health but have received harsh criticism for offering extreme solutions to young kids. Beyond actual numbers on a scale, one of the biggest changes over the past couple of generations is a semantic one, with a growing chasm between the different camps. It's hard to imagine consensus will be reached anytime soon.

What follows is the most recent data that invokes medical terminology, the language used by doctors and scientists but not necessarily embraced by all. Obesity rates in kids and teens have gone from 4 percent in the 1970s to over 20 percent today. More than one in every five kids is obese, a shocking statistic until you consider that more than twice as many (42 percent) of all adults in the United States fit that description. And these are just obese adults; another 31 percent of the adult population is overweight (defined as an elevated BMI, but not as high as with obesity). This means that close to 75 percent of the adults in this country carry more weight than is recommended by medical professionals— worldwide the figure is 39 percent. All of this is to say that when adults grow concerned about a kid's weight gain, it's not without reason . . . and it's not only the kids.

Once a person of any age carries excess weight, their hormonal balance shifts. We covered this in chapters 3 and 6, but here's a brief reminder: Excess fat tissue results in higher levels of circulating sex hormones because of peripheral conversion. In bodies that haven't entered puberty yet, these hormonal shifts and surges are thought to play a role in accelerating puberty's start, either by directly telling breast tissue to grow or by stimulating the brain's hypothalamus to begin releasing GnRH, kicking off puberty's feedback loops. The data looks a bit mixed here, with some studies pointing the finger at higher androgen levels tipping kids into puberty rather than (or in addition to) estrogens. But either way, we know that excess body weight affects the timing of puberty in all genders.

Adjacent to conversations about excess weight: Many kids (and adults) who don't want to become an overweight statistic work hard— sometimes too hard—to keep their weight low. We have dedicated a whole chapter to body image and eating disorders (chapter 14) because this is a massive player in the field of puberty. But it should be said here that our image-dominated culture has exacerbated these issues over the past several decades. Social media has fanned those flames, not only idealizing body types for all genders but also offering up endless solutions to achieve them, an overwhelming rabbit hole of information. One dramatic example is pro-ana content, which promotes behaviors associated with the eating disorder anorexia nervosa. A subset of people following dangerous online trends can get labeled as healthy or aspirational until it becomes clear they are actually ill.

Another big change in the opposite direction is access to plastic surgery and particularly the enhancement of curves. Cosmetic procedures have become standard worldwide. Plenty of arguments exist in favor of injections, lifts, and full-blown surgeries that can profoundly change a body and improve self-esteem. But beauty goals become especially dubious when Brazilian butt lifts define a new ideal—a shape, by the way, that defies written description, so if you've never seen one, you ought to just go look it up right now. Implants from head to toe make dramatic curves more achievable, but never naturally. The Kardashians single-handedly catapulted this trend, but to their credit, over the months that we have been writing this book they have been very publicly removing many of their implants. Perhaps as their own kids push up against the lower limits of puberty, they have started to see the impact of surgery-dependent body goals on young kids themselves starting to transform.

While male body image ideals have always existed, these days they are far more publicly recognized. We've come a long way in recognizing that boys feel many of the same pressures girls feel—the six-pack-abs standard can be as soul-crushing for males as the teeny-waist standard is for females. But, our culture hasn't done much yet to ease the pressure on boys. In fact, quite the opposite: they too see plastic surgery as a solution. They lean into other strategies to bulk up as well, like consuming protein powders, herbal supplements, and other additives promising to add muscle mass, with little or no data to back up their claims. The market for—and marketing of—these products has ballooned over the past few decades, as the quest for largeness earned a new name: bigorexia.

Beyond male and female bodies, one final tectonic shift has been the recognition of how trans and gender-questioning kids feel while sitting at the intersection of growth spurts, weight gain, and the appearance of curves. We get deep into the topic in chapter 19 but would be remiss if we didn't nod to it here because the issues covered in this chapter represent some of the most obvious outward manifestations of gender expression. For kids considering or taking hormone blockers, note that when these medications tend to slow growth plate closure, they result in continued height gain. Depending upon the gender in question, this can have its own complicated implications as a kid continues to grow and grow and grow.

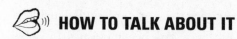 **HOW TO TALK ABOUT IT**

Tweens and teens could make a profession out of comparing themselves to other people. As they grow and change, they also closely monitor the transformation of others around them, determining minute by minute where they fit on the spectrum they consider "normal." This routine is exhausting for both kids and the adults around them.

Even if we repeatedly remind kids that there is no *one* normal but rather a broad range of possibilities, most don't buy it, instead carrying on with their constant comparisons. Which is fair when considering that the word *normal* loses all credibility during the adolescent years (as it should!) when everyone seems to take on a different size, shape, weight, and build and they're all supposed to be okay with where they are at. This is a tall ask, no pun intended.

In a middle school classroom, the tallest kid might tower 18 inches above the shortest, or the heaviest kid might have 40 pounds on the lightest; full-breasted kids wearing adult bras sit next to flat-chested ones; kids with fully defined biceps play at recess with kids whose arms have no discernible musculature. It is completely reasonable for every kid in that class to wonder why: *Why am I so tall? Why am I so short? Why am I the only one with breasts? Why am I so skinny? Why do I weigh more than everyone?*

So when we talk to kids about where they fit into the *Star Wars* bar of puberty, it helps to be aware of the internal monologue coursing through their minds. No kid, not a single one, sits in their bedroom at night thinking, *My body is just right. I am developing exactly how I am supposed to, and I look exactly how I want.* This is why, even if we adults look at a kid and think, *Whew, we're all good here—everything is happening right as it should!*, chances are extremely high that the kid is not riding on the same wavelength. They see themselves as out-of-sync or imperfect in one way or another.

The most impactful thing we can do is to normalize that there is nothing standard about growing up. Frankly, we need to throw out the word *normal* altogether and define what's happening in all-inclusive, vague, but realistically broad terms. We're taking suggestions for what the word to replace *normal* could be. In the meantime, here are some ways to both show and tell kids that there's a huge range of what is—wait for it—normal.

Acknowledge rather than dismiss

It's tempting to dismiss kids' worries as we try to reassure. The trick with reacting to concerns about their lengthening, widening, thickening, or thinning bodies is to make kids feel heard and seen while keeping the temperature low on the conversation. If they come in hot, shouting things like *I'm going to be short forever . . . My hips are so wide . . . My shoulders are too narrow . . .* do your very best not to react at their level of intensity. Instead, listen, nod, *mm-hmm* them. Which is no easy feat and, let's be honest, will not help kids feel any less dissatisfied with the place they occupy in the panorama of puberty. But at least it will remind them that they can lean on you when they need to let it all out.

Keep your mouth shut. Yup, shut.

If you're looking at your kid thinking, *They're going to be so short . . . Their stomach has rolls . . . Their arms are so skinny . . .* it is your job to zip your mouth closed until you can avoid saying anything about your kid's body. This is not easy! It seems nearly impossible to stop from making side remarks when there's real concern about growth or lack thereof. But resist the urge, because no matter how casual you think those comments are, kids hear and hold on to everything.

And along the same lines, do not disparage your own weight gain or body shape in front of your kids. This creates a family culture valuing how bodies look, rather than what bodies do or how they feel. Kids have a hard time believing "it's all normal and everyone is different" when they hear rounds of self-criticism from you. Sometimes the best approach is to follow the "no body talk" rule: don't talk about how people's bodies look, including height and weight. Find other, less third-rail topics, to comment on. More on this in chapter 14.

Address timing when it's early

Someone always has to go first. On the planet of puberty, these are the early bloomers. Some tower over friends; others develop breasts while everyone else stays flat. Going first—going it alone—is deeply challenging. But a few reminders:

- Continue to treat kids the age they are, not the age they look, even as they grow taller and heavier, curvier and hairier. We can still cuddle with them and play silly games with them— they're not adults, not even close, even if they smell and look as if they are.

- Become their empathic sounding board when they need to talk about what it feels like to go first, to have people treat them as older and place unfair expectations on them.

- Remind other people who make comments about your kid's changing body that you won't tolerate it. And keep reminding them if need be.

- If you're worried that your kid is developing *too* early, check with your doctor. The term *precocious puberty* describes pubertal changes that happen far enough outside of the normal window to require a medical evaluation. Anytime there's a worry about any of this, reach out to someone trustworthy and knowledgeable for help. At the very least, they can reassure you everything is fine.

Address timing when it's late

Being last in line feels hard too. The late bloomers on the caboose of puberty ride at the back, watching everyone else get bigger while they wait their turn. Some would say these kids have it the hardest because it can feel like the train has left the station without them.

- Worried that nothing's changing physically? Check in with a doctor before reflexively telling a kid it's all fine. This helps them feel heard. It also reassures you that all is happening as it should.

- While they are in the puberty waiting room, they're likely experiencing friendship shifts and changing athletic realities. This is a great time to help them diversify their interests and activities to include things that don't require a body already in puberty. Art, cooking, improv, martial arts—lots of new and fairly cool options present themselves when people go poking around for them.

- If friends have stepped up their clothing style to fit a taller or curvier body, help your teen shift their style in a way that works for them too, honoring the fact that they may be physically smaller but they're socially and emotionally in step with their pals.

- Never guess a kid's age—always ask. Between today's much earlier puberty and the perennial late bloomers, two kids the same age can look like they're 10 years apart. Playing the guessing game will undoubtedly make at least one of them feel crappy, so don't do it. Just ask.

Puberty can look different even under the same roof

People develop along different time lines, even in the same house, even with lots of genetic overlap. This can result in sibling comparisons, especially during puberty. One might gain more weight and less height while the other grows long and lean. Or sometimes a younger sibling develops first, catapulting past the older one. Let the comparison Olympics begin, with participation from every grandparent, aunt, uncle, and family friend. *Oh my God, you've grown so tall! Oh dear, you've gotten so big! I have a good diet for you to try! We need to put some meat on those bones. Wait, which one of you is older?*

- Instead of watching this play out, step in and nip those comments in the bud, especially the thoughtless ones that can stick around for a lifetime, and not in a good way. Be the advocate here.

- Normalize the situation. If you're noticing tension brewing, don't bury it. Help everyone acknowledge what it feels like to be living in the bodies they inhabit. You can laugh together, and inevitably someone (or everyone) will cry. But then it's out there, a perfect opportunity for kids to articulate feelings, develop empathy, and learn from a sibling that the grass isn't always greener.

Remember that weight gain happens before, during, and after puberty, or not

We live in a culture obsessed with dieting and fitness on the one hand and facing an obesity epidemic on the other. The topic of weight is tough stuff. It is common for some kids to gain a noticeable amount of weight just before puberty—this phenomenon earning the questionable nickname "prepuberty pudge." We're not fans of that phrase, or another aphorism on adolescent bodies, that kids "grow out before they grow up."

The word choice leaves lots of room for improvement because it doesn't apply to so many. Some ways to handle kids' (and adults') reactions to body transformation include the following.

- Steer clear of puberty platitudes: they may or may not turn out to be true, and they don't reassure kids anyhow. Plus, they're often tone-deaf.

- Instead, as dissatisfying as it might feel to them at the time, simply tell kids the truth: bodies grow on different time lines—they start when they're ready, and they land where they're going to land. *Just like people have different personalities, they also have different body shapes.* Your kid might roll their eyes or huff away in exasperation, but at least you're not setting up unfair expectations about their body.

- Always remember that you have no clue how they are going to look when they finish puberty. You may think you have a clear sense of height or build, but trust us when we say that bodies develop far less predictably than most people think.

- A healthy diet, reasonable portion size, and regular exercise all help to maintain healthy body weight. However, all of these things can become sources of stress or obsession too. Keep a close eye on the kids in your life, and get help quickly if you start to see any red flags. Much more about this in chapter 14.

- As we all know, weight fluctuates throughout a person's life. The end of puberty isn't a destination, it's a milestone.

Watching kids grow taller, gain weight, and acquire curves can be equal parts mesmerizing, thrilling, and uncomfortable—for us and for them. And because we all went through similar transformations, we often can't help but project our own growth experiences on them, the good, the bad, and the awkward. Moving away from *How tall are you? How much do you weigh?* toward topics like *How does your body feel this week? What are you noticing?* helps kids learn to listen to their bodies and take care of themselves as they change. Ultimately, we help them more by shifting the conversations away from quantifiable topics like height and weight, toward qualitative ones like body knowledge and emotional insight.

FROM PEOPLE JUST OUT THE OTHER SIDE

R.F., he/him, age 17

I am now a pretty normal height, weight, and size, but when I was 12, I was a lot taller and bigger than everyone else my age. It was never a bad thing, but I wouldn't say it was fun either. It was awesome being able to get rebounds, block spikes, and dunk on higher basketball hoops, but what nobody ever thinks is about is the awkwardness of hitting puberty before everyone else.

The leg hair, voice cracks, and height difference between me and everyone else my age made hitting puberty early a little painful for me. But the most painful thing was the bad coordination that came from a quick growth spurt. I was never bad at sports, but my newfound height made sure I wasn't good enough to be the best at basketball or soccer. My kicks were too hard when I didn't want them to be, and my shots hit the backboard relentlessly.

One specific thing I did notice a lot is how differently I was treated compared to others my age. I looked older than a middle schooler, so I was treated as older than a middle schooler. This did not help or hurt me, but I think it had more of an effect on the other kids who were treated like children while I was not. My looking the oldest did not make me act the oldest, but it made me feel like I had to act the oldest.

Hitting puberty early didn't change too much in my life, but it did feel like a big deal in the moment. If someone had told me that everyone was going to get where I was at some point soon, and that it may even be a gift to be done with puberty before everybody else, I would have laughed but also felt reassured. And I think that is right: it may not have been the easiest time to live through, but I got through it before anyone else. And even though it is also tough for people in the opposite situation, it is good to know that everyone catches up.

R.E., she/her, age 21

When growing up, I was smaller than everyone else around me. I was told children's clothing sizes correspond to age, so why did my clothes say 6 to 7 when I was 12 years old? Why were my friends wearing clothes from the women's section, yet I still had to go to the teen section when we were in high school? I was told that I was short because of my genetics and that I needed to eat more to make sure that my low weight didn't become unhealthy. My doctor told me that I was a late bloomer. I was constantly being told what was "normal" for my age and that I wasn't hitting those marks but that I shouldn't be concerned and that it would happen for me at a later time.

Then, late in high school, the doctor said I had my growth spurt and gained more weight than I ever had. The nurse and doctor would not stop talking about how I gained so much weight and the ways in which my body was developing. If I was small and late, why did my body decide to change now? I felt embarrassed and irrationally thought I did something to cause these changes. I had always been labeled as the small girl, the late bloomer, the tiny one—there was so much attention being paid to my physical appearance, and once these changes were brought to my attention, I feared it would draw even more attention from those around me. Because I was experiencing this later than my peers, I felt like I was in the spotlight and that I had to go through it alone.

I wish I could tell my younger self that I had nothing to be ashamed of. Puberty can feel awkward, and body changes are uncomfortable. Everyone goes through it, just at their own pace and their own timing. Kids just need to know they will get through it and the changes are normal!

CHAPTER 10

Sleep

It's a funny thing when a biological necessity of life is treated like a luxury, but that's often our relationship with sleep. As a result, everyone seems to have an opinion about it: the amount that they're *supposed* to get, the amount they *really need,* ideal mattress specs, pillow type, how dark the room should be, open door, closed door, and on and on. People take sleep very personally. That's because we spend about a third of our lives doing it—or at least we're supposed to. Sleep is something we need and crave, and if we defy it for long enough, our bodies revolt and demand it. But its quantity is not binary because people can get a wide range of hours resulting in a restfulness spectrum. It *is* binary, though, in the sense that deep, long sleep feels great, plus it's good for you, while fitful or too little sleep is awful on both fronts.

 LET'S START WITH SCIENCE

The primacy of sleep has led to a burgeoning field of science examining ideal quantities. Here's what researchers have proven repeatedly: depending upon age, there's a range of sleep each of us should be getting in a 24-hour cycle breaks that looks like the following.

> Newborns and babies: 14–16 hours
> Toddlers: 12–14 hours
> Elementary schoolers: 10–12 hours
> Middle and high schoolers: 8–10 hours
> Adults: 7–10 hours, depending upon who you ask

Newborns, babies, and toddlers are generally very good at getting the sleep they need because they demand it: when they aren't put to bed, they scream and cry. Sometimes new parents don't recognize this cue for what it is, but when a baby yells at you, rubs their eyes, refuses to eat, and fights every other effort at distraction or consolation, chances are they're tired. Not always, but almost always.

It's as we get older that we begin to deny our need to sleep. Sometimes there's too much to do and we feel compelled to stay up; other times, the fun stuff is only getting started when it's time to go to bed. Because life—especially school and work life—tends to be set to a fairly rigid clock starting relatively early in the morning, if you want to achieve the sleep you need, something's got to give. Otherwise, suffer the consequences.

In the dormant hours of life that are often labeled as "doing nothing," the body actually accomplishes a great deal, but this tends to be underappreciated because we're (literally and figuratively) not conscious of what's going on deep inside. For any of us who need to be convinced about the value of sleep, it helps to know what sleep actually does for the body. This list is so long that, in its most detailed form, it can feel overwhelming: an endless laundry list never helps sell lifestyle interventions. To simplify, below are four of the most significant biological impacts of sleep that seem to matter the most to tweens, teens, and twenty-somethings. Tell them about these four things—or invite them to read this chapter—and they're more likely to go to bed a little bit earlier.

1. **Memories are stored during sleep:** While we sleep, our brains sort through the events and information of the day, deciding what to hold on to and what to toss. Some data gets stored in easily accessible memory banks; some gets tucked away into the deep recesses of long-term memory; and some gets wiped altogether. This is why pulling an all-nighter before a test is less effective than just going to bed: late-night information cramming while depriving yourself of the sleep needed to integrate that information into memory makes that same information harder to retrieve the next day.

2. **Sleep resets mood:** Everyone has lived this, but it's important to label it, especially for kids with other drivers of mood swings at play. After a particularly short or bad night's sleep, some people feel edgy, others whiny, and others silent. Some are incredibly resilient, able to spring back, but even these people will report not feeling themselves or not on their game. We've all been there.

3. **Sleep affects metabolism:** There has long been an association between extra body weight and shorter or poorer quality of sleep. Historically, late-night snacking was blamed—people who were up must have been eating. While this might be true for some, it turns out not to be the reason why most people carry more weight when they undersleep. Rather, this phenomenon is caused by two hormones, leptin (a hormone made in fat cells that signals satiety or fullness) and ghrelin (a peptide made by the

stomach that stimulates the feeling of hunger). Leptin and ghrelin operate like two pals on a seesaw.

During waking hours, leptin drops and ghrelin rises; during sleep, balance is restored as leptin levels rise and ghrelin levels fall. When you don't get enough sleep, leptin doesn't rise high enough and ghrelin doesn't fall low enough, so the next day the body feels hungrier than at baseline. This is how getting adequate sleep directly affects our feelings of hunger and satiety.

These hormones work at the cellular level too, affecting the way individual cells use energy. Leptin increases energy expenditure, essentially allowing a person to use the calories derived from recently eaten food, while ghrelin does the opposite, decreasing energy expenditure in order to store away food calories for use another day. So with enough sleep, leptin is high and ghrelin is low, and food energy is spent freely on all of the activities of the day. You feel great; you have "lots of energy." But with too little sleep, leptin isn't as high and ghrelin isn't as low, signaling to the body to sock away energy in the form of fat. Save it for a rainy day, and don't trust this body to take good care of itself, to be well rested *or* well fed. An unrested body takes steps to pack away future fuel stores and conserves energy but leaves you feeling exhausted.

4. **You grow when you sleep!** Perhaps the number one motivator to get kids into bed earlier is the fact that they grow when they sleep. Growth hormone comes from the pituitary gland, the very same gland responsible for LH and FSH. Fun fact: despite its name, growth hormone plays a bunch of roles throughout the body, many of which have nothing to do with growing, but instead affects

everything from heart function to glucose balance to bone mineralization.

Sleep triggers a specific pulse-like pattern of growth hormone release. Growth happens when there is a minimum baseline amount of growth hormone in the body and then more of the hormone surges in bursts, with concentrations getting high enough to tell the long bones to grow. (Important sidenote: the growth plates must also be open—if they are closed, then no lengthening can happen.) Growth hormone surges occur during sleep, which is why a parent can—and should—explain to their kids that they grow when they sleep. Not at night. Not when they lie down. *When they are asleep.*

No explaination of the biology of sleep is complete without mentioning melatonin, the hormone produced in the pineal gland, deep within the brain. As the surrounding world grows darker, the pineal gland secretes melatonin, cueing the body that it will soon be time for sleep. Light does the opposite, inhibiting the release of melatonin. These feedback loops form the basis of our circadian rhythms and sleep/wake cycles.

Melatonin does not work like a switch, but more like a dimmer: it can take a couple of hours of rising melatonin levels before the body feels sleepy. For some people though, physiological winding down is key to being able to fall asleep, which can be a problem in modern life with its plugged-in, artificially lit conveniences which are direct rivals to melatonin secretion. Being in a bright space tells the brain to stay awake and alert, even if it's pitch-black outside. Add to this all sorts of other stimulants—from music to TV to caffeine to sugar—and melatonin suddenly has lots of competition. Researchers have taken a particular interest in the impact of screens on melatonin secretion, especially as devices have become more portable and more ubiquitous. The blue light emitted from phones, iPads, and laptop screens has been associated with a reduction in melatonin secretion, which is why screens may keep some brains awake for longer. It turns out adjusting the light to yellow ("night mode") minimizes the interference, allowing for more typical circadian rhythms. It's also important to point out that no matter the color of the light emanating from the screen, many people stay up later because of the content itself: texting with friends, watching videos, flicking through social media posts, or doomscrolling. All of this contributes to the blame heaped on devices, and with their multiple obstructions to the onset of sleep for both kids and adults, it's well deserved.

One more note about melatonin secretion that's specific to teenagers: as kids progress through the teen years, their pineal gland releases melatonin increasingly later in the night, explaining why many of them complain about not being able to fall asleep even when they get themselves into bed at a reasonable hour. While it's absolutely true that their chemical trigger to wind down may be delayed by an hour or two, they can train their pineal gland to get into their desired rhythm. So a teenager who gets in bed most nights around midnight but decides to go to bed one night at 10 P.M. might not be able to fall asleep very easily, but if that same kid brushes their teeth and gets into PJs and turns down the lights around 10 P.M. each night, eventually the melatonin release will catch up with this schedule.

Sleep is important, and not getting enough can be problematic. Emerging new data ties insufficient sleep to physical shifts in brain structure, affecting attention and inhibition control. This seems to be especially true for grade school kids who don't hit a threshold of nine hours per night. Studies show that as these sleep-deprived kids get older, they face higher rates of depression, anxiety, and impulsive behavior, as well as challenges with problem-solving and decision-making. No doubt, between the writing of this book and your consumption of it, there will be more data supporting the virtues of high-quality, long-lasting z's, what wonky researchers and pediatricians like to call "sleep hygiene"— tuck that snazzy term away.

WHAT'S CHANGED OVER THE PAST 20, 30, 40 YEARS

Over the past several decades, a deep appreciation has evolved for the importance of sleep. Research dates back to the 1700s but took a giant leap forward in the 1950s with the identification of rapid eye movement (REM) sleep. Up until this point, much of the study of sleep had revolved around understanding dreams, but toward the end of the twentieth century, many researchers shifted focus and started to explore sleep disorders like narcolepsy, sleep apnea, and insomnia, all of which has led to a newly robust understanding of the biological implications of sleep.

Clarity has also emerged around the idea of circadian rhythms. When we were growing up, the term *body clock* hit its stride. The idea was that the entire body was synced into some sort of 24-hour rhythm, which made good logical sense. Now, though, researchers have documented individual clocks for each organ in the body. Some cycle every 24 hours, but for others it's 23 or 25, and some even shift with the season or the sun. Sleep in general and melatonin in particular are central to keeping the body's clocks in sync.

The biggest change, though—bigger, even, than understanding sleep's benefits—is that sleep has become coveted . . . at least by the older set. While almost every kid remembers being told over and over about the virtues of a good night's sleep, it has taken until the twenty-first century for this concept to catch on socially. Sleeping has attained cool status: Workplaces recognize the need for shorter workweeks and incentives to take breaks. Likewise, many schools are rolling back start times in an attempt to let kids sleep later into the morning. Some states, like California, have folded later school start times into law. Ultimately, it's a lot easier for a parent to convince a kid to get into bed when the rest of the world normalizes and even celebrates that act.

HOW TO TALK ABOUT IT

From day one, sleep can be a battleground, starting with desperately try-ing to get a newborn to sleep, then coaxing a toddler into bed, which feels like nothing compared to negotiating with a grade schooler about bedtime or doing battle with a teenager about staying up late for work and play. Each age has its developmental and situational reasons, but the adolescent years seem to embody a particularly gnarly tangle of sleep issues: access to social media, increased socializing (online and in per-son), heavier academic pressures, and changing circadian rhythms. Not to mention, adults lose their power to simply tell kids to go to bed when those kids are now often the ones tucking in the adults.

We don't need any more data to prove the importance of sleep—there's no study out there saying that sleep is unimportant and should be reclassified as low priority—so the question becomes: How do we com-municate the importance of sleep in a way kids can hear? How can we convince them to go to sleep when every bone in their bodies is condi-tioned to push against our rules and advice?

Address one thing they really care about: growing

Most adolescents become intensely focused on how tall they're going to be. Not to gender the issue, but it's a particular focus among boys. Some of that stems from the very real societal value placed on a man's height, with the absolute goal varying from place to place and family to family. You can't promise a kid that sleeping a certain number of hours each night will guarantee a precise stature, particularly if his parents hover several inches below the dream altitude. But you can tell kids—and this is the truth, not parenting BS—that getting enough sleep will help them grow as tall as their genetics will allow. This doesn't have to be a long lecture, and in fact it's better if it's not. Just keep things short (sorry) and sweet, saying in a quiet moment when it crosses your mind (but not in the middle of an argument about getting into bed), *I read this wild thing—apparently kids grow when they sleep—so if you want to grow as much as you can, you should probably start getting into bed earlier.*

Target the late-night cramming sessions

We hear from families all the time that the battle over reasonable bedtime goes hand-in-hand with intense academic pressure. The burden kids feel to get good grades weighs so heavily that they are staying up into the wee hours of the morning working on homework, studying for tests, churning out projects. The stress itself is bad for kids for so many reasons, emotional and physical, and now, on top of that, these stressed-out kids cannot clock the hours of z's that they need. The big four benefits of sleep—mood reset, memory filing, metabolic rebalance, and growth—become unattainable if they're regularly burning the midnight oil. We need to give them permission to go to sleep. Convince them with science (because your opinion certainly won't sway them): *You literally store memories while you sleep, so at a certain point you're actually better off going to sleep and storing what you just learned rather than continuing to cram.*

Fight the device battle (and win!)

The push and pull of devices is real. On the one hand, adolescents socialize on their devices, with social media, video chat, and texting as important to them as the corded telephone was to some of us. Their devices connect them in ways we don't understand, even if we think we do. And emerging from a pandemic that so deeply affected their ability to socialize and connect with other kids, many of us have become particularly sensitive about demonizing devices because we've seen how helpful they can be! On the other hand, the data tells us that kids should be off screens an hour (if not two) before they go to bed, giving their brains a break from stimulation and blue light, encouraging their melatonin to rise. What's more, every one of these devices—not just phones but computers and iPads and gaming devices, too—should charge outside the bedroom because every person sleeps better without the dings and buzzes of notifications. (Fun fact: this advice is not just for kids.)

But good luck to everyone involved. These rules need constant monitoring and reinforcement because they will be broken more than they will be kept. It's tough to finish grueling homework and forgo the fun part of the night in order to get more rest. And when something thrilling is going down, when a text volley picks up speed and turns intoxicating, putting that device down proves nearly impossible. While it's a drag, it's really worthwhile to repeat yourself on a weekly (or daily) basis, because kids need to be reminded (over and over) why you want them off devices: *I know I sound like a broken record, but it's my job to keep you healthy and make sure you get enough sleep, so time to get off your device and get ready for bed.* And then, model the advice you give and do the same thing.

Demonstrate the impact on their mood

Adults know how crappy they feel when they don't get enough sleep—irritable, short-tempered, unproductive—so when we notice those behaviors in kids, consider that they're not getting enough sleep. Rather than call them out for acting like jerks, get curious as to what's actually happening after you say goodnight. Some sneak onto screens, others grab a book, and many lie in bed unable to doze off, their minds spinning as they process their day. It might seem like a no-brainer to you (of course they're moody, they're sleep deprived!), but they may not have connected those dots. So help them: get granular, pointing out how lack of sleep affects moods. It works much better when you throw yourself under the bus and say something like *Remember last week when I was so crabby and snappy with you? I stayed up late the night before binge-watching a new show on Netflix. I was in the worst mood the next day because I didn't get enough sleep! Sometimes I can tell when you're not getting enough sleep. Can you?*

The sleep challenge never ends for some. But understanding the why of it all—why sleep is important, why it makes you feel better, why it changes your energy level and school or work performance—goes a long way toward self-awareness. Eventually this turns into a better nighttime routine for many kids and adults alike. Until then, brace yourself for a nightly mocking as you repeat yourself endlessly: *It's time for bed. It's time for bed, honey. Hey, dude, time for bed. TIME FOR BED!*

FROM PEOPLE JUST OUT THE OTHER SIDE

R.E., she/her, age 21

When I was in high school, I did not prioritize sleep. I would come home from school, take a nap or get started on homework, go to dance practice, come home, and then do homework all night. By the time I was a senior in high school, I was getting six hours of sleep a night if I was lucky and usually was getting closer to four or five hours. On nights before big tests or presentations, it could get down to three hours. I was *always* tired, which also contributed to my difficulty in doing work during the day.

Lack of sleep negatively affected my sleep cycle and sleep habits, and not to mention my immune system, but what it most affected was my mood. I was constantly on edge and my emotions were heightened. When I got to college, I found myself in the same routine. I was able to sleep later in the mornings so I was getting more sleep overall, but I still went to bed pretty late. Believe it or not, I get tired a lot earlier now. My poor sleep schedule from high school has carried on throughout college, and it is not sustainable. Now, as a rising senior in college, I wish that I had practiced better sleep habits in high school.

Beyond needing sleep so that I can be a functioning human being,

I've realized how important sleep is to just be happy! I can predict the exact meltdown I will have at the end of a week when I do not get enough sleep. It makes it hard to enjoy my classes and spend time with friends when I can barely keep my eyes open and all I want to do is get some sleep. As someone who would tell myself, "Sleep is for the weak" so that I could study for one more hour or get one more assignment done or even waste time on my phone to relax after a long night of working, my advice is go to sleep! It's so important, and I never believed that I needed it because I thought I was fine without it. Looking back, I realize how prioritizing my sleep would have helped me, and I see why it was so important to build healthy sleep habits earlier on!

CHAPTER 11

Brain Development

Understanding the confluence of what's happening both above and below the neck during puberty—basically in the brain versus in the groin— helps clarify why kids might look like they're maturing even when they don't act like it. Or, said another way, kids often appear older than their behavior would suggest, and with puberty beginning earlier and earlier, these looks and actions can seem ever more out of sync.

 ## LET'S START WITH SCIENCE

Brain development starts well before puberty begins, it lasts *much* longer, and it is governed by completely different forces within the body. Other than the brain housing a couple of glands involved with sex hormone cycling—like the hypothalamus and the pituitary—its maturation doesn't have any direct impact on the body's physical shifts toward reproductive capability. Looking at the situation from the opposite perspective though, puberty profoundly affects the brain and its development. Puberty-steering hormones like testosterone and estrogen bathe the brain's neurons, changing how they signal one another and, in turn, how adolescents act and feel. When puberty first starts, the brain is not even half-way done on its journey toward maturation—namely the ability to make reliably smart, consequential, "adult" decisions. This barely half-baked staging, in turn, influences everything else about the social and emotional experience of puberty in spectacular ways. Not necessarily good spectacular, mind you, but not always bad.

Let's start at the beginning. At birth, human babies have approximately 100 billion neurons packed into their brains. A *neuron* is a nerve cell that sends messages to other nerve cells. Neurons communicate by releasing tiny doses of *neurochemicals*—like dopamine, epinephrine, or GABA, to name some of the better-known ones—that jump from the end of one neuron to the beginning of another. Some neurochemicals are excitatory, turning "on" the next neuron in the chain, while others are inhibitory and send a "stop" signal. Neurotransmitters create an intricate system of communication among nerve cells packed impossibly close together inside the head.

Each neuron has a central cell body that houses its nucleus, basically its command center and the storage hub for its DNA. Branching out from the cell body are strand-like arms extending to other neurons in the local area. These arms come in two types: long, spindly axons designed to send signals away from the cell body, telling other neurons what to do, and shorter, branch-like dendrites designed to receive signals from neighboring neurons, then shuttle them toward the cell body. Each neuron has only one axon, but it can have anywhere from one to several hundred dendritic trees, allowing for thousands of connections.

Neurons communicate with one another at their tips, the axon spraying a whiff of neurochemical toward the receiving dendrite. Once the neurochemical fits into its receptor, it's translated into an electrical current that shoots up the dendrite, through the cell body, and down the axon. Electrical impulses travel extremely quickly through a single neuron, much faster than the chemical signals between two cells. So why the two different strategies in tandem? Because an electrical impulse is essentially analog—either it happens or it doesn't. Meanwhile, chemical signaling can vary depending upon the type, dose, and duration of neurochemical release, making it more nuanced. By relying upon two different modes of communication, one within a single nerve and the other between different nerves, neurons have found a way to balance speed and message. It's kind of like sending the same letter by both snail mail and text (except neurochemicals don't take five days to reach their destination and almost never find themselves returned to sender!).

Understanding this combination of chemical and electrical signaling is key to wrapping one's head (sorry, bad pun) around brain maturation in general. That's because one of the measures of brain maturation is the ability to send signals quicker than before. While chemical messages between the tips of two neurons require a fixed amount of time, electric signals can be sped along when the environment becomes more conducive, literally. Which is precisely why the brain builds a layer of insulation around each axon: to help speed the transmission of their electrical signals. This layer, made from fat cells, is called myelin, and the process of covering the long arms of the nerves is called myelination. If two signals are sent to different parts of the brain at the same time—one signal slowly cruising along an unmyelinated neuron and another zipping down a myelinated one—the one traveling fastest will likely prevail because, when an impulse gets to a specific area of the brain rapid-fire, then the body can act on that signal just as fast.

The brain begins its process of myelination before birth, starting at the very bottom and deep inside. It takes decades—about 30 years, no exaggeration—for the myelin to work its way from the bottom to the top and from the inside out, nerve cell by nerve cell. By the time a kid hits the tween years, myelin has traveled about halfway up and out, reaching the limbic system, which is the part of the brain that controls risk and reward, thrill seeking, and motivation. The limbic system is the impulsive, feel-good center, and it can send and receive messages exceptionally quickly by the start of middle school. On the other hand, the prefrontal cortex—the consequential, long-term-oriented area nicknamed "the brain's CEO" for its supposed smart decision-making—sits all the way at the top and outermost part of the brain, tucked right underneath the forehead. It will not be fully myelinated for another decade and a half, maybe two. In other words, all through middle school and high school and college and beyond, messages are sent to and from the limbic system faster (up to 3,000 times faster!) than they're sent to the prefrontal cortex.

It's worth repeating the *30 years* part here. Thanks to improvements in brain imaging and studies of people with no known medical issues, research shows that the prefrontal cortex is not fully myelinated until a person is somewhere between 25 and 30 years old. This explains *a lot* about how young "adults" act throughout their twenties.

Back to brain maturation in the tween and teen years: Let's say you're sitting at the dinner table asking your teenager about a party happening later that night. You bring up drinking and drugs, hooking up and sex. You have an amazing conversation that covers *all* the worrisome bases, and your kid tells you absolutely everything you ever wanted to hear about their anticipated behavior. It's more than that, because the conversation is open and raw and honest, and you're getting truthful back-and-forth about what could happen and how to handle each scenario. This feels like a colossal parenting win! When dinner ends, the kid heads off to the party.

Each scenario you discussed is front and center now, just a couple of hours after this deep and meaningful conversation. But as decisions are made, some land in precisely the opposite direction of earlier promises. What gives? It turns out that friends light up a teen's limbic system in a way that adults simply don't. So at the dinner table, your kid was honestly sharing intended behaviors, but using the prefrontal cortex to do it. Yes, they have prefrontal cortices and they can access them in the right setting, but those neural pathways are not yet myelinated, so messages get there more slowly. When kids are with adults, their limbic systems aren't amped up, allowing more time for messages to reach the prefrontal cortex before they act or answer. But at a party filled with peers their age and lots of novel, pleasure-seeking opportunities, impulses fly across the neurons of the actively engaged limbic system—this is fun, after all! or terrifying! or a little of both—while the prefrontal cortex cannot keep up. When peers turn up the mental volume of the limbic system, there's no incentive for a kid to wait patiently for a signal to crawl all the way out to the unmyelinated prefrontal cortex. That's how the plan not to drink or hook up or fill-in-whatever-blank-you-want-to-fill-in gets up-ended: the presence of myelin in the limbic system but not at the pre-frontal cortex results in an unfair fight between the impulsive and rational parts of the brain.

What about the kids who *do* make good decisions? Remember, all kids have a prefrontal cortex—it's right there under their foreheads—and some are remarkably capable of accessing that part of their brain no matter what happens to be going on around them. These kids are hard-wired (literally) to give themselves a little extra time for messages to get all the way to the outer edges of their brains. Their limbic systems still dominate, but because they don't act immediately, other areas of the brain hold sway. Now these same kids also tend to have different risk/reward thresholds, with many describing themselves as not loving the feeling of living on an edge. Their temperament clearly plays a role too; they're often not the life of the party and almost always more risk-averse. The ones who give their brains a little bit more time to shuttle impulses from place to place ultimately wind up with the title of the "responsible one," which is it's own complication.

So now is it a little clearer why tweens and teens and, yes, most cer-tainly twenty-somethings do the (sometimes idiotic) things they do? There's a race inside their brains, and the path to the limbic system is faster than the path to the prefrontal cortex until the time when all roads are paved with myelin. By age 30, the race is tied between signals reach-ing the emotional limbic system and the consequential prefrontal cortex. This biological phenomenon that we call brain maturation gives consis-tently good decision-making a fighting chance.

Before moving on from biology, it's important to acknowledge that myelin isn't the only determinant of a mature brain. The other, equally key piece of the puzzle is called neuronal pruning, a biological version of

"Use it or lose it." Remember that at birth the brain has 100 billion neurons, a number that increases through the toddler years. Eventually, though, the brain starts trimming down the number of neurons packed inside. The way it determines which to keep and which to toss is simply based upon use: neurons that have been used are saved. And the more frequently they are used, the faster a signal moves among them. It's as if the neurons are like footpaths through snow, with the most walked-on paths becoming the flattest, easiest to follow.

It's the combination of pruning and myelination that creates expertise: the more often certain pathways are used and the sooner they are myelinated, the more efficiently a message makes it from point A to point B, which, in turn, means more messages will travel along that route.

 ## WHAT'S CHANGED OVER THE PAST 20, 30, 40 YEARS

Brain development hasn't changed—at least as far as we know. But then again, scientists have been able to look at images of "normally developing" brains only for about 25 years, when magnetic resonance imaging (MRI) machines first became widely accessible, allowing researchers to peer into the structure of the brain. Positron emission tomography (PET) scanners, invented in 1975, made it possible to measure brain activity by visually documenting the amount of energy consumed by different neurons in different areas. In the late 1990s, PET and MRI scanners could be used in conjunction—a scientific marriage of the ages!—catapulting brain research massively forward.

The results of these studies are well known, and they've been mentioned several times in this chapter already: brains aren't fully myelinated until nearly age 30. This knowledge helps adults reconsider how kids make decisions. But more profoundly, it has led to a fundamental shift in what we consider a "grown-up" to be. When today's parents were graduating from high school, they were largely considered capable of making adult decisions. It wasn't as if they behaved much differently back then, but the social convention was that they *were* classified as grown-ups. Today, armed with the knowledge that the prefrontal cortex has another decade to go from grad night until full maturity, we think of older teens quite differently. It's not a biological shift, but rather a perceptual one.

The other big change, again not to brain development but to surrounding circumstances, is the earlier onset of puberty itself. Today, sex hormones begin coursing through brains at younger and younger ages. Myelin has always marched steadily along neurons, millimeter by millimeter, its presence in some areas and absence in others explaining away typical tween and teen behavior. Layered on top of that slow process are surges and dips in hormone levels circulating through the bodies of middle and high schoolers.

Because those hormone tides are now rising a couple of years earlier than they used to, but myelin still accumulates year by year, the partially myelinated brain is *less* myelinated at the time of puberty's onset. How has this affected the degree of mood swinging? Or the way decisions are made during grade school? And how do added layers of modern life, like cell phones, play into the functioning of young brains? These studies are just getting started. But even without formal research, we can see quite clearly that it affects how our kids feel. Chapter 12 takes a deep dive into mood swings, which are intimately connected to these past few sentences. Plainly put: a child in third or fourth grade experiences emotional ups and downs that used to be the hallmark of middle schoolers.

 ## HOW TO TALK ABOUT IT

As brain research has progressed over the last few decades, so too has adult humor about adolescents' poor decision-making. It used to be *My teenager makes the worst decisions because he is an idiot,* and now it's more like *My teen makes the worst decisions because his prefrontal cortex isn't mature.* In theory, many adults now understand that given brain development, adolescents can't entirely help but make dumb and unsafe decisions. Sometimes we put that knowledge into practice when we deal with kids . . . and sometimes we don't.

In the past, adults might have been frustrated by the fact that kids looked old enough to make mature decisions and then failed to do so. This disconnect has grown even more challenging as puberty has marched earlier, the gulf between their appearance and developmental capability widening, creating a (sometimes) giant chasm between adults' expectations and kids' behavior. The result: pure frustration that we can move past by remembering a few basic facts.

They can't always help it

When kids are little, we ask them to accomplish a certain task over and over, and they do that one thing with varying degrees of success. Hanging up their coats when they come home or putting their shoes in the closet—these aren't hard for most of them to master, so when they don't do them, it can feel like they're ignoring us or flexing their oppositional muscles. But sometimes they just don't do it, even with repeated requests. This doesn't mean they are being jerks; it means they need help accomplishing the task, like having a stool nearby so they can reach the coat hook. Or, they can't remember to do what you're asking because another thought floated through their mind at that precise moment.

The same can be said for tweens and teens. Yes, they might be purposefully defiant, refusing to call you at the designated time when they're out at a party, but it's possible they need some scaffolding to help: *I know it's hard to remember to call me when you're in the middle of a party, but I need you to check in, so can you set a reminder on your phone at 10 P.M. to call?* Or maybe you have a kid with limited executive functioning and when they're around friends they become even more scattered. Then you can add: *I get that it's hard to remember to call, so can you ask a reliable friend to set a reminder too?* We have to parent the kid we have, not the kid we wish we had.

Having conversations about good decisions isn't futile (despite how it might feel)

It's astounding when a kid lists every responsible answer to questions about managing tough situations, only to turn around and do something terrifying later that night. No, they're not professional BS artists; they are simply living with brains under major construction. This raises the question: Is it even worth having these conversations in the first place? If, when push comes to shove (or when limbic system comes to prefrontal cortex), the limbic system will win out, why bother?

The biggest reason why these conversations matter boils down to muscle memory. Okay, the brain isn't actually a muscle, but walking through scenarios and even role-playing can help kids anticipate what's coming instead of being surprised by pretty predictable situations. That said, these are conversations, not monologues—they need to be active, not passive, experiences for kids. Take the example of what to do when drugs are offered up at a party. Lectured kids receive the information passively (they're also probably bored and annoyed), but kids who are asked for their input are actively engaged. Better yet, querying kids what they would do rather than telling them what to do reveals what they know and what they don't; whether or not they have a plan; when they need help and when they're good. If you can convince them, do a role-play. It is an effective way to work through difficult scenarios ahead of time. But be forewarned: asking a teen to role-play will likely elicit massive eye rolls and brutal mockery. It's an exercise almost everyone loves to hate.

Explain the science

It sells kids short when we assume they don't find the science of their bodies compelling. Many are fascinated by watching a tampon expand in water; realizing that there actually are little balls inside the scrotum; grasping why popping pimples actually makes things worse. Besides, they wake up in a different body every day for nearly a decade, and they tell us all the time that they're a lot less confused when they understand what's happening inside.

The same goes for helping kids understand the neuroscience behind their moods and decision-making. If they're into it, share this chapter with them. If they need something more basic, start with a simple analogy: *At your age, your brain has a superhighway to your limbic system (the area that controls pleasure-seeking and risk-taking behavior), but the road to your prefrontal cortex (which controls thoughtful decision-making) is under construction, so traffic heading there moves slowly. That's why sometimes you do some pretty silly stuff or you make choices you kinda know you shouldn't. Understanding this can help you make better decisions.* Explaining the situation helps them make sense of why they sometimes make (very!) subpar choices, even if they mean well—and it might remind you of the same. Also, explaining to them that *their friends light up their limbic system and their parents don't* can relieve their guilt when they find you incredibly dull!

Teach the importance of taking a pause

There's more than just power in knowing that a tween or teen (or twenty-something!) brain needs extra time for messages to reach the prefrontal cortex—there's a solution. While hardly foolproof, pausing before acting literally allows time for messages to travel across the entire brain, providing a fighting chance for kids to make better choices. This time technique benefits pretty much everyone, by the way. Have you ever needed to take a couple of deep breaths or count to 10 to cool off? Same principle.

It's no light lift to teach kids to take a breath without being cringey. Start by helping them reconsider where they went wrong in a past situation. *If you had it to do over again, what would you do differently?* Then ask how taking some time might have affected their behavior or the overall outcome. *How could you have paused to think for a few seconds?*

Then bring it home with a strategy that works for you: *I know it sounds dorky, but the first thing I do is take a deep breath because it helps me calm down and it buys me a little time.*

As maddening as it is to witness kids make wrong choices even (especially!) if we've warned them, discussed it, and role-played, remember they are works in progress. They can't always help it. Don't give up, because eventually the endless brain construction project will finish and they just may shock you with their ability to consistently do the right thing.

FROM PEOPLE JUST OUT THE OTHER SIDE

B.H., she/her, age 21

I remember the first time my drunk friend offered to drive me home. I was in high school, and it was one of the first few times I drank with friends, so I was feeling nervous but excited to be at one of my first high school parties. Sarah, with a red Solo cup filled to the brim with way too much vodka and a tiny bit of Sprite in her hand, told me she was ready to go home, but she drove her car here and wanted to drive it back. She asked me, "Will you drive with me? I don't want to go home alone. I live *soooo* far away and I don't want to come back to get it tomorrow. I also don't want to pay for an Uber." I was afraid to say no. I heard my parents in the back of my head telling me to never get in a car with a drunk driver and to call them to pick me up. At the same time, I was worried that my friends would be annoyed and mad at me for not getting in the car with them.

I felt stuck and then suddenly had an adrenaline rush. My face felt hot and I could feel my heart beating faster. I decided, in order to appease them and feel comfortable within my own boundaries, I would lie that I had already ordered an Uber five minutes before and that I could add a few stops to make sure my friends got home. And I did just that.

They were drunk, so they believed me, and we got in an Uber and I made sure they all got home.

In the heat of the moment, I decided that it would be easiest to think about the consequences of a little white lie versus letting them drive home drunk. Something that I felt was extremely helpful in making this decision was that I knew my parents would not be upset if they came to pick me up at 2 A.M. or paid for my Uber home. I was split between two choices: risk pissing off my friends and order an Uber, or risk getting into a bad accident that I'll regret forever. The choice became easy for me in the heat of the moment because I took a step back, thought hard, and knew that I had a safer option that had zero consequences.

CHAPTER 12

Mood Swings

By definition, moods swing. Literally: the definition of *mood* is "a temporary feeling or state of mind." We all know how much—and how quickly—these states can change, but shifts range from small, subtle, and graceful to drastic, jarring earthquakes of feeling that come out of (almost) nowhere. That second group contains the mood swings we're talking about in this chapter, the ones synonymous with puberty.

Moods swings are particularly front-of-mind for the adults caring for the 44 million kids in the midst of puberty in the United States and the approximately 1.4 billion around the globe. Once mood swings are better understood, perhaps they can be avoided or at least addressed more effectively. This turns out to be high on the wish list for everyone involved. Over the years, we have never met a kid who likes how mood swings feel or an adult who enjoys being on the receiving end.

 LET'S START WITH SCIENCE

Let's actually start with the word *mood*, to level set. Moods can show up as whiny, irritated, or agitated for sure. But they can also appear as fits of laughter and giddiness; with contemplation and silence; and even frustration too. Moods are simply states of mind. Even though conversations about adolescent moods often land on negative (and gendered) descriptors, when we talk about mood swings we're including them all: the good, the bad, and the oh Lord, here we go!

Adolescent-mood science is limited because only a handful of researchers have studied the connection between brain maturation and moodiness. The few studies that do exist describe the biology behind classic tween and teen moods like this: immature behavioral control centers in young brains make adolescents more emotionally reactive, thanks largely to one particular part of the limbic system called the *amygdala*. This piece of the brain is notably less regulated than its adult counterpart, explaining why kids tend to be far more responsive to negative emotional information than their parents (but not always). In other words, when you say something that rubs a tween or teen the wrong way, they tend to react with bigger feelings than an adult receiving the same words (though not always!). Another big contributor here is the immature prefrontal cortex, which lacks the ability to help teen brains regulate emotions once they are feeling them. That explains the spiral in response to a mildly critical comment, a drama consuming an hour of your life you won't ever get back (*But all I said was that they might want to change their shirt!*).

Understanding mood swings requires baseline mastery of the structure and function of the brain. (Chapter 11 goes into detail about how neurons fire and how different parts of the brain communicate with each other.) In this chapter, we focus more on what's floating around and inside the brain, its microenvironment. You're probably not surprised to read that hormones are the stars of this story.

Here are the bare bones of what you need to know: The brain is a bundle of billions of neurons wrapped tightly together and protected by the skull. This configuration means that the brain wears its own bony armor all day every day, some of the strongest protection in the body. The skull fits the brain nicely but not tightly, kind of like a bike helmet over a head. If the skull were perfectly fitted, molded to the precise dimensions of the brain, then any swelling or bleeding or increased pressure would quickly turn catastrophic: an unyielding bony skull would exert tremendous force on an expanding organ underneath. As a result, and very much by evolutionary design, the brain is noticeably smaller than the skull—fitting inside it but by no means snugly. This mechanism allows for the brain to expand and contract just a little bit.

In order to cushion the brain—because the slightly squishy brain would repeatedly bang itself against the firm skull if there were no cushion, possibly damaging its neurons with each bump and blow—the body makes a fluid called cerebrospinal fluid (CSF), a natural shock absorber. Fun sidenote: certain types of headaches are caused when the CSF cushioning shrinks, like when someone is dehydrated, and the brain knocks against the skull. The CSF bathes the brain, so whatever is in the CSF surrounds and affects the brain's neurons, kind of like marinating a chicken. It also plays an important nutritional role, allowing neurons access to certain nutrients that maximize brain function.

But the precious neurons of the brain would be vulnerable if exposed to everything that comes into the body, so the CSF has a bouncer-style setup, a special filter called the blood-brain barrier. This barrier provides an extra layer of defense against potentially devastating visitors, like infections: if the body's immune system doesn't wipe out a bacterial or viral invader quickly enough, the blood-brain barrier aims to make sure it doesn't infect the brain (but other organs, you're on your own). Like everything else inside the body, the blood-brain barrier is imperfect by design, because in order for the brain to function, lots can (and must!) cross the blood-brain barrier. This includes oxygen and glucose, which fuel brain cell activity, and also less helpful molecules (well, depending upon who you ask) like caffeine, alcohol, intoxicating drugs, and, you guessed it, hormones.

Remember that hormones circulate through the bloodstream, coursing up and down the body from head to toe. When they cross the blood-brain barrier, they become part of the chemical CSF stew bathing individual neurons. It turns out that estrogen hanging around the CSF can make neurons behave in certain ways. Classically, but not always, estrogen magnifies emotional reactions, from giggles to tears, creating a wear-it-on-their-sleeve reactivity. Meanwhile, testosterone affects neuronal firing in other ways, which explains to some extent why male moodiness tends to swing between introverted quiet and sparks of rage—again, not always and not for everyone. You can probably see where this story is headed, and it's no surprise because we all live a version of it: when estrogen or testosterone first begins to surge in a pubescent body, hormones also surge in the pubescent CSF. And when hormone levels plummet, thanks to feedback loops in the sex organs resulting in hormonal peaks and valleys, it drops in the CSF too. The net impact of high highs and low lows is a dramatic hormonal roller coaster with even more exaggerated moodiness.

Well, sort of. Hormones only explain half the story because the tween and teen brain is mid-maturation. Adolescent brains are aggressively myelinating and pruning, two facts that deeply affect the way hormones—and any chemicals floating around in the CSF—change the behavior of neurons. There's much more on this topic in chapter 11, but by way of quick review, here goes: By the tween years, the neurons of the limbic system are covered in a layer of insulation called myelin, allowing this part of the brain to send and receive signals very fast. The more thoughtful, rational, and still largely unmyelinated prefrontal cortex sends and receives signals far more slowly. Scientists describe the impact of this myelin imbalance as "heightened responsiveness to rewards," which makes sense since motivation and feeling good and *hell yeah!* are the bread and butter of the early-to-be-myelinated limbic system. This explains why tweens and teens are far more likely to make risky choices than older, more mature adults. The prefrontal cortex, designed to regulate these reactions and hold them in check, cannot yet keep up with the limbic system's game of neural ping-pong. The presence of myelin in the limbic system and its relative absence from the prefrontal cortex make middle and high schoolers more reward-centric and less able to rein in their emotional responses to these rewards.

Neuronal pruning plays a role here too. The brain is designed to identify neurons that are not used, and then literally to kill them off. This neuronal pruning—named for the process that resembles pruning an overgrown tree—reduces clutter in the brain space, increasing efficiency. It's what makes any of us, old or young, get better and better at a given skill: when we use and reuse certain pathways, we improve our ability to do (or think about) something. Practice makes perfect . . . or at least better. We also spare that pathway from extinction. This is the origin of the neuroscience mantra *Use it or lose it*, referring to selective pruning throughout our entire life span. Because the adolescent brain is only beginning this long process, it's open to lots of new skills but expert at very few, if any. One thing it's not great at is making rational decisions instead of impulsive and feel-good ones.

Putting this all together: Myelination determines the speed of signal transmission, pruning determines which pathways will persist in the brain, and hormones play a (sometimes *big*) role in the way nerves interact. In a half-mature brain suddenly exposed to surging and then dropping doses of hormones, one result is wildly swinging moods.

As kids make their way through puberty, mood swings usually improve, partly because the hormonal peaks and valleys level off and partly because the brain gets accustomed to managing these shifting levels. Continuing myelination certainly helps too, but it won't be done until a kid comes close to reaching 30.

While we encourage adults to be understanding and patient with kids' mood swings, there are times when these behaviors indicate something more going on. Mental health professionals encourage caregivers to be on the lookout for a sudden and then lingering change in mood, like a usually cheerful kid who withdraws and seems persistently down for a week or more. Spotting the difference between a mood swing and a clinical disorder can be extremely difficult, especially with tweens and teens. For instance, anxious teens can present as angry, irritable, and aggressive—not necessarily qualities one immediately associates with adult anxiety. Another example: it can be hard to differentiate normal adolescent chafing against rules, guidance, or mere adult presence from something more concerning. As ever, if you're in doubt, it's always best to check in with a pediatrician, guidance counselor, or mental health provider.

WHAT'S CHANGED OVER THE PAST 20, 30, 40 YEARS

Here's the biggest shift: puberty is starting much earlier than it used to, which means that hormones like estrogen and testosterone are making their way into younger brains. Since we know that the brain's maturation is purely chronological, the onset of puberty doesn't affect its ability to think in an older, more sophisticated way. A nine-year-old with breast buds may *look* slightly older than another kid in their class, but their brains are all basically at the same place in terms of myelination and pruning; that said, she will have a much higher load of hormones bathing a less mature, less myelinated brain compared to a classmate who doesn't start to develop for another couple of years.

Does this affect mood swinging or decision-making? Does it change how they feel, their emotional ups and downs? Right now, the deeply dissatisfying answer is that we don't know. We would need to conduct a study with 8-, 9-, and 10-year-olds in which we examined them to identify their stage in puberty, drew their blood to measure their hormone levels, and gave them a survey to assess their emotional lability. In a perfect research setup, the kids would enroll before they ever experienced a hormone surge—let's say around age 6 or 7—and then we would evaluate them at regular intervals every few weeks or months, documenting their physical changes and hormone levels along the way. And even that wouldn't necessarily tell us what we want to know, because hormones rise and fall throughout the day, so taking a single measurement at a random time every so often might result in very misleading data.

We have yet to meet a parent or adult caregiver or teacher without an anecdote about how the age of mood swings has shifted downward. The most common comment we hear is surprise over the early onset of eye rolling and door slamming. Almost no one used the word *tween* when most of us were between 8 and 12, and maybe for good reason. Back then, that age group didn't have its own moniker and mood swings didn't make their debut until right around the charming age of 13. But now, with the downward shift of hormonal surging, moods show up closer to 8 or 9. It's fitting that there's now a descriptive term that sounds so much like *teen* because their behavior mimicks that stage of life.

When we teach kids in the classroom, we always ask about moods: *How many of you have either laughed uncontrollably or sobbed without being able to stop—even when what you're laughing or crying about isn't that funny or that sad?* One hundred percent of the hands in the room go up. Then we ask: *How many of you like how this feels?* Zero. There is never a hand in the air. This indicates that kids are aware of earlier mood swings, and they don't like them any more than we do. If you need a reason to start talking about how to handle these big emotions, now you have one.

 ## HOW TO TALK ABOUT IT

The moody teenager has been replaced by the moody tweenager, which is why when parents say, *My 10-year-old is acting like I did when I was a teenager,* they're right! The good news is that there are things we can do to help them—and ourselves—chart a course through the hormonal storms of adolescence.

First things first: Remember that kids cannot help their moodiness. If this chapter has taught you nothing else, hopefully you got that message loud and clear. Kids can't control their surging and plummeting estrogen or testosterone. Adults find this maddening, a few even calling pubescent kids assholes out loud, most just silently judging them that way. But this isn't fair, because though they might *act* like assholes, they're not doing it willfully. They're victims of circumstance, the circumstance being puberty.

So make a concerted effort not to flip *how* kids act into a characterization of *who* they are. Do your best to avoid labeling them on account of their emotional outbursts. Kids hold on to these labels long after they outgrow the behavior, and if you need proof, just pause for a second and recall a searing comment said about you back in the day. Didn't take you long, did it? These things stick. It's our job to support kids while they're riding an emotional roller coaster with no safety bar or seat belt and to provide them with reassurance and comfort, not ridicule and judgment.

Surging hormones can make kids laugh hysterically, cry uncontrollably, get in your face aggressively, or go utterly silent. Regardless of how a particular mood might swing, it can be extremely difficult to avoid a less-than-constructive reaction. But check yourself: we're the ones with fully developed brains and (generally) more stable hormone levels, or at least a longer track record of managing our own chemical ups and downs. Keep in mind that kids feel pretty powerless when they're at the mercy of their hormones—they don't like being exceedingly unpleasant or unreachable either. Your best move here is to offer up empathy. How? Especially in the heat of the moment, try some of the following strategies.

Avoid engaging and escalating

Easier said than done! However, as with 99 percent of the advice in this book, practice makes better (never perfect). So how do you refrain if every fiber in you just wants to rail at an ungrateful, unpredictable, out-of-control child? First, take a deep breath. Yup, that again, because it helps. Second, find a neutral and empathetic response that can work in the face of an emotional hurricane: *I'm so sorry. That really sucks. That must have felt really crummy.* And third, when a kid goes on the offensive and, in their anger or frustration or sadness, starts to attack you, do *not* engage. You can simply say: *I can see you're very upset. Let's take a break and talk about it later.*

Phrases to avoid

It's not our style to go negative, however we strongly recommend avoiding some of the following antagonistic phrases.

> **Do not tell them to calm down:** Whatever you do, DO NOT TELL THEM TO CALM DOWN! It never works. When under-construction brains are flooded with hormones, calming down presents a gargantuan challenge that takes time on their part and patience on yours. What you can do is take some deep breaths of your own, which will help your brain reset and might coregulate your kid a bit too.

> **Do not tell them to stop crying:** There are two reasons for this. Maybe they can't stop crying because the estrogen flooding their body is telling them, *Keep crying.* Or, maybe crying feels good, a pop-off valve for their strong emotions. Just because it makes you uncomfortable to see them cry doesn't mean tears are bad for your kid. Instead of telling them to stop, you might say: *Would it help if I sat here with you? Would you like a hug or is it easier if I don't touch you right now?*

> **Do not say that it's not a big deal:** An adult might not think it's a big deal when their kid is disinvited to walk to Starbucks after school, but to that kid, it feels like a really big deal—it's hurtful and lonely. So when we turn around and say, *Get over it, it's not that big a deal,* it invalidates

their feelings. What's more, this response makes them not want to share with you in the future. To avoid this, consider saying something like, *Such a bummer. Is there anything you want me to say, or is it better if I just keep you company?*

Do not tell them it'll be fine tomorrow: We as adults might know that the C on their history test will not dictate the next 50 years of their lives, but kids don't have the lived experience or the developmental maturity to look very far down the road. When they are railing against the injustice of an exam, instead of minimizing their emotions, find something empathetic and simple to say instead: *That must feel really unfair. You sound really disappointed.*

Avoid meeting anger with anger

Sometimes pubescent moodiness comes out as anger or aggression toward adults, siblings, or even friends. The temptation to meet their anger with our own is so strong. Our internal monologue can sound like *Who does this kid think he is? He is so ungrateful, and now he's treating me like garbage—I'm not going to stand for that.* Our frustration might be completely valid, sometimes resulting in shouting back, saying unkind things, slamming doors, and storming out of the room. We are only human, after all. But we're playing a long game here where the goal is to help teach kids to regulate their big emotions, and fighting fire with fire doesn't model emotional regulation. So what can we do?

Set boundaries around behavior without losing our crap: Aliza Pressman, host of the *Raising Good Humans* podcast, has a brilliant line: *All feelings are welcome, all* *behaviors are not.* Just because they are angry doesn't mean they get to beat on their younger sibling or belittle you. Make it clear that certain things are unacceptable.

Show them a way out: When older kids throw tantrums, they often dig themselves into holes and can't climb out. We can throw a ladder down the hole to offer an escape route. How? Pour them a cold glass of water and put it in front of them; call the dog over and start petting it, and maybe your kid will follow suit; ask if they want to take some time alone and offer to check back in a few minutes (but then show up after a few minutes!).

Try new strategies: tolerate silence

Some kids go quiet during puberty. One minute they are chatty snuggle-bunnies, and the next minute they seem to be living on a remote island in the middle of your house. This shift can be confusing and worrying, sometimes provoking a knee-jerk reaction to double down on efforts to engage them. Resist this urge, because it will likely push a kid to retreat even further into their shell, like a hermit crab on the beach. Practice the skill of asking a question and then waiting for a response. If the quiet isn't getting you anywhere, you can try some of these strategies instead.

Get interested in their interests even if they're not the least bit interesting. Show them that you value what matters to them (even if you're faking it). Wendy Mogel, author of *The Blessing of a Skinned Knee* and *Voice Lessons,* advises parents to "become enchanted with their enchantment."

Ask open-ended questions that leave room for elaboration. Instead of *How was school today?,* you can try

What's one funny thing that happened in class? It won't work every time, but intermittent success is better than none when the standard response is *Fine*.

Help the silent kids talk about stuff when they aren't sure how to start. Let them know the door is open by saying things without judgment, like *I'm always here to listen to you without judgment. I know there's a lot going on in your life, and sometimes it's nice just to get it out.*

One final note on the quiet kids: If your spidey sense is telling you that all is not right with your kid and you simply cannot get the conversational door cracked open, find someone for them to talk to, like a guidance counselor, a pediatrician, or a therapist. Don't assume you're overreacting; trust your instincts.

No magic pill eliminates tween and teen moodiness. And wow, can it be supremely annoying. But it won't last forever—in fact, the dynamic will start to improve the sooner we constructively engage with moody kids. This means not rising to the bait, avoiding meeting their anger with our anger, and finding new ways in with the quiet ones. The sooner we get past the most pendulous mood swings, the sooner we can help them navigate all the other confusing highs and lows of puberty.

FROM PEOPLE JUST OUT THE OTHER SIDE

J.S., she/her, age 20

As I was growing up, my mom would half-jokingly and half-seriously ask me if I was in "mood A" or "mood B," meaning was I feeling moody or not (and if I was in mood B, watch out). Even though I hated this at the time and didn't find it at all funny, in hindsight, this was a really direct and accurate way for my mom to gauge how I was feeling. In middle school especially, my moods were up and down and up again, sometimes a hundred times in just one day, and I never knew why I was feeling the way I was feeling. Looking back, I understand now that my mood swings were a normal part of growing up, but I wish I was able to have that perspective during the time in which I felt that they dominated my life.

Though I wasn't aware of it at the time, many of my friends also experienced moodiness and irritability at the same time in their lives. My best friend jokes that if someone even breathed the wrong way or chewed too loudly when she was in eighth grade it could set her off, and she would have to isolate herself in her room until her mood passed. Listening to music, cuddling her dog, and drawing in a coloring book all helped reset her mood when she felt like this. Another friend experienced moodiness a little later in her life, in the beginning of high school, and would snap at her friends and family if anyone tried to talk to her, even if nobody was doing anything wrong. She said that she would spend a lot of time on her phone to avoid human contact when she felt this way; she hated that her moodiness took hold of her and made her mean to people she cared about.

Even though mood swings must be really overwhelming and frustrating to manage from a parent's perspective, remember that they are equally as overwhelming and frustrating for your child! Nobody wants to be feeling that way, and your child probably feels out of control of their own emotions, which is no fun. Sometimes you just need to give your kid a little space and time to cool down, even if you might want to yell at them. Other times, they might need a hug and a shoulder to cry on. Always ask what you can do to help and provide options, and remember that moodiness doesn't last forever.

B.H., she/her, age 21

Emotional regulation was extremely difficult for me ever since I started puberty, and I felt like I was riding an emotional roller coaster every day. Mood swings became an almost daily thing for me. My mom, even to this day, still tells me I'm extremely emotional and sensitive. I later realized that there's nothing wrong with that. My emotions are a large part of who I am, and I have come to realize that it makes me unique. But growing up with these strong emotions was hard, especially for my parents and my closest friends. Looking back, I felt like my bigger mood swings took control of and dictated my mood for the rest of the day. For instance, anytime I got into an argument with my parents, it would blow up. It felt like there was a ticking bomb inside me and it was bound to explode every time I pushed down my feelings, which would slowly build up and go off to any small trigger.

I learned that mood swings happened more often when I was tired, felt hormonal, or was overwhelmed and frustrated by something. It was hard for my parents to help me too, because they would also feel tired and overwhelmed by my emotions. What helped me was that over time I learned to accept myself and others for our emotions and mood swings. But I couldn't have achieved this without the help of a therapist. Going to therapy made me understand just how big my emotions were. It's normal to feel strong emotions, and you should never shun yourself or others for it. As soon as I came to realize that, my family dynamic was much more stable. A product of leaving for college and growing up was that there was much less yelling. I stopped yelling back and learned to sit with my feelings, allow myself to process them, and then figure out a solution. I was also much better at regulating my emotions and dealing with explosive personalities when I decided to remain calm during an argument. The bomb exploded sometimes—we're not perfect—but it was much easier to handle as I grew older.

CHAPTER 13

Mental Health

This is not a chapter about mental illness so much as it's a chapter about mental *health.* While we walk through many of the terms casually bandied about these days—starting with stress, anxiety, and depression— our focus is on the forces that affect tweens' and teens' emotional status both positively and negatively at the same time that they're grappling with puberty. It's important to identify hardships, but just as critical to dig into the self-care that protects against them.

The mental well-being of adolescents often feels fragile—and it certainly can be. Their partially mature brains, bathed in a chemical stew of hormones (and sometimes sugar or alcohol or drugs), have to handle friend dramas and school pressures and us, the adults who love them but also hold them accountable. As with everything else during this stage of life, it's protective to understand what's going on inside the body, including the brain, at any given moment and to prepare for what might come next. In the world of pediatrics, this is called anticipatory guidance: the what (put on a seat belt when you're in the car) followed by the why (just in case there's an accident) keeps everyone safer. So buckle up as we dive into mental health.

LET'S START WITH SCIENCE

The term *mental health* includes psychological, emotional, and social well-being. *Psychological* means arising in the mind, things like thoughts, feelings, and ideas. *Emotional* refers to feelings exclusively, though obviously they can be (and often are) tethered to thoughts and ideas. And *social* resides outside of the brain, the events and interpersonal dynamics in someone's life, the part of this triad that represents external forces. Mental health is deeply influenced by all three: when we interact with someone or go somewhere or endure something, our brain processes the experience and then filters and translates it into a feeling. Getting into a fight with a close friend generates one set of emotions; climbing to the top of a hill and soaking in the view of the landscape below takes the brain in an entirely different direction.

One goal of this chapter is to walk through the most common mental health terms swirling all around us, defining each one clearly. Later in the chapter we'll offer pointers about how to talk about them, as well as when to get help from a healthcare provider. We begin with the most oft-used mental health terms and the science behind them. *Stress, anxiety,* and *depression* are three words uttered together so often, they sometimes sound like one. The three conditions are quite distinct, though.

Stress is the mental or emotional strain that results from either adverse or demanding circumstances. Taking a test is stressful. Breaking up with a significant other, stressful. War, homelessness, and abuse are all stressful. Losing your keys—stressful too. Stressors come in all shapes and sizes and intensities, but once they arrive they trigger a common physiologic response: a neurochemical cascade starting with the amygdala deep inside the brain signaling the nearby hypothalamus to rally the adrenal glands (one sitting atop each kidney; and yes, because glands can multitask, also the epicenter of adrenal androgens that make skin sweaty, oily, and hairy). The stress pathway triggers the adrenals to release adrenaline (aka epinephrine), which in turn raises the heart rate, blood pressure, respiratory rate, and more. This coordinated response is called the sympathetic nervous system, and we all know what it feels like in action when it turns on and off in response to an active threat. The "look" of stress can vary widely from person to person, which is why not everyone appears stressed out, like great poker players and trauma surgeons who wear it well. Regardless of outward appearances, internally, the stress response should modulate depending upon the magnitude of the scenario, with minor issues generating less of a physiologic reaction than major ones.

Anxiety is stress's first cousin. They share the common ground of mental or emotional strain, but the difference is that anxiety comes not from an active circumstance but rather from approaching, theoretical, lingering, or imagined ones. A test causes stress; the symptoms of worry in advance of a test or after it's over, with the result still pending, are thanks to anxiety. Getting fired causes stress; the thoughts about telling family members, paying bills, and finding a new job create anxiety. Essentially, anxiety results in persistent, excessive worry even when the stressor is gone (or hasn't yet arrived). But both stress and anxiety engage the sympathetic nervous system, which is why the words *stress* and *anxiety* are used interchangeably: both make the heart race, the palms sweat, the face flush, the bowels move, thoughts run, concentration plummet, or whatever your unique constellation of adrenaline-induced tells may be.

Depression, meanwhile, is a whole different phenomenon. It's completely normal for everyone to feel sad, downtrodden, or worthless from time to time. The diagnosis of depression requires a mood disorder marked by some combination of ongoing low mood, reduced energy, and decreased activity or interest or self-esteem, frequently interfering with sleep, appetite, or concentration. Depression is classified along a scale of mild to moderate to severe, with people at the farthest end often contemplating or attempting suicide.

It makes sense that stress and anxiety are treated as if they're synonymous (even though they're not) because they share so much common ground. But why does depression get lumped in—especially with anxiety, which these days is almost always called anxiety-and-depression, said in a single breath? It's because they are causally linked: People with anxiety are far more likely to experience depression and vice versa. *Co-morbidity*, which just means the coexistence of two different diagnoses at once, is common among psychiatric issues, especially anxiety and depression. During adolescence, anxiety tends to appear first, most often in the form of social anxiety and typically in middle school—which may sound very familiar to anyone who has ever attended middle school, the center stage for the meetup between peer pressure and identity formation—and within a couple of years, depression can follow. This one-two punch can happen at any time during the life span, but it's especially common through adolescence and into the early adult years.

COMMON MENTAL HEALTH DIAGNOSES AMONG ADOLESCENTS

Mental health incorporates much more beyond stress, anxiety, and depression. The following list presents some of the most commonly talked-about ones. For those hungry for more information, we've got a slew of resources listed—and periodically updated—on our website.

Addiction: This refers to the use of substances or participation in behaviors that become chronic and habitual (usually because they cause dopamine hits in the brain, which feel amazing), even though they have known harmful physical, psychological, and social effects. Some people use substances to self-medicate their identified or not-yet-diagnosed mental health challenges, like smoking weed or self-prescribing anxiolytics to manage anxiety. No matter how they landed there, a person who is addicted to something will experience symptomatic withdrawal when the substance isn't available, with symptoms ranging from anxiety to irritability to nausea to tremors.

Anxiety disorder and panic attacks: Anxiety disorder is defined by excessive and persistent worry that is difficult to control, causes significant distress or impairment, and occurs on more days than not. Panic attacks are sudden episodes of intense fear that trigger severe physical reactions when there is no commensurate danger or apparent cause. These clinical terms are often used casually by tweens and teens self-pathologizing normal feelings of anxiousness or worry.

Eating disorders: This group includes body dysmorphia, anorexia, bulimia, binge eating disorder, and more. Each diagnosis can exist as a stand-alone struggle or coexist with some of the other issues on this list. For instance, a person with body dysmorphia might also struggle with depression. Chapter 14 takes a deep dive into each of the eating disorders.

Obsessive-compulsive disorder (OCD): People with OCD have uncontrollable, reoccurring thoughts (obsessions) and/or behaviors (compulsions), with an insuppressible urge to repeat them over and over. A little bit of compulsion—to complete tasks, keep oneself organized, study or train just a tad more—can go a long way toward success. But when thoughts tip into debilitating fears or invasive ideas, crowding brain space, they become more destructive than constructive. Kids talk about OCD a lot these days, but it is only diagnosed in 1 to 3 percent of all children.

Now for the science around self-care. Almost everything your grandmother ever told you to do in order to live a healthy, happy life not only turns out to be true, it's backed by data.

Exercise

Exercise has always been credited with improving mood—runners call it a runner's high, but most sports and physical activities have their own celebratory term for that certain point during exercise when a rush of euphoria hits. This feeling tends to get attributed to the endorphins released during intense physical activity, but researchers have gradually debunked this theory, instead attributing the rush to endocannabinoids.

Like endorphins, endocannabinoids are naturally produced hormones. However endorphins don't easily cross the blood-brain barrier the way endocannabinoids do. Once in the brain, endocannabinoids can bring a sense of joy. They can also induce calm and reduce anxiety—endorphins, not so much. Regardless of the mechanism, it's pretty clear that moving the body turns on the production of chemicals that make us feel better in every way. It is nature's own antidepressant.

Exercise generates long-term mental health benefits, especially regular cardiovascular workouts, which can stimulate the growth of new blood vessels in and around the brain and can also multiply brain cells in certain locations (scientific term: *neurogenesis*). Memory researchers believe this slows or even prevents cognitive decline. The part of the brain associated with memory and learning, the hippocampus, actually increases in volume with regular exercise, improving memory, focus, and task-switching ability (a skill formerly called multitasking, but renamed because the brain is incapable of doing two cognitive things at once—it can switch back and forth between tasks pretty darn fast, though!).

Working out works for mental health. People without depression are more likely to exercise than those with it. That said, depression itself lowers energy levels and increases apathy—who wants to exercise when they feel blotto?—but structured physical activity can actually reverse depressive symptoms. Unfortunately, working out doesn't seem to protect against becoming depressed in the first place, but it boosts mood in just about everyone, with and without the diagnosis.

Nutrition

No news flash here: what we eat deeply—and quickly—affects how we feel. There's a way to eat well regardless of dietary philosophy, so it doesn't matter if you're a carnivore, pescatarian, vegetarian, or vegan. Important aside here: no dietary path guarantees smart, healthy choices. A healthy diet contains fruits and vegetables of all colors; a variety of proteins and carbs; many more whole foods than processed ones; natural sugars over refined sugars; moderate portions; and lots of water during and in between meals. Eating this way makes us feel energized, and our moods are more stable. Fear not! A healthy diet includes comfort foods from fries to chocolate to straight-up sugar for a quick energy surge or a moment of self-soothing—just keep it in moderation. Food is deeply powerful, which makes nutrition a big player in self-care.

It's also no great surprise that balanced diets tend to benefit long-term mental health. When a person eats well, several things follow: weight is usually maintained and doesn't fluctuate wildly; skin tends to be less reactive (translation: fewer pimples); and the body feels satiated but not painfully stuffed or bloated. All of these drive a positive self-image, confidence, not to mention a happy mood. Of course, things don't always work out this way, and sometimes those who eat well-balanced diets still struggle to feel good, but with poorer nutrition, the struggle would arguably be greater. If the thought has crossed your mind that the science supporting nutrition and exercise applies as much to kids as it does to adults, you are right. In fact, there's no self-care strategy that works well just for one age group—these tips span all generations.

Chapter 14 goes deep into eating disorders in particular, so we'll keep this part short. But suffice it to say, the benefits of balanced nutrition contribute to positive mental health, and on the flip side, many mental health issues involve food. Sometimes this topic feels like a third-rail, generating fears of tipping food-related conversations with tweens and teens into an actual eating disorder. There are gentle yet constructive ways to cover this territory—a worthwhile endeavor given the endless data connecting our moods, self-confidence, and overall wellness to diet.

Sleep

We've got a whole chapter (chapter 10) dedicated to this topic, but we're going to beat the drum once more here, this time as it relates specifically to mental health. Simply put, getting sleep fundamentally affects mood. It's the easiest form of self-care to practice, because it doesn't even require being awake!

Multiple studies have documented the benefits of sleep. In one, researchers at the University of Pennsylvania sleep-deprived a group of people, allowing them just 4.5 hours of sleep per night for a full week, and found (to no one's great surprise) that they were more stressed, angry, sad, and mentally exhausted; but when normal sleep resumed—voilà!—their moods improved.

Getting a long enough stretch of uninterrupted deep sleep requires figuring out how to get the minimum number of hours needed and still balance a busy schedule. Easier said than done. Some people plan late wake ups so they can sleep in, picking up their hours there, but the body doesn't always comply and instead of grabbing extra hours on a lazy morning, it still wakes up at its regular time. This is highly annoying but makes perfect sense because the body's circadian rhythms are entrenched by design, and harder to break than most imagine. Plus, a good night's sleep requires lots of details many people take for granted, like bedding suited to the ambient temperature; a pillow that's not too soft, not too bulky; a decent mattress on a solid, nonsqueaky frame; quiet; a dark enough room to allow for falling and staying asleep, which can mean lots of different things to different people; and feeling safe and secure. The list of sometimes expensive or unattainable variables goes on.

The relationship between sleep and mental health is bidirectional, meaning that each can help or hinder the other. Mental health issues can make sleep harder to come by, sometimes caused by medications keeping people awake, other times because the underlying issue itself causes insomnia. Both anxiety and stress, for instance, increase agitation and arousal which is not super conducive to lying down and conking out. And vice versa: lack of sleep leads to poor mental health—or at the very least, a nasty mood with a short fuse to boot.

An important note about teenagers indulging in sleep for self-care:

Melatonin is a powerful natural chemical released by the brain's pineal gland, whose job it is to tell the body it's time to wind down for sleep. We get into the nitty-gritty in chapter 10 about how lots of variables interfere with melatonin release, especially overhead lights and the blue lights of computer and phone screens. Because teenage brains tend to produce melatonin later into the night compared to younger or older brains, these kids are literally not tired even when they intellectually want to go to bed. It's insanely frustrating to try to do the right thing for yourself, putting the devices away early and getting into bed just to lie there unable to fall asleep. As we preach in our sleep chapter, while circadian rhythms are powerful, they're also trainable. Getting into bed around the same time every night helps the body adapt to routine, but if it's a new adjustment, the shift might take some time. An occasional late-night outlier is fine, by the way. That said, the body rarely complies when the schedule gets totally out of whack.

Mindfulness and meditation

The science supporting the benefits of mindfulness and meditation is booming, particularly with respect to mental health, so much so that what was once a hippie fringe technique is now a mainstream approach to addressing everything from routine challenges to mental illnesses. Study after study proves its benefits, including reduced emotional reactivity, improved behavioral regulation, and increased subjective well-being. In other words, meditators feel less moody, make better choices, and report being happier than they were before they went down the mindfulness path.

Convincing kids to use meditation can be a steep climb because it requires patience and quiet, not exactly everyone's forte at that age. But short breathing exercises that settle the brain—and the body—for just a couple of minutes have proven benefits. Even for the adults in the room, patterned breathing (like square or 4-7-8 breathing) for 15 to 30 seconds provides enough of a mental break to reset mood and reframe a reaction.

Lots of other life hacks fall under the general mindfulness umbrella and benefit mental wellness. Friendships play a tremendous role in happiness (see chapter 20), as do romantic relationships and deep connections with family members. Picking up new skills or hobbies can also provide a boon to mental health, thanks to both the mastery of something new and the social connections made with like-minded people. In fact, the list of techniques that work to buffer mental health could run pages—we've barely scratched the surface.

WHAT'S CHANGED OVER THE PAST 20, 30, 40 YEARS

The need for mental health care has escalated across the board. Rates of anxiety disorders, eating disorders, ADHD, and addiction have all climbed steadily, making the mental health landscape barely recognizable from a generation ago. Hospital in-patient facilities are packed, many with waiting lists for the acutely ill needing around-the-clock care. Then a global pandemic only exacerbated an already exponentially rising phenomenon of mental health issues among adolescents. Talk to any psychiatrist, psychologist, social worker, marriage and family therapist (MFT), or other mental health professional and they will tell you that they've never been so busy. They are with patients who need their help, and they are turning away new referrals. Here's why:

- Just under half of all teenagers in the United States—49.5 percent—have been diagnosed with a mental illness or mental health struggle at some point in their life.

- Between 2005 and 2017, the rates of major depressive episodes among 12- to 17-year-olds increased by 52 percent—in 2005, 8.7 percent reported major depression over the preceding year, but by 2017 the number had increased to 13.2 percent. That's more than 1 in 8 teenagers with major depression.

- Anxiety disorders were already hitting new heights in 2016, when approximately 11 percent of all kids ages 12–17 carried the diagnosis; today that number has multiplied nearly threefold, with 32 percent of all teenagers diagnosed.

- In 2021, more than a year into the COVID pandemic, the U.S. surgeon general and the American Academy of Pediatrics declared a youth mental health emergency because that year:

  44 percent of high school students reported feeling persistently sad or hopeless.
  15 percent of all kids between ages 12 and 17 had one or more major depressive episodes.
  10.6 percent grappled with ongoing severe major depression.
  4 percent struggled with substance abuse.

Perhaps some of this increase comes from doctors and researchers getting better at asking about these issues and from respondents/patients being more honest when they answer. One sure factor increasing the numbers has been the general destigmatization of mental health issues. A generation ago, the subject was barely whispered, but in 2021, when Simone Biles stepped off the mat mid-Olympics citing mental health, her willingness to share openly created a watershed moment in which public figures, celebrities, and other professional athletes felt free to reveal their journeys. Shifts in conversation about mental health were already apparent well before this, but now the stigma had officially lifted.

Moments like these increase the likelihood that anyone—celebrity or average Joe—will talk about their mental health with a doctor, a researcher, or a friend.

A ton of emergent data backs up the fact that mental health has taken a nosedive, not over several decades but just over the past 15 years (and escalating especially during COVID lockdowns). These days, unhealthy stress seems to have become ubiquitous among tweens and teens. Ask them how they're doing, and it will be as likely you hear "stressed" as "fine." So when we try to quantify what has changed since today's parents or grandparents were living their own puberties, the prevalence of almost every mental health issue has grown by at least an order of magnitude.

Social media has both hurt and helped. While the internet has been hailed as a great connector and is home to a variety of mental health support communities, it's also associated with rising rates of depression, anxiety, and eating disorders corresponding to the amount of time spent on various social media apps.

ADOLESCENT SUICIDE

Suicide is the most catastrophic consequence of depression. The CDC has been closely following rising suicide rates among tweens, teens, and twenty-somethings, documenting a grim prepandemic trend: a nearly 60 percent increase in the decade between 2007 and 2018. COVID magnified the problem, further increasing rates of emergency room visits for suicidal ideation or attempts, most notably among tweens 10 to 13 years old. And among people 15 to 24 years old, suicide is the second leading cause of death. In 2022, a shocking 20 percent of high school students reported suicidal ideation and 9 percent reported a suicide attempt. The Trevor Project flagged even higher rates (as high as 25 percent) among kids identifying as LGBTQ+ compared with their heterosexual cisgender peers.

This data is frightening. In response, a mental health emergency was declared in 2021 and a new national 988 Suicide Prevention hotline was established. Who is at risk? A bigger subset of kids than ever before, especially ones who have endured physical or sexual abuse, substance use, or bullying; who have a history of mental illness; who lack access to mental health care; and who have access to lethal means like an unlocked, loaded gun. But there *are* proven ways to help prevent suicide. The most important protective factors turn out to be family and community connections, social-emotional coping skills, and access to mental health care. See the resources section on our website for more information.

The generational shift in self-care brings welcome relief. More people than ever use—and talk about—self-care strategies like meditation and journaling, exercise and sleep. The digital landscape serves here as well, offering up apps to make all of these more accessible. Most people are well acquainted with the neuroscience data promoting the benefits of longer sleep, and the word *melatonin* is not foreign anymore—in fact, people don't just know it, they buy it in the vitamin aisle.

A new self-care strategy that has evolved from necessity is the advice to remove all devices (computers, iPads, phones, you name it) from the bedroom overnight. Two decades ago, there *might* have been a computer in the bedroom, and possibly a phone (likely cordless, not cellular); four decades ago all of that was unimaginable—the TV was in the family room and the corded phone in the kitchen. But today pings and rings and endless streams of email and texts interrupt sleep, so much so that most people looking for a good long stretch of it are all too willing to plug their devices in somewhere else overnight. Yes, even kids, particularly when adults in the house model the behavior.

HOW TO TALK ABOUT IT

Adults often feel uncomfortable addressing kids' mental health, especially the ones who didn't grow up in families that openly discussed feelings or who were advised to "toughen up" when struggling emotionally. But as with so much in this book, discomfort is not reason enough to avoid conversation. And remember that looking out for mental health goes beyond speaking, it's not only about what we say or do but also about keeping our eyes and ears open.

If you have any concern that a kid you care about is struggling with a mental health issue, don't wait to see if it's a passing phase or will get better with time—go talk to a professional. Getting an appointment quickly with a healthcare professional may be difficult, but there are lots of layers of help available to start: school psychologists, guidance counselors, local religious chaplains, and pediatricians, all of whom can lay eyes on a kid and help assess the situation, stabilizing things until more can be done or pointing you to emergency services if necessary.

Worry about emotional wellness exists on a spectrum, with extreme cases far at one end. A more crowded area of the spectrum is populated by kids who worry us just a little . . . enough to raise a yellow flag but not nearly five-alarm-fire-worthy. Here are some ways to foster an environment that promotes their mental health.

Help kids differentiate between normal reactions and pathology

Thanks to social media and the internet, today's adolescents self-pathologize like it's going out of style. How many times in the last week have you heard a tween or teen talk about having a "panic attack" or about their friend who they think has an "anxiety disorder"? On the one hand, cheers to the normalization of big, difficult feelings, ones that have traditionally been hidden in a school bathroom stall or under the covers at night. We're all for bringing the whole spectrum of human emotion out into the open. But kids need help differentiating between clinical diagnoses and typical-yet-challenging feelings. Feeling stressed out doesn't equal an anxiety disorder. Sweaty palms and a racing heart doesn't mean a panic attack. Organizing the desk before starting homework isn't a sign of OCD. Feeling sad for a week about a breakup doesn't flag clinical depression. It's on us to help kids normalize more difficult feelings that come along with growing older and, at the same time, teach them to distinguish between tough emotions and mental illness.

Don't dismiss their emotions as "drama"

Our culture tends to dismiss adolescents' big emotions as "drama"—overreactions to minor situations that don't warrant the temperature of feelings expressed. Our own internal monologue may say *Been there, done that, get over it!* but discounting our kids' feelings can put them in peril, especially when they take the cue that we're not interested in hearing what's going on. Or they may be fine now, but choose not to share down the road as life escalates.

What doesn't *seem* like a big deal to us *feels* like a big deal to them. As neuroscientists explain, adolescent brains experience emotions more strongly than younger and older ones do. As tweens and teens build the skill of emotion management, they simultaneously ride out highs and lows. Some kids express feelings in a way that sounds like the person at the gym who grunts loudly while lifting heavy weights—yes, it's annoying, but if it makes them stronger, who are we to judge? Most important, if we dismiss their feelings as trivial or label them as overblown, our kids are less likely to come back to us another time. If they don't trust us to treat their feelings with respect and there's something serious going on, they will go to someone else or, worse, to no one at all.

Keep lines of communication open

We say this in every chapter, but that's because it is *so* important, particularly when kids are struggling emotionally. By keeping lines of communication open, we don't mean you should talk more. Quite the opposite—in many cases it's more about sitting quietly and listening. Different personalities communicate differently, so a few suggestions:

The kids who are talkers might talk a lot, but they don't necessarily talk about the things going on beneath the surface. With chatty kids, it can be in the moments of quiet when they delve deeper, so create space for them to find some stillness. Or just resist the urge to fill the silence with your own words.

The naturally quieter kids most definitely won't open up if adults in their lives keep talking, constantly occupying the verbal space. Those kids need time—at home or at breakfast or in the car or on a walk with the dog—to find breathing room to open up more, especially if there always seem to be lots of other kids around.

The kids who are stressed or anxious need help from adults, particularly with bringing their emotional temperature down. Calm can take the form of providing quiet company or sitting near a kid who is spiraling and taking slow, deep breaths. Kids often follow the lead here, helping their pot go from a boil to a simmer.

None of this is to say that adults should be utterly silent, but we should be judicious when opening our mouths. It's what works. Open-ended curiosity goes a long way in creating opportunities for kids to start talking: *I'm wondering . . . I'm noticing . . . What do you think about . . .* all give kids the opportunity to lead the conversation rather than follow the direction adults choose. This can be particularly hard if you're feeling worried about a kid, in danger of losing your self-control, or desperate to dive right into the issue. But it works wonders to help kids share more substantive responses, not to mention build the muscle of self-reflection, learning to look inward and then express what they see.

Be a kid's release valve, not their source of pressure

Many kids will share openly and bluntly about the extreme amount of pressure they feel to get top grades and scores or to excel at sports or band or theater. The college process dogpiles expectation upon expectation, making many kids feel that no matter what they do, it's never enough. Adults have two choices: add to the pressure or be their release valve. Spoiler alert! There's only one right answer here.

So what does it sound like to be the release valve? Instead of asking a kid at the end of the day, *How was the test? How much homework do you have? Did you talk to the teacher about your paper? How much playing time did you get in the game? When do you find out about the play?* try asking things like this: *Did anything funny happen in school today? Wondering if you want to watch a movie with me this weekend? Did you notice what the dog did with his bed while you were gone? Do you want to taste this new cheese I bought?* Low-stakes questions that have nothing to do with an assignment or a looming task can help flip the mood for kids. Finding other things to talk about besides school and obligations helps kids feel like whole human beings, not just the sum of their accomplishments or failures.

Important sidenote: We all bring our own anxieties to the table. So reflect and take stock of yours. If you find yourself looking to your kid to calm *you* down, that's a sign the conversation isn't really about them. Go find your own release valve.

Enforce the habits that lead to good mental health

As kids get older and gain more independence, so much falls outside of adults' control. That is just a fact of life. But this doesn't mean that *nothing* is within our control, particularly when kids are living under our roofs. While the enforcement of rules and expectations can become particularly challenging in the adolescent years, sometimes tempting us to just give up, these are the years kids need our limit-setting the most. All of that data about sleep, exercise, and balanced nutrition goes a long way toward promoting mental wellness—it's our job to help kids follow through (even if it's a painful slog).

Sleep. Make sure they're not up at all hours, regardless of whether they're socializing on devices or studying endlessly. Helping kids set limits can ensure they get to bed at a reasonable hour. Moving devices out of their rooms overnight goes a long way to accomplishing this, as does getting them off their phones ideally a full hour (or two!) before bed. We know, it's a constant battle, not to mention one you might not be up for (literally, if they go to bed later than you do), but it's worth fighting.

Exercise. Not every kid loves to play sports or work out at the gym, but every kid needs to move their body for *at least* 60 minutes every single day. This can feel burdensome to kids who don't consider themselves "athletes," so help them find ways to exercise that are comfortable and authentic to them: walking the dog, taking an online dance class, going to yoga with a friend. The emotional benefits of even moderate exercise cannot be overstated, but kids often need help finding the right fit and getting into a routine. Be patient because creating a lifelong habit of physical activity is a marathon, not a sprint (pun fully intended). And no, it does not matter one iota if they change the thing they are "into" every week, so long as they are moving.

Balanced diet. And by balanced, we mean *balanced:* fruits and vegetables and, yes, chocolate and ice cream.

Different kinds of foods play different and important roles for physical and emotional wellness. Some fuel our energy, some comfort us, some help us build muscle. It's on the adults to ensure that a wide variety of foods are available. And it's just as important that we not demonize certain foods while making sure kids are getting what their bodies and brains need.

How to know if a kid is in crisis

Adults worry 24/7 about the kids they love, and there is *nothing* worse than watching a kid suffer. However, certain outward signs require immediate action, including self-harm, suicidal ideation, alcohol or substance abuse, and purging or ongoing caloric restriction. Sometimes it's hard to categorize subtle (or not-so-subtle) shifts in behavior: what's simply part of the regular adolescent emotional tsunami versus a call for professional help? If ever in doubt, get help. And if any of the following appear and persist for more than a week or two—or if you just have a strong feeling in your gut that you need more hands on deck—reach out to a professional. These are signs a kid might be experiencing more than a rough patch:

- Consistent sadness or worrying, inconsolable tears

- Apathy (indifference)

- Lethargy (exhaustion), including sleeping too much

- Inability to sleep

- Loss of interest in hygiene, self-care, or presentation—like not showering or changing clothes

- Avoiding social interactions by not speaking to friends, not leaving the house, or withdrawing completely from the people around them

- Shifting eating habits, with either far less or far more consumption than usual

- Ongoing irritability or anger, including sudden outbursts

- Observed or disclosed heavy drinking or substance use

FROM PEOPLE JUST OUT THE OTHER SIDE

B.H., she/her, age 21

I have struggled with mental health issues for a lot of my life. In middle school, I was severely bullied for years, and I suffered anxiety and depression, which have followed me to this day. I lived in Hong Kong for seven years from my elementary to middle school years, and discussion about mental health was stigmatized, so much so that I never understood how I felt or why I was feeling a certain way. As a 10-year-old, I felt so alone. I was isolated because I couldn't talk to friends about it and was scared to bring up the bullying to my parents because they would just call me emotional and moody, a common accusation against me in my family. As a consequence, I dealt with the trauma alone. It was my aunt who intervened when she found out about it through my cousin, who also went to the same school and who told my parents about it. They moved me back to California, where things started to look up for me. I think they realized that I was turning into someone they didn't want me to be and thought moving back to a culture that I felt much more connected to would benefit me.

A few years later in high school, another traumatic event happened to me. I was sexually assaulted during senior year. My mental health had never been this bad before. School used to come so easily for me, but I was finding myself getting Cs on tests for the first time in my life.

I had to become a different person; I wasn't the emotional and full-of-life kid that everybody knew. Rather, I was a shell of a human being, burying myself in schoolwork and not confronting what had happened to me. But this time things were different: I wasn't alone. I told my parents and my best friends about it. It was difficult for my parents and the people who loved me to hear that this had happened to their only daughter and their good friend, and it was not an easy topic of discussion right off the bat. My parents and I had never really talked about mental health before this, but I guess the silver lining was that it was finally something we discussed at the dinner table.

I started seeing a therapist, and my parents finally stopped seeing my emotions as a hoax. With the help of my awesome therapist, my loving family, and my caring friends, I learned to discuss my feelings and to come to terms with my trauma. It took me some time, but I was finally able to talk to my peers, parents, and trusted adults about it. I no longer felt ashamed that I was dealing with mental health issues, and I wasn't doing it alone. The biggest difference between my success with overcoming trauma and other mental health issues was the ability to talk about it with the people around me. I was able to lean on friends and family who wanted to help me and didn't judge me for who I am and what had happened to me. It was the support that I got from the people around me that made me feel safe for the first time in my life.

Unfortunately, terrible things happen to everyone, and it's important to be able to acknowledge and notice the changes in your kid's mood and temperament. For me, I think my parents didn't want to believe that their perfect daughter could be suffering from mental health issues. This affected me so much to the point I was gaslighting my own feelings, and that's where it got dangerous. I sought a sense of validation from outsiders for so long, and the first person to give it to me was one of my best friends that I trusted and opened up to. Be that person for your kid!

In hindsight, my parents did the best they could, given the situation. Both occasions were difficult for them to handle; however, there was a large shift in how they helped me with the bullying and the sexual assault. They allowed outside intervention, for one, and did not dismiss the idea of therapy and mental health, despite their upbringing. My best friend in high school, who supported me the most throughout this experience, was a product of a liberal Los Angeles upbringing that valued mental health. I consider myself lucky, because I'm grateful for the support that I had.

CHAPTER 14

Body Image and Eating Disorders

One of the great cruelties of puberty is its deep unpredictability, not just the path through but also where everything will settle out in the end. If we had to pick a single hallmark of puberty that best epitomizes this, it would be body shape and size.

Pubescent bodies shift profoundly. During the pubertal growth spurt alone, kids gain 20 percent of their height and even more of their weight. Some seem to transform overnight, while for others a barely visible metamorphosis unfolds over months and years. This discrepancy alone would be enough for any of them to handle, but then there's the fact that the body will continue to morph throughout their life span. Sometimes adults still look very similar to the way they did at the end of puberty, but many live in profoundly different shaped bodies. It's easier to manage a transient stage on a time-stamped journey with a knowable end point, but body shape turns out to be precisely the opposite. It's the facet of puberty that lingers longest.

LET'S START WITH SCIENCE

Body image refers to a person's relationship with their own body: what they see in the mirror and how it makes them feel. A negative body image can be fueled by body dissatisfaction (not liking part or all of what they've got) or body dysmorphia (fixation on external appearance) and can ultimately lead to an eating disorder. It makes perfect sense that the shape-shifting changes of puberty can trigger these challenges; what's surprising is how long these painful feelings can persist, lasting through the teen years for some, decades for others.

DEFINING THE MOST COMMON TERMS

Body dissatisfaction: When a person has persistent negative thoughts and feelings about their body; this is an internal, emotional, and cognitive process but is influenced by external factors.

Body dysmorphic disorder or body dysmorphia: A mental health condition characterized by one or more self-perceived defects in appearance that others see as minor or don't see at all.

Eating disorder: Any of a range of mental health disorders—including anorexia nervosa, bulimia nervosa, and binge eating—characterized by atypical or disturbed eating habits.

Anorexia nervosa: The triad of abnormally low body weight, intense fear of gaining weight, and a distorted perception of weight.

Bulimia nervosa: Recurrent episodes of binge eating followed by compensatory behaviors such as vomiting, ingestion of laxatives, or excessive exercise to prevent weight gain.

Binge eating: Episodes of eating an excessive amount of food, which may take place in a short span of time or may be more of an extended grazing.

Sources include mayoclinic.com, uptodate.com, NEDC.com.au.

Culturally we've gendered the phenomenon of eating disorders, assigning it largely to females. This turns out to be a big mistake, but an innocent one that evolved because many girls and women aim to be thin. Weight loss in an attempt to reach this goal is an easy tell. Body dissatisfaction often starts when the midsection fills out and begins to accumulate fat around the waist—this happens to many tween girls shortly before or at the very start of breast development. Some remain blissfully unaware, but many take notice, labeling themselves with words like *fat*, *chubby*, or *big-bellied*. As puberty progresses they acquire curves in their hips, butts, and breasts, shifting from rectangular to fuller-figured, and they are suddenly, simultaneously sexualized for their curves and criticized for their lack of thinness—unless they remain stick-like, in which case they are criticized for their lack of curves and many are still sexualized nonetheless. It's complicated stuff for anyone to manage, but particularly the tweens and teens living it.

Guys, on the other hand, have their own body image challenges. They usually feel intense pressure to get bigger or "jacked," striving for musculature, which manifests as gaining weight in order to add more muscle mass. Their bodies transform through puberty too: some add pounds to their midsection, butt, and upper thighs especially; others gain slowly while stretching and stretching, thinning out evermore; and still others start puberty on the heavier side. Some in this last group seek to lose weight while gaining muscle, which gets hailed as "becoming healthy," even though sometimes it's not.

And so, we have landed at a place of profound body pressure for all, saddled with a lingering double standard: when females try to shed pounds, they're identified as pathological; when males do the same, they're getting in shape. Until recently, genetic males barely lit up the body image radar—almost no one gave them credit for feeling all the same ways that girls feel about transforming, sharing many of their dissatisfactions just in opposite directions. But today (finally!) there's a growing appreciation of the fact that the male body ideal exists and exerts a ton of pressure.

The current state of body image issues is best described by the data, some of which may surprise you.

- A 2022 national poll of parents of 8- to 12-year-olds reported that 57 percent of their daughters and 49 percent of their sons felt self-conscious about their appearance. Among 13- to 17-year olds, those numbers were 73 percent and 69 percent, respectively.

- Body dissatisfaction starts young, with some studies suggesting that up to 78 percent of kids are unhappy with their bodies by the time they are 17.

- Male body image issues abound, with 43 percent reporting dissatisfaction with their appearance—their skin, hair, nose, genitals, body shape, or muscle mass.

- Female body image issues persist, with some studies reporting dissatisfaction levels as high as 91 percent, though others put it closer to 40 percent.

- Nearly 30 million people in the United States have a full-blown eating disorder (anorexia, bulimia, or binge eating), and it's estimated that 95 percent of them are between the ages of 12 and 25.

- Approximately 10 million people in the United States have body dysmorphia, likely a gross underestimate reflecting the fact that *body dysmorphia* is a new term with little data behind it.

- Eating disorders are among the deadliest mental illnesses, second only to opiate addiction—10,200 deaths each year are attributed to eating disorders, and 26 percent of people with eating disorders attempt suicide.

While the risk for body image issues spans all genders, it's far higher for LGBTQIA+ people. Kids and adults identifying as nonheterosexual are two to four times more likely than their heterosexual peers to engage in weight control behaviors (like fasting, consuming diet pills, or purging via vomiting or laxative use) or to develop a full-fledged eating disorder. Transgender people report some of the highest rates, driven by the body ideals of male muscularity and female thinness that may be even harder to attain when their chromosomal sex does not align with their gender identity. Those who have not transitioned often feel trapped in the wrong body, further propelling dissatisfaction and lowering self-esteem. Add to that victimization from bullying or discrimination (often both), and it becomes clear why this group faces stacked obstacles when it comes to body image.

The fact that every gender is affected here reminds us to look for body dissatisfaction, body dysmorphia, and full-blown eating disorders across the board. No kid—no person, for that matter—is immune. There are subsets of kids, though, to keep a particularly close collective eye on.

The earliest bloomers, especially genetic females. These kids have bodies that mature well before their friends' do, becoming taller and noticeably curvy ahead of everyone else their age. Many of them report feeling bigger than their classmates, and in fairness, they often *are* bigger: in height and bra size and sometimes waist size too. This translates into self-consciousness and body dissatisfaction. Some studies show that the perception of their weight matters more than the actual number on the scale, reinforcing the importance of how they feel.

Athletes, especially ones who wear leotards or swimsuits or do sports that involve standing in front of a mirror or weighing in. Athletics wields a double-edged sword with regard to body shape and self-perception of that shape. On the one hand, many athletes love their strong, fit frames. On the other, sports can generate tremendous pressure to be bigger (football, hockey), to be smaller (ballet, cheer), or to live right on a weight cusp (wrestling, rowing), all of which can drive overly aggressive or overly restrictive eating choices. Sports that require leotards, bathing suits, and/or mirrors (we're looking at you, dance, diving, and gymnastics!) are associated with particularly high rates of restrictive eating or purging. Sports that value bulk can inadvertently (or purposefully) encourage young athletes to consume body-building supplements and even to use anabolic steroids.

Social media regulars. Kids scrolling through social media posts see all sorts of imagery. Time spent on these apps correlates directly with low self-esteem and body dissatisfaction. The platforms prioritizing selfies and likes—most famously Instagram, with its culture of image perfection—reinforce hard-to-attain body ideals. Other platforms use algorithms to feed extreme body content like pro-anorexia (pro-ana) videos and websites with chat rooms meant to "educate" people on how to "successfully" pursue eating disorders.

Once a person heads down the slippery slope of being dissatisfied with the shape of their body, they may choose to try to do something about it. Some restrict the amount of food they eat or limit themselves to certain food categories—the ones who are "successful" go on to lose weight, sometimes significant amounts, with the most restrictive ones becoming anorexic. Others attempt to restrict food intake but give over to urges and consume massive quantities instead. Some add purging to this cycle: restriction followed by binge eating and then an attempt to get rid of the calories they have overconsumed via self-induced vomiting, consumption of laxatives, or intense exercise. Within this group, there are people who lose weight, people who gain weight, and people who maintain their weight and defy suspicion that something's going on. There are also people whose desire to bulk up drives them to increase their calorie consumption, sometimes unhealthfully, and others whose low self-esteem pushes them into a cycle of overeating, gaining weight, feeling worse about themselves, and eating more. All of these scenarios—and there are plenty of others that fall under the category of disordered eating—share a deep mental health component.

A final note about the term *eating disorder.* It implies that three separate things are going on: (1) unhealthy behavior with respect to food; (2) obsession with food, eating strategies, and body shape, to the point where these thoughts are constant and all-consuming; and (3) impaired normal social function caused by fears of eating, judgment, or missing exercise. An eating disorder is a lot for anyone of any age to carry.

 ## WHAT'S CHANGED OVER THE PAST 20, 30, 40 YEARS

There's good news and bad news on this front. On the positive side, body image and eating disorders are far more talked about now than ever before. Body dissatisfaction is understood as an early flag for low self-esteem and corollary risks. Body dysmorphia is no longer dismissed as "all in her head"—it's also no longer considered an exclusively female issue.

Beauty standards have ricocheted over the years, but today there exist multiple body ideals, at least for females: thin is still in; fit and strong is also seen as sexy; and thanks to celebrities, curves have made a gigantic comeback. Plus-size models now occupy the ranks of the mainstream, and thinness is not necessarily a determinant of celebrity or success. The body positivity movement has transformed the way people think of weight, helping remove some of the implicit bias heavier people have had to contend with for much of their lives. The fact that females have more than one body type they can consider ideal marks an improvement, but there's clearly a way to go here.

Males, meanwhile, remain at the starting line, waiting for progress on this front. Guys find themselves with a singular set of goals, relatively unchanged since GI Joe debuted his plastic six-pack abs in the 1960s: broad shoulders, well-defined muscles, narrow hips, ripped thighs, and smooth, hairless skin from the neck down. Today's main beauty standard difference is the hair on the top of the head, which was once only sexy if full but now ranks if it's fully shaved too.

Even as the definition of beauty has shifted over the decades, dissatisfaction has grown. It's almost as if there's broader acceptance of every body type except one's own. Data suggests that these trends are on the rise, largely driven by a recent acknowledgment that body dissatisfaction, body dysmorphia, and eating disorders affect males in numbers far higher than ever recognized: these days 25 percent (not the oft-quoted 10 percent) of all people diagnosed with anorexia are male, and a third of all people with eating disorders of any type are male. Of people who do things like try to lose weight by restricting their food intake or exercising compulsively, a full half are male. Perhaps recognition of the issue among the male half of the population increases the number of cases being picked up, but it's also very possible that the actual number of people with body image issues is rising.

Another new term on the horizon, sure to identify even more people living under the umbrella of body dissatisfaction, is *orthorexia*. This term doesn't have a clinical definition as of yet, but generally speaking it refers to an unhealthy focus on healthy eating and exercising that in some cases borders on obsession. Keep your eyes peeled, because you're going to hear this term a lot in the future.

If we had to pick the biggest driver of the recent acceleration in body dissatisfaction and everything that flows from there, it would be social media. Data released in an investigation of Instagram in 2021 revealed that the social media app was well aware of its impact upon young viewers. This exposé earned Instagram lots of bad press and a new moniker: Thinstagram. Instagram is not alone, of course—a parade of social media apps bear responsibility for redefining how viewers, especially kids who aren't supposed to be on those platforms in the first place, feel about themselves. But it's a perfect example of how a medium unimaginable a dozen years ago has singlehandedly transformed the landscape of mental health issues and body negativity.

 ## HOW TO TALK ABOUT IT

Struggles with body image, rooted in puberty, can stay with people throughout their lives. Any adult who has wrestled with this issue knows how complicated the feelings become when a child in their life gains or loses weight. Frankly, old feelings reemerge even when the kid's growing body simply looks just a little too much like theirs did. No matter how difficult it is, though, we *must* leave our baggage at the door.

For starters, the adult in the room needs to (constantly) remember that it is normal for kids to gain weight before, during, and after puberty. In fact, with very few exceptions, weight loss is *not* a good thing for growing kids. Chapter 9 is packed with information about this if you need a refresher.

Pubescent kids ride a wild body roller coaster, literally waking up in a (slightly) different body every day. Imagine how confusing and overwhelming that feels. You know what's helpful? Having the adults in their lives love, support, validate, and encourage them. You know what's not helpful? Shaming, humiliating, and dumping all over them. Fostering positive body image in kids takes ongoing inordinate self-control from the adults, who need to keep their mouths shut and their hearts open.

Which is not to say that adults don't have a *brutal* internal monologue running through their minds, with devastating judgments pinging as they clock a kid gaining weight or staring unhappily in the mirror or avoiding the tiniest morsels of food. As Zoë Bisbing, cofounder of the Full Bloom Project, advises, "it's okay to register your disgust" in response to your child. Rather than self-censoring those thoughts, be aware of reactions to kids and then reflect on where they're coming from. But don't turn those thoughts into words directed at the child—instead find another adult, a friend, a partner, a therapist, *anyone* other than the kid, and share those thoughts with them.

This advice to parents must be blunt because it can literally save lives. Fostering a kid's positive body image is exhausting, and addressing an eating disorder can require a massive undertaking, but both are must-do's, not may-do's, otherwise the consequences may turn dire. It's never too late to lean into a culture of body positivity even if you know you've blown it in the past. We won't get to all the possible scenarios here, but these are some of the best ways to address these issues.

Avoid "you're not fat, you're beautiful"

When a kid comes home announcing *I'm so fat!*, a common knee-jerk response sounds like *You're not fat, you're beautiful.* There is nothing wrong with telling a kid they are beautiful, but that doesn't make the reply helpful in this circumstance because without meaning to say so, it conveys the message that fat people can't be beautiful, which is not true. Plus, it addresses the complaint (*I'm so fat*) rather than the underlying issue. A better response would be a curious one: *I'm wondering where that comment is coming from. That's an unusual thing to say—what made you say that?* This avoids a quick dismissal with blanket reassurance, focusing instead on what's driving the statement.

Teach kids to be cultural critics of the media's body ideals

We all know that kids are bombarded with imagery of unrealistic body ideals courtesy of social media and clickbait digital content—we get versions of the same in our feeds too! Delaying access to their own device(s), setting screen-time limits, and restricting their apps and platforms all minimize the onslaught. But let's face it: these ideals are *everywhere,* even in old-school TV shows and print magazines. Photoshop is taught in school for God's sake! So the best way through is to encourage them to be cultural critics of what they see, explaining (or if they're older, asking them to explain to you) how influencers take hundreds of photos in order to create the "perfect image" or how editors use photo-editing tools to give people the "right" body shape. Awareness removes some of the pressure, revealing these as unattainable goals and hopefully shifting focus away from trying to reach them. Grab a teachable moment, describe what's going on, and then move on without a sanctimonious lecture.

Remove scales from your house

When we say that tweens and teens are meant to gain weight throughout puberty, we mean it. There's no need to have a scale to document that trajectory. Even though weight gain is healthy and expected (and in most cases needed), ours is a society where weight gain often causes distress, especially when it passes into triple-digit territory, crossing 100 pounds. And when weight loss is the goal, scales can be even more problematic, fueling a desire for thinness. If someone in the house needs to check weight for health reasons, keep a scale out of sight and put it away after use—but trust us when we say that kids will eventually find that scale, so if possible, ditch it altogether and weigh in elsewhere. As hard as it is for some of us to let go of ideals tethered to a number on a scale, it's not a healthy habit, so take the opportunity *not* to pass it along.

Skinny people can be self-conscious too

It's easy to assume that thin people are thrilled to be thin, but that's not always the case. Some are uncomfortable with their size, and even more uncomfortable when everyone feels the right to comment on it: *Aren't you lucky to be so skinny? Boy, I wish I had your metabolism.* This is especially true for teen boys, who tell us that being skinny is *not* considered a good thing. Be aware of the pressure to bulk up and get "ripped" or "jacked," especially among athletes. This isn't just a guy phenomenon, by the way—these days girls complain that their butts are too small, a sentence rarely uttered in the 1980s or 1990s. If you see a kid you love on the receiving end of thoughtless comments about how skinny they are, step in and say something. Those passing remarks can have lasting effects on kids, fueling body dissatisfaction or worse.

Keep your eyes open to the "getting healthy" kick

Eating disorder specialists often discuss the missed inflection point when a kid who has been unhappy with their body suddenly decides to cut out food groups, exercise obsessively, or restrict food intake in an effort to "get healthy." Sure, making conscious choices about food and exercise can be legitimately good for you depending on what those choices are, and almost every kid could stand to make better choices without our nagging. But sometimes it's a warning shot across the eating disorder bow. As uncomfortable as this advice might be, it's not okay to ignore this behavior. Here are some ways in, but if nothing feels right, reach out to your healthcare provider for other suggestions.

> **For the kid who is cutting out food groups:** *Hey, I noticed you haven't been eating the pasta I made for dinner. Has something changed?*

> **For the kid who is on a workout kick:** *It seems like you're spending a lot of time in the gym, and it's great to exercise, but I want to make sure you're eating enough to balance all the exertion.*

For the kid who is skipping meals: *I see that you haven't been eating breakfast lately—wanted to check in on that. Do you need some other options?*

When you find empty wrappers hidden in drawers

Eating something yummy, salty, sugary, or chocolaty can feel really good. They're celebratory fun foods or they're comfort foods that cheer us up. Unfortunately, they're also the foods people sometimes consume secretly because they are labeled "junk." It can be incredibly hard to address secretive or binge eating without shaming kids for wanting those foods in the first place. (Who here doesn't have some chocolate or ice cream at the end of a long day?) One way to address secretive eating without vilifying it would be *I noticed some wrappers in your bedside drawer. Those snacks are really delicious (I love them too!), and it's fine for you to have them sometimes, but with ground rules. There's no secret eating in our house because there is no shame in wanting to have something delicious. You don't have to hide it. Since it's my job to make sure you get enough nutrition in your body, I need you to have a say in when you eat those foods. What do you think, is this a fair plan?*

Bingeing and purging doesn't always have a tell

Many health issues have a tell—a fever, vomiting, rash—but eating disorders can be much easier to miss, especially when weight doesn't fluctuate. Bingeing and purging, the combination known as bulimia, is the classic example. Many bulimics maintain their weight, and for all the world their eating habits appear thoroughly unrestricted. But look closer and there may be signs: going to the bathroom right after eating (to vomit or use laxatives); expressing profound unhappiness about their appearance; engaging in punishing behaviors like obsessive exercise or fasting in response to eating too much. People who purge by throwing up can have a perennially sore throat, shredded fingernails, and eroding enamel on their teeth caused by the acid in vomit. Over time, even though they may not appear deprived, bulimics become malnourished, and eventually they face dramatic health risks. They're also more likely to battle comorbidities such as substance abuse, anxiety, and mood disorders.

This is a scary topic because one wrong step in the conversation and a kid becomes even harder to reach. But given that eating disorders like bulimia carry with them tremendous physical and emotional ramifications, we must reframe this worry. Besides, it's very possible that a kid wants help and doesn't know how to ask for it; or they're ashamed of their behavior and see themselves as disgusting; or maybe they just need some nonjudgmental help to change course. Talk to a healthcare provider to get resources, support, and guidance—eating disorders are best handled by a team. In the meantime, one simple sentence to a kid can go a long way: *I am always here if you want to talk, no judgment.*

Get kids clothes that fit

We hear from kids that as their weight and height change, it's really important to have clothing that fits. They feel less self-conscious and more comfortable. And yes, we know that it seems like just yesterday you got them new pants, new T-shirts, new shorts, you name it. But positive body image also means taking joy in our bodies and expressing ourselves through style and movement—it's hard to do that when clothes feel too small. A simple *Want to get some new clothes?* works wonders.

FROM PEOPLE JUST OUT THE OTHER SIDE

B.C., he/him, age 16

On body image

As someone who's naturally pretty skinny and has funky proportions, body image is a weird topic for me. I'm about 5 foot 11 (not 6 feet) and have longer legs than my brother, who's 6 foot 3. I have a small torso with wide hips, ribs that stick out, and the abs that skinny people have, not abs that I've worked out for because I don't really work out. Are there things I wish I had that other people have? Of course. I don't have super-broad shoulders, or a big chest, and I have pretty skinny arms. With all that being said, I don't really care that much.

Every day on my social media feed I see really good-looking men with chiseled abs and white smiles posing for videos and pictures, and I'll admit they look amazing. If I could look like them in that very instant I probably would. However, there are some flaws in what we see on social media. Even though they may look a certain way online, in real life they could very easily look a lot less muscular. On social media, we only capture a glimpse of the person's life. In this glimpse, the lighting is perfect, and oftentimes the person will have worked out just before in order to get what's called a "pump." A pump happens post workout where the muscles get bigger for a short period of time.

Also, thinking about the amount of time, stress, and work that goes into their lives just to look a certain way doesn't entice me to be like them in any way. As a big sweet tooth, the diets of the people online are my worst nightmare. Part of what gets me through the dark New York winters are the many chocolate-covered almonds I eat with my mom around 10 P.M. most nights. Or in the summer, being able to enjoy a Shake Shack caramel milkshake without any stress is so important for my overall well-being. Now, I'm not saying people should just be constantly eating bad foods and never be active because it gets to the point where it's unhealthy. Having said that, it's important to let loose once in a while and relax. One of my friends over a year span went from being overweight to being one of the most in-shape kids I know, but when talking about his transformation he said that although he's incredibly proud, everything he went through in order to be so in shape was not necessarily worth it. He found his mental health significantly declined in the year span. From the outside, having a flattering body may sound good, but the side effects are not always positive.

As a parent there are a few things your kid should know. The first would be to not always feel the need to look exactly like influencers online because they often don't even look the same in real life. Another piece of advice is to remain active and eat healthy, but sometimes the most healthy thing to do could come in the form of eating something unhealthy. A "healthy" person doesn't need to have the biggest arms or the best abs, but can simply be a happy person who has a solid routine. The final thing a kid should know is that there's certain things they can't control about their body. As stated before, I have ribs that stick out and can't control how they look. However, the best thing to do is to embrace how they look and wear it confidently.

A.N., she/her, age 22

On eating disorders

Last week, I went to the beach with friends. The moment we parked our car, I threw my towel on the sand and ran straight into the cold Atlantic Ocean. It's a pretty common thing to do—it gets hot outside, we go swimming. But as I dunked my head underwater, I thought about a version of myself four years ago. I was on a beach trip with friends to learn how to surf. But I barely made it 10 minutes in the ocean before I had to get out. I was struggling with an eating disorder at the time, and my body had stopped doing a lot of the things it was supposed to do—like keep me warm. People rarely talk about that aspect of eating disorders, but I wish it was something I had known. My heart rate was low, I was constantly anxious and irritable, my hair fell out, and I felt tired all the time but couldn't sleep.

Growing up, the ocean was my favorite place—any kind of swimming brought me so much joy. But as I went into middle and high school, I started thinking more about how I looked at the beach compared to my classmates, or in my clothes. And it felt like my friends were always getting compliments about how they looked, and never seemed to worry. So I started to think more about what I ate, and how I exercised, but it very quickly became obsessive. Over time, I realized I wasn't able to do anything except think about food and my body. I lost laughter, time with friends, my ability to focus at school or really focus on anything at all. I was anxious all the time, drowning in the conviction that I needed to look a certain way in order to be worthy of love or care.

It's a long process—and continues to be—but I wish I could show that version of myself how proud I am to have learned to care for and appreciate my body again. And in this process, I got back so much more than a functioning body (although that part is wonderful). I rediscovered laughter, the beach, dinners with friends and family, even birthdays. These are all things I would tell myself a few years ago, because I am so happy to have them back.

R.W., she/her, age 21

On eating disorders

My summer before college, I heard many fears and comments about the "freshman 15."

The freshman 15 refers to the 15 pounds that first-year college students supposedly gain. It's basically a myth, but it was my personal nightmare. I remember when my favorite, everyday jeans stopped fitting during my first semester. So I started wearing my "loose" jeans—they were no longer loose. I thought to myself, "Oh no. The freshman 15 is hitting." It was as if the world was ending.

When I came home from college for spring break, I knew I looked noticeably different. I felt myself yearning for a body that I did not have, a body that I did not even know how to achieve. I had always been told I was so small and tiny, and my doctor would tell me I was underweight. I thought that was how I was "supposed" to look, and now I felt the opposite. A week later, I was sent home from college because of the COVID-19 pandemic. I was stuck at home all day, fixating on my appearance. My bottled-up feelings toward my image erupted, and I sat on my kitchen floor and sobbed to my mom about how I had been feeling. After a year of trying to figure out how to feel more confident, I decided to start working with a trainer. I had grown up as a dancer, and I missed feeling strong and confident. The program I was given included a meal plan. The trainer wanted to help me learn how to eat balanced and healthy. Well, "balanced and healthy" turned into "restrict and binge" for me. I would restrict myself all week and then get one cheat meal, where I would end up overindulging to the point of feeling sick. I was torturing myself and soon realized I had to stop following the meal plan. In gaining control of my meals back, I noticed that the restrict and binge habits continued. I had just been trying to fix my poor body image, and now I was equally focusing on my appearance and had formed a bad relationship with food.

Lucky for me, I am a nutrition science minor, and in the semester that I felt the lowest about my body image and eating habits, I happened to be in a class about properly fueling the body. I learned what restricting my diet was doing to my metabolism, and how the binge and restrict cycle was affecting hormone production, which in turn impacted my mood. Once I realized what I was doing to my body, I concluded that I needed to heal my relationship with food and with my appearance. I am grateful to have been enrolled in a course that helped educate me on how nutrition and health were linked in terms of diet and eating patterns.

CHAPTER 15

Youth Sports Overspecialization

Two truisms distill the science of exercise down to its core

Everything in moderation, including moderation.

(Oscar Wilde)

If you don't make time for exercise,
you'll probably have to make time for illness.

(Robin Sharma)

Since almost no one would refute either of these, what the heck went wrong with youth sports? What started as an effort in community-wide, good-for-you fun, youth sports has evolved into a voracious machine that pushes many kids out of team-play (and even plain old exercise) altogether, and the ones who remain in the game are driven toward injury, exhaustion, and burnout. Many youth sports, especially at the high school and college levels, know no moderation. This chapter covers a topic so broad, so socially and financially powerful, it could fill an entire book. In fact, it has—among others, we're thanking you, Michael Lewis, for writing *Playing to Win* about the youth sports industrial complex. Oddly, though, the topic of overspecialization almost never makes it into health-oriented books, which seems absurd because exercise in general, and sports in particular, deeply affect the shifting bodies and surging hormones of adolescents. So game on!

LET'S START WITH SCIENCE

Beginning with the broadest possible view, there are four basic pillars of health: exercise, nutrition, sleep, and hygiene. Of course, many other drivers of wellness exist, but these four categories, alone and together, form the basis of self-care.

When we move our bodies regularly, eat balanced diets, sleep soundly through the night, and care for our skin, our hair, and our breath, each one of us, regardless of age, is less likely to be sick, injured, even marginalized. More than that, these ablutions and routines increase the likelihood of wellness in the larger sense and make us feel (and often, look) good. In fact, without attention to these four pillars, nothing else on the quest for wellness really matters: you can take all the vitamins you want, meditate like a monk, and swear off french fries or all intoxicating substances, but without regular exercise, balanced nutrition, adequate stretches of deep sleep, and good basic hygiene, you will not stay healthy.

Research demonstrates that the earlier in life these health practices are introduced and ritualized, the more habituated and sustainable they become. This deeply virtuous cycle is especially true for exercise, which feels like a gift when it's routinized and enjoyed but a painful chore when shoehorned into daily life as a must-do on the checklist. Exercise sets in motion a long list of benefits that we've all heard a hundred times, probably more: it helps maintain body weight, build muscle mass and bone strength, release happiness-inducing chemicals, and improve overall mood.

When most of us think about exercise, our minds go right to working out. But exercise among kids looks different, falling into two distinct but overlapping categories: play and sports. It's easy to forget that play often translates into a strenuous workout, but think back to the last time you huffed and puffed your way through a full-out game of tag with a bunch of kids . . . or a dance party . . . or a pillow fight. They're all cardiovascular challenges masquerading as straight-up fun. Beyond the exercise piece, free play turns out to be a tremendously important part of growing up because it allows kids to think creatively without an adult telling them what to do. This unstructured environment forces kids to set goals, make rules or tweak existing ones, manage one another, solve conflicts, and develop empathy, all of which prove crucial to their interactions outside of the playground as well. Kids who don't master these skills generally aren't invited back into the game.

Organized sports offer many of the same social and physical benefits as play, just with different rules and spectatorship. Like free play, sports provide social and emotional development, creative thinking, and problem-solving. But these days, sports are generally highly-structured, governed, and attended by adults.

This isn't to say that organized sports have no value, because of course they do. Tremendous value! They carve out time for kids to move their bodies; provide safe outlets for congregating; teach fine and gross motor skills ranging from rudimentary to highly specialized; offer an environment for camaraderie and leadership; develop team-building skills; and provide mentoring relationships with coaches. Any form of exertional movement—but especially organized sports, with their warm-ups and drills and goal-oriented motor skills—can enhance muscle development, hand-eye coordination, flexibility, footwork, agility, strength, endurance, and stamina. And beyond all of that, on the whole the kids who play them have higher self-esteem and better self-discipline than kids who don't.

In theory, sports participation should be entirely positive. Just rewind a couple of sentences to that long list of the benefits. It's hard, actually, to overstate the positive impact of engaging in physical activity in a social and safe setting, particularly for kids living in less well-resourced communities. Or for kids who would otherwise be left to their own devices—literally, they'd be on their devices if it weren't for organized sports. But the mantra *Everything in moderation* needs to prevail here, and thanks to the modern-day phenomenon of overspecialization, it doesn't.

Overspecialization (used interchangeably with *specialization* when it comes to youth sports, a statement in and of itself) doesn't have a hard-and-fast definition: sometimes people use it to describe playing a single sport too often, while other times it's meant to connote the repetitive motions of playing one specific position in that sport. Both, it turns out, are problematic. Why? Here are a few reasons:

- Specializing in a single sport earlier is associated with a higher risk of injury, and as a result, kids are now landing in operating rooms for procedures like ACL repair and Tommy John surgery, which were once considered adult operations.

- Overspecialization in a given sport can lead to fatigue or even burnout, either mental or physical.

- The expectation of expertise at increasingly young ages creates psychological stress for many kids.

- Overspecialization can flip the benefits of being on a team upside down, with studies showing some young athletes becoming less likely to share with their peers or to help others.

- Sometimes overspecialization can lead kids to quit a sport altogether, often at surprisingly young ages.

- Athletes who specialize in certain sports are at higher risk for eating disorders, depression, and anxiety.

This list—and the last one especially—explains why the American Psychological Association has said emphatically: "Intense training in a single sport to the exclusion of others should be delayed until late adolescence to optimize success while minimizing risk for injury and psychological stress." The American Academy of Pediatrics has its own version of this statement, warning that "burnout, anxiety, depression, and attrition are increased in early specializers." Every professional child advocacy organization seems to agree that delaying sports specialization—in most cases until late adolescence—increases the likelihood of athletic success.

How common is specialization? It depends upon the sport, but in a word: *very*. One example is found in a 2011 study of 519 U.S. Tennis Association junior players where 70 percent acknowledged specializing by the time they reached 10.5 years old. This study was published more than a decade ago, and the rates have only climbed from there. Add to that the other consistent research finding across different sports: as focus on a single sport increases, enjoyment drops.

Parents get—and deserve—a fair amount of the blame for the new status quo. In studies surveying coaches about parental behavior and involvement, nearly three of every four coaches report a high level of concern, with about one-third feeling significant direct pressure from parents. But let's be clear that the issue isn't limited to parents. While overspecialization may begin with them encouraging one sport over others, coaches and the focused programs they represent become powerful influences along a kid's path. They demand ever-increasing time commitments and physical achievement, and penalize those who don't toe the line either by reducing playing time or dropping them from the program altogether. Lots of adults bear some responsibility for this sorry situation.

WHAT'S CHANGED OVER THE PAST 20, 30, 40 YEARS

A lot.

On the upside, youth sports have grown into thriving microcommunities for kids across the country, with many leagues becoming staple institutions—some engaging kids before they even start kindergarten—and Title IX–driven participation resulting in a massive influx of girls, especially at the entry level. It's a phenomenal achievement that sports like tennis, golf, gymnastics, and football each count more than a million registrants between ages 6 and 12 nationwide. The American Youth Soccer Organization (AYSO) boasts 400,000 grade school players in 850 leagues across the country, a big number to be sure, but just a fraction of the 2.2 million youth soccer players. And if you think *that's* a big number, as kids age up, both baseball and basketball count more than 4 million of them on their rosters.

While the raw numbers seem enormous, the Aspen Institute's 2016 *State of Play* report noted that the percentage of youth participating in sports on a regular basis has actually declined over the past 15 years, falling from 44.5 percent in 2008 to 40 percent in 2015. The report points to females of color in particular, who have the lowest rates of participation in sports of any population segment in the United States. So while many communities have outstanding youth sports programs in place for young kids to gain basic skills, this isn't enough: over time youth sports have fallen victim to both overspecialization on the one hand and under-resourcing or under-engagement (or both) on the other.

Participation has declined and, right along with it, a commitment to let kids be kids. Somehow it has become increasingly intoxicating to encourage them to "choose" their sport at younger and younger ages. This has created a phenomenon whereby the ones with "natural gifts"—and mind you, these are often seven- or eight-year-olds crowned with these accolades—who dominate on the court or field get swooped up and shepherded along an increasingly steep path toward the promise of youth sports greatness. This assembly line has picked up speed over the past couple of generations, with more and more teams declaring phenoms, then inviting these kids to play a level up. It's a badge of honor to be the youngest on a team of older (generally bigger and stronger) kids, but it's also often physically or emotionally stressful. *Never mind,* the adults around them say as they shuttle these kids when they move on to league championships and All-Star teams, then club and travel teams too. Maybe the adults see potential; maybe they are living out their own childhood fantasies; maybe they are counting on college scholarships years down the road; maybe they just want to win a game of parental one-upmanship. Whatever their reasons, and even when a child is legitimately *not* a standout, a growing number of adults push kids to improve their skills by practicing and competing more and more and more.

At some point in the near-recent past—though it's hard to say precisely when this inflection point occurred, because the shift happened slowly and insidiously over decades and it was slightly different depending upon the sport—it became almost impossible for a kid to succeed in a youth sports program without specializing. Eventually, an activity that might have been practiced a couple of days per week and played in a Saturday morning matchup turned into a four- or five-day-per-week commitment, with holiday weekends spent on the road, the commitment stretching from a season to nearly the whole year, all of this beginning as early as grade school. And to what end? Most of these kids do not go on to professional careers. In fact, these days fewer than 2 percent of high school athletes even go on to compete at the Division I level in college athletics.

Here's where American society has landed: youth sports have almost entirely lost their free-play component. RIP, pickup games in neighborhood parks. Pure exhaustion from all that organized play on multiple concurrent teams combined with underfunding of community resources that once made fields and blacktops safe and accessible proved to be an insurmountable combination. And as crazy as this sounds, it feels like many adults don't mind this shift because (they think, but they're deeply mistaken) free play interferes with kids' progression to excellence, as if letting kids horse around without drilling or training won't get them there. Of course, the opposite is almost certainly true because enjoyment and cross-training turn out to be two keys to sports success.

Today's overspecialization also means that if an athlete hasn't mastered a sport by middle or high school, it's often too late to try it for the first time. And even if they can get in that entry-level door, the expectations are likely the same as for every other sport they may or may not have engaged in, with multiple practices each week, year-round play, and concurrent commitments to the school team, the local club team, and maybe a travel team too. So if a soccer phenom blows out their ACL and wants to try something else, good luck. Ditto for the baseball pitcher who has already had his elbow repaired and the football player who has been concussed one too many times. The net result is that many of these kids go from regular physical exercise to barely moving at all.

The COVID pandemic didn't help youth sports one bit, relegating most students to their homes for online learning for several weeks at a time or, if you lived in a state with stricter mandates, for up to 16 consecutive months. Club teams thrived in this environment, skirting regulations from local authorities and school districts during the peak COVID days. On the plus side, many kids were still able to enjoy their sports; on the minus side, that's some pretty hypocritical modeling about health.

Here's another increasingly insidious aspect of sports overspecialization: it is available to those who can pay, often costing thousands of dollars per year just to participate, a setup known as the "pay-to-play" model. Over the past few decades, when it came to youth sports, the socioeconomic divide between resourced and under-resourced communities grew steadily wider. Today, it's generally the kids whose parents can write the checks and take time off to travel to tournaments and arrange childcare for the other children left at home, who get to play.

If all that isn't enough, we need to talk about how college factors in.

Tuition for the average four-year college grew by 180 percent in inflation-adjusted dollars between 1980 and 2020, and prices continue to rise. For families who cannot afford these skyrocketing prices without significant scholarship money or financial aid, an athletic scholarship offers a ready solution. We've never met a parent who doesn't want the best for their kids, so if athletics paves a way to an affordable college education and a better future, why not invest in their sport to get them on the recruiting track? Even for parents just hoping to get their children into the most prestigious colleges possible, why not double down on specialization if it can mean the difference between admission or rejection to their college of choice? Of course, the calculus is not nearly as simple as a competitive admissions advantage, given the price that kids pay physically and emotionally. Fewer than 7 percent of high school athletes even go on to play a varsity sport in college regardless of the NCAA division. And once the demanding requirements for playing college sports are taken into account, the physical and emotional costs to them may be too steep.

The ceaseless surge in earning potential for professional athletes has become a powerful motivator to barrel through. Pros live a not-so-new-fangled American dream lifestyle dripping with wealth, on display for all to see (thanks, social media!). If turning pro is a path to riches and fame, then early specialization feels like a cheap price to pay for a shot at it. Certain colleges have cashed in on the business opportunity too, selling the promise of a sports career that effectively begins when they're still in school. At the top of this funnel sit the companies (often younger than the athletes) promoting youth sports specialization and a path to NCAA recruitment. Especially in sports like soccer, lacrosse, and volleyball, where playing on travel teams and enrolling in showcase tournaments have become mandatory for ascent to the next level, this leg of the journey to college can be prohibitively expensive—not to mention absurd, with kids as young as 12 courted by college Division I programs! But at least some will become high-net-worth, high-visibility celebrities, and for those rare few, the early investment pays off.

Youth sports overspecialization feeds on itself, making bigger and bigger promises but with higher and higher stakes. In general, kids who participate in team sports enjoy boosted self-esteem and lower rates of depression and anxiety, which are layered on top of the already well-known benefits of regular physical exercise. But kids who *overspecialize* in sports suffer more adverse effects than positive ones, both emotionally and physically. The physical toll was covered earlier in this chapter, but to refresh your memory—Tommy John surgery, which was once solely for major league baseball players, is now far more common among teen athletes than among professionals. And consider this: mental health issues like burnout, depression, anxiety, and eating disorders are now so frequently seen in adolescent specialized athletes that researchers have called out this subset of kids as a particularly high-risk group. In 2022, widely publicized suicides of several collegiate student-athletes within months of one another highlighted the pressure specialized student-athletes are facing.

To say that things have changed in the world of youth sports is a gargantuan understatement. If you're overwhelmed by all of this information, now think about the kids who feel all of this pressure. Data shows that the more money families pour into youth sports, the more stressed the kids and the less they enjoy their sport. And here's the amazing bottom line: it turns out, being a multisport athlete, not a one-sport athlete, has always been—and is likely still—the best path to playing in college or even turning pro. Specialization doesn't get most kids what they think they want. Case in point, 71 percent of Division I men's football players were multisport athletes in high school.

HOW TO TALK ABOUT IT

Everything we write about in this book is based on science; it's also all close to our own hearts, drawing on bits and pieces of our personal journeys raising tweens and teens.

Vanessa has spent her entire life as an athlete. The beneficiary of the Title IX world, she was a three-sport varsity athlete in high school and a Division III college soccer player (until she realized she just wanted to play for fun). As an adult, while she shepherded her two older children through early specialized soccer careers, Vanessa built Dynamo Girl, a company dedicated to using sports to build girls' self-esteem, *not* to build elite athletes. Dynamo Girl is a multisport program rooted in social-emotional learning—in effect, an antispecialization program. And yet, when she wasn't coaching school-age girls to love moving their bodies simply for the joy of it, Vanessa spent hours and hours driving her own kids to their practices and games, sacrificing holiday weekends as a family to take one or another to tournaments. This split identity was not lost on her and her husband until, one by one, her children entered high school and quit their club soccer teams. They left for the best reason possible: each one became enamored with the possibility of playing a different sport each season. They went from specialized to generalized. In full disclosure, Vanessa still has one child still playing club soccer, but she is praying this one decides *not* to play in college.

Cara has spent the past 25 years as a pediatrician preaching—okay, occasionally ranting too—against overspecialization. She has sent kid after kid to sports medicine doctors for avoidable overuse injuries. She fields calls about return to play (not to mention return to class) after concussions. And yet, as Murphy's Law would have it, her own son fell in love with a single sport toward the end of middle school. He began sculling, a form of crew in which rowers each pull a pair of oars in a boat, a detail relevant only because three-quarters of the way through eighth grade, he and the rest of the world were sent home thanks to COVID. In Los Angeles, where Cara lives, COVID restrictions remained strict and in force for 16 months. While her kids Zoomed their schooling from home during that entire stretch, her son was able to row because kids could scull in individual boats (those poor rowers who opted for sweep rowing, in which the rowers pull one oar each, had no single-boat option unless they wanted to go in circles!). Rowing became his true passion, one of the few activities he could do during an exceptionally formative time. As a result, he evolved into the very thing Cara swore she would never encourage: a specialized youth athlete.

Does this make us hypocrites? We hope not—partially because we have always insisted that our kids cross-train in order to protect their bodies, but also because we, like you, parent a generation of kids overwhelmed by the mental health impacts of achievement culture. And while we see clearly the specific issues tethered to sports specialization (like depression, anxiety, low self-esteem, body dysmorphia, and eating disorders), we also know just as keenly the issues tethered to *not* having a physical outlet (an eerily similar list).

For those of you whose athletic past—or lack thereof—powerfully informed your identity, you may find yourselves struggling to leave your baggage at the door, a concept covered in detail in chapter 2. When navigating youth sports, or really any other topic about raising kids, the most important thing to remember is that it's not about us; it's about our kids, who deserve to write their own stories. Leave your sports greatness in your rearview mirror unless your kids want to talk about it. But don't lose sight of the fact that your stories generate some degree of awe that can flip quickly into pressure, even if you don't mean for them to. By the same token, leave your own sense of athletic inadequacy in the past. Our kids do not exist in this world in order to rewrite our own failed histories.

It's so easy to press hard on the overspecialization gas pedal, especially given how much our culture values athletic achievement, sometimes a springboard to professional success and other times a solution to financial stressors solved with an athletic scholarship. It's natural to lean into something they're good at when our own kids seem happy—truly happy—building tight bonds with teammates and thriving across the board.

Overspecialization isn't all bad; it's just not good without moderation. Yes, you can specialize and find balance. But to do this requires tempering some of the forces at work in order to protect our kids' emotional and physical well-being. Here's our best advice, whether your kid is an elite athlete or a recreational player.

Keep your mouth shut on the sideline

After decades of coaching kids at all levels, we can confidently say that when parents coach their kids from the sidelines, no matter their age or ability, it is *not helpful*. There are two important reasons for this:

1. **Coaches have a philosophy and an approach that they deliberately and carefully implement over the course of the season.** If you also instruct your kid from the sidelines (no matter your own level of skill and experience), you're going to confuse the hell out of them. They won't know who to listen to or, frankly, who to please. Let their coach do their job. If you have concerns or questions, speak privately and calmly to the coach after the game. If you are a parent-coach, treat your kid with the same empathy and generosity you give to other kids on the team, and leave your coaching on the field—don't bring it to the car ride home or the dinner table.

2. **The best way for kids to learn is by doing and by making mistakes.** Yes, we all pay lip service to that concept, but it's true. Physical actions tried, failed, and tried again are critical to establishing a mind-body connection. We learn by trial and error, not when our every movement is dictated by someone else. When a parent acts like they have a joystick on the sidelines controlling a kid's play, their kid truly doesn't learn the physical or tactical lessons they could.

Don't ignore it when a kid looks like they're in pain

How many times have kids been encouraged by an adult to play through the pain? Please don't do that. Their bodies are still growing, their growth plates make their bones more vulnerable, and their ligaments are like rubber bands—kids don't live in adult bodies, so don't treat them like they do. Get an injured kid off the field and to a doctor. And please don't push them to go back to play before they're healed. No game, no recruitment opportunity, no meet is as important as your child's health. Full stop.

If a coach is abusive, find a new coach

Those of us who played competitive sports 30 years ago were used to a certain kind of aggressive, and in some cases abusive, coach. We now know that while that behavior might motivate kids to perform well in the short term, there are long-lasting negative impacts on kids' emotional well-being, not to mention short-term implications like a lack of willingness to continue to play the sport. Nothing is more important than keeping your kid healthy and safe, and often you are their greatest advocate. If their coach is verbally or emotionally abusive, it's time for a new coach. Enough said.

Be your kid's refuge, not their biggest critic

For many competitive athletes, their sense of self-worth lives and dies with performance. But body changes during puberty can profoundly affect that performance: their strength, speed, agility, and endurance will fluctuate, sometimes wildly, affecting their ranking, placement, playing time, and self-esteem. Don't pile on that already heavy weight by making your kid feel like crap. Instead, be their light in the darkness, their refuge in the storm. Support them and love them, no matter how well (or poorly) they play. Down the road, how you care for them in that moment will have a far greater impact than how many minutes they got.

It's their dream, not your dream

This one is hard. Really hard. The struggle not to live our lives through our kids is *so* real. But they have to be the ones who want "it," whatever "it" is. The motivation needs to come from inside them, driven by a passion for a sport that allows them to willingly make the sacrifices and commitments required to improve and even excel. If they are doing this to please us or fulfill our dreams, they will only come to resent us and hate the sport in the end. No exaggeration. But if they do want it badly enough, then our job is to somehow help them find balance in their lives, not add to the pressure.

This chapter might be as preachy as we get in this book because we know how damaging sports overspecialization can be, physically and emotionally, and how tilted the system is toward benefiting those with the resources to pay to play. We also know that superhuman strength is required to avoid getting dragged into the mud of it all. So if you are allowing, or even encouraging, your kid to specialize, just do it with your eyes and heart open, and with as much balance and moderation as possible.

 FROM PEOPLE JUST OUT THE OTHER SIDE

C.A., she/her, age 20

I am an NCAA Division I athlete in the Ivy League, where I play field hockey. I have been playing field hockey for upwards of 10 years. In addition, throughout my childhood, I played soccer for 6 years, lacrosse for 7, crew for 3, and have been weightlifting (for strength and conditioning purposes only) for 4 years.

I probably spent roughly 10 to 15 hours a week, on average, playing field hockey before I went to the NCAA. As I grew up, however, the numbers started to increase until the summer before my first season at college, where I was probably spending roughly 20 hours a week—this is the same amount of hours that Ivy League field hockey athletes abide by in season.

As an athlete, I have come to understand that parents often hold the most influence over child athletes. Since they are the ones that pay for the teams and provide transportation, they hold the power, and so often parents can abuse it and push their child too far. There is a difference between pushing your child to be the best that they can be with regard to their physical and psychological well-being, and pushing your child to the brink of their athletic ability without regard for their well-being. The latter can make them susceptible to burnout, anxiety, depression, low self-esteem, a sense of disappointment, too much pressure, et cetera. Be a quiet force in your child's athletic journey. Let them take the driver's seat and decide their aspirations, and then give them the motivation, inspiration, and resources to do so.

It is important for caregivers, coaches, and teachers to accept the fact that if kids specialize in athletics, they will not have the same time, energy, or motivation a nonathlete will have for other normal things. There is a common misconception that athletes are lazy when it comes to academics, chores, work, et cetera. This isn't the case. Our concentration, mental strength, and physical abilities are simply divided differently from people who aren't specialized athletes.

On a related note, adults need to understand that children who are specialized athletes need their sleep and rest. Pushing your child too hard, spreading their mental and physical capacities a mile wide and inch deep, will result in a dip in athletic performance, your athlete's mental and physical health, and their overall enjoyment of the sport.

Some of the most common issues among athletes, however, are body image issues, particularly among female athletes. This has to be understood. I was often told that the only reason I wasn't fat or severely overweight was that I was an athlete and therefore burned the excess off. There is always that constant, nagging thought in the back of my mind: If I lose two pounds, will I be two seconds faster?

Eating disorders are a real threat to an athlete's physical and mental health. Do not, I repeat, do not force your child to stay on a diet or regimen in order to "improve" or maintain their athletic performance. Athletes need to eat pretty healthily, but constantly reminding your child is not beneficial. Trust us. You telling your child they can't have a piece of cake on a birthday because they have a game the next day is not fair or right. Trust your child to make the right decisions regarding food. Try not to comment on what they eat or how much they eat. Not even just a comment, but a little glance or the projection of judgment was enough for me to walk away from food. Nothing is more annoying or upsetting than indulging a little once and a while—for instance ordering a large ice cream cone when you go out—and hearing your parents say, *You're going to eat that? With a game or practice tomorrow?* I beg you, please do not comment on how your child eats unless it is becoming hazardous to their health.

The running theme of parental advice with regard to their specialized children is trust and understanding. A great way to show support to your child if they are specializing is by being completely supportive of their choices. Whether they choose to continue their sport or if they decide to quit, let your child navigate their way through the process themselves and make their own decision while having you to fall back on for support and direction if they need it. Sometimes all an athlete needs from a parent is a supportive message, a shoulder to cry on, or a presence at a game.

CHAPTER 16

Sex, Hookup Culture, and Porn

We have both spent a fair amount of time teaching kids about sex. One of us might have even taught her own kids in a packed classroom, which she thought went swimmingly well but they would describe in terms 180 degrees opposite. Despite that hiccup (let's call it a grit-builder!), as our kids have grown older we find ourselves talking about sex a lot, with them and with their friends, and most amazingly not always initiated by us. These days, a conversation around the kitchen island about contraception or chlamydia is as much a nothingburger as running through the logistical plan for the weekend. Yes, we are well aware this is not typical.

Our own experience may not be standard fare, but it can be, and hopefully by the end of this chapter we will have proven to you that the bar to get there sits remarkably low. Abide by some guiding principles, and these conversations will get more productive and easier as time goes on: Offer up some basic terminology at the start, ask nonjudgmental questions, answer what you know clearly and forthrightly, and then listen. Respond when prompted or open up about your past when asked, but otherwise zip it and listen. If you do this, you will learn a ton of priceless information (not to mention several new words) while establishing yourself as someone they can come talk to—which, we promise, they will do, eventually.

LET'S START WITH SCIENCE

Talking about sex involves two sets of conversations: one about science and a parallel one about humanity. The subject cannot be limited to one or the other without serious consequences, physical and emotional. Ultimately, this required combination explains why so many people don't know how to begin The Talk (more on that later): they're either fumbling for the right level of biological explanation or flying blind when it comes to talking through relationships and respect and consent. Many adults tell us they feel completely at home with only half of this conversation; some describe being raised in families where the topic of sex was forbidden, leaving them overwhelmed on both fronts all these years later.

Even those most comfortable though, need to learn a new looming landscape that includes hookup culture, in which young people have a variety of sexual partners outside the bounds of a committed relationship, and today's nearly ubiquitous exposure to porn, often graphic, hard-core, and readily available on laptops and phones everywhere. The ground beneath our collective feet has shifted dramatically, making it more, not less, important to have factual, candid conversations with kids, teens, and young adults about sex.

The science of sex is fairly straightforward. Our favorite way of approaching the biological aspects goes like this: *There are four different kinds of sex: vaginal sex, oral sex, anal sex, and masturbation. I'm going to explain each one, and then I am here to answer any questions you have, today and always.* From there, we break down the four types:

1. **Vaginal sex,** also called vaginal intercourse, usually refers to the insertion of a penis into a vagina. However, some people use the term *vaginal sex* to describe anything penetrating the vagina, things like fingers or sex toys.

2. **Oral sex** means one person's mouth on another person's genitals. It's as simple as that.

3. **Anal sex** describes the penetration of an anus. Often the term implies that a penis is doing the penetrating, but much as with vaginal sex, other objects (fingers, sex toys) can be used as well.

4. **Masturbation,** which is self-pleasure, or, as we like to say, sex with yourself. Masturbation can certainly be a solitary activity, but it doesn't need to be—sometimes people do it together, in the same room or on two ends of a phone or computer screen.

So that's it, the conversation starter that may drive some kids running and screaming from the room but almost always opens up amazing dialogue, even if it takes a while. When sex is defined in clear, nonjudgmental terms, kids feel empowered by the language. And when they have questions, they are able to use accurate words to ask an adult, which makes it much easier for the person on the receiving end to give them the information they need.

There are, of course, a few extra terms worth throwing out before wrapping the science-y part of this chapter. First: *abstinence,* which means the choice to abstain from (i.e., not have) sex. Then there's *safe sex,* which refers to sex that involves protection from both pregnancy and sexually transmitted infections (STIs). In order to have safe sex, at least one participant must use a barrier like a condom or a dam—unless there's only one participant in the room and then the sex is "safe" in the pregnancy and STI sense of the word (we get into all of this much more in chapter 17). Next: *rape,* which is sex without consent. It's important to note here that vaginal, anal, and oral sex all involve penetration, a key component to rape. When penetration is not involved (and also when it is), a nonconsensual act is referred to as *sexual assault.* In other words, any nonconsensual sexual act—physical, verbal, audible, or behavioral—can be sexual assault, but the definition of rape involves penetration—an object or body part entering another person's body without their consent. And finally: *pornography*, more commonly just called *porn*. This is professionally produced or amateur-generated imagery intended to sexually arouse the viewer. While it's voyeuristic, and therefore sex-adjacent, it can also have a direct impact on when and how people have sex; and for sexually naive adolescents, porn can define their idea of what sex is supposed to look like from the outset before they ever experience it in real life.

 ## WHAT'S CHANGED OVER THE PAST 20, 30, 40 YEARS

The evolution of sexual attitudes and behaviors over the past few decades looks more like a serpentine river than a straight line. Many of us were raised by the children of the sexual revolution, whose own activities in bed (or in the back of a car or at Woodstock) were at least partially driven by the Supreme Court's legalization of birth control, first for married couples in 1965 and then for all in 1972. The next 50 years saw dramatic growth in contraception options, with so many new forms: foams, gels, diaphragms, rings, intrauterine devices (IUDs), and implantable hormones. The pill has been iterated and reformulated dozens of times, using different types of estrogens and progestins (synthetic forms of the hormone progresterone) in varying doses to cater to the sensitivities of different bodies. And condoms have evolved into countless colors, shapes, sizes, flavors, and textures available in gargantuan displays at almost every drugstore and even in supermarkets. Chapter 17 takes a deep dive into each of these, but it's important to note them here because they have driven many of the cultural shifts in sexual activity: as contraception boomed and pregnancy risk dropped, the consequences of having sex changed dramatically, increasing sexual activity outside of marriage across the board—or at least social acceptance of it.

At the same time, though, many forms of birth control in this country are (and have always been) limited to people with access to health-care and some combination of medical insurance and spare cash. In fact, other than condoms, few forms of protection have been available over the counter. And the emergence of deadly STIs like HIV (also covered in depth in chapter 17) and shifting abortion laws have certainly affected sexual freedom in their own, dramatic ways. Hence the back-and-forth of how sex is talked about, not to mention who's having it.

Which prompts the question: When are kids having sex these days? According to the biennial Youth Risk Behavior Survey, conducted in 2021 by the U.S. Centers for Disease Control (CDC), far fewer high schoolers are doing it compared with a generation ago. In 1991, well over half (54.1 percent) of U.S. high school students reported having sex, but by 2021, that number had fallen to 30 percent. It's worth noting that the 2021 study took place during the COVID pandemic, so it's a fair bet that remote schooling and social distancing impacted these numbers.

This data has a major flaw, though. When kids are prompted about sex in the *Youth Risk Behavior Survey,* they are asked if they have had any "sexual contacts" or if they have had any "sexual intercourse," with nei-ther term defined in any specific way. Did kids answer what the re-searchers thought they were asking? Across the three decades that this survey has been conducted, have kids maintained the same implicit un-derstanding of what the survey was kinda, sorta hinting at? In other studies, when researchers ask kids whether they have ever had sex, they rarely add the word *vaginal,* even though vaginal sex is usually what they mean—or what they mean to imply. Generalized questions about "sex" or "sexual contacts" breed confusion, leading to murky data. Clearer and more specific ones—like *Have you had vaginal intercourse? Oral sex? Anal sex?*—would offer up a far more robust set of results about whether kids are truly delaying the act or just engaging differently than their parents and grandparents did.

Not all researchers get it wrong. For instance, the CDC published a study in 2018 asking teenagers specifically about oral and anal sex: 39 percent answered yes to having had oral sex, and 11 percent answered yes to having had anal sex. If nothing else, this shows that lots of teenagers are completely willing to answer detailed questions about their intimate activities. Also, a lot more teens are having anal sex than people might think.

Here's something neither the *Youth Risk Behavior Survey* nor most of the studies out there have ever covered, though it's high time they did: hookup culture. This is a big ask, though, because hookup culture refers to a confusing, hard-to-define new set of expectations and behaviors upending an old-school way of thinking about romance, relationships, and sex. Flash back to the "bases" of your own childhood, which varied slightly by geography but generally implied a linear path from kissing (first base), to feeling up (second base), to giving or getting a hand job (third base), and then going all the way (home base, almost always refer-ring to vaginal intercourse). Today's hookup culture has almost no linearity—the steps through sexual exploration can feel less like a game of baseball and more like Mr. Potato Head, with different pieces placed in unexpected spots, his mouth sitting where his ear should be.

To some people hooking up means having sex; to others it's every-thing *but* having sex, making for a communication nightmare. Some people who describe themselves as "just hooking up" have been sexually active for many years without the supportive adults in their lives realiz-ing this; others claiming the same status are only kissing or lightly fool-ing around, and some of those end up slut-shamed (a term that derides someone for having multiple sexual partners). Hookup culture has re-ordered linguistic, relationship, and sexual norms, stripping them of both order and clarity. Which is why our own flashbacks to young love—starting with dating for a while, then committing to relationship status, and finally deciding to have sex—don't resonate with many kids in the twenty-first century. These days, it's common to hear teens and twenty-somethings describe having sex with a specific partner for weeks or even months; *then* possibly going out on dates (or not); *next* choosing to be exclusive, meaning not having sex with anyone else (but don't confuse this with dating!); and then maybe, eventually, entering into a committed relationship . . . or not. Or some combination of that in a very different order. When it comes to predictability, all bets are off.

Part and parcel with hookup culture, there's new language floating around. *Friends with benefits* is a phrase most adults know, and it's still a thing, but the term *situationship* is taking over. This term (full disclosure: our favorite new word that we learned while writing this book) embraces the cloudiness of relationship status for a new generation, a baffling norm that's equally confusing to the people living it. Situationships include any and every type of relationship up to a committed one. Hooking up can absolutely fall into the situationship category, as do the following terms, which you may have never heard before: *getting with* (hooking up without sexual intercourse), *tapping* (vaginal sex), and *dogging* (vaginal sex or possibly anal sex—and note *raw dogging* means no condom involved). People who are "dating" can do all of these things too.

Completely separate but layered on top of hookup culture is a trend toward outward sexual fluidity, in which someone's sexual orientation is not fixed but changes depending on attraction and circumstance. Many adults—certainly Boomers and Gen Xers, but also most Millennials—came of age when people were expected to define their sexual orientation in clear terms. A huge number actually had to hide their true identities because of rampant hostility and legal inequities. But these days, middle schoolers in many parts of the country comfortably refer to a friend as bisexual or pansexual. We explore sexual orientation in more depth in chapter 18, but sexual fluidity bears noting as we list what has changed in the world of sex because it informs how we talk to the kids in our lives. If we don't use inclusive language and we don't educate ourselves about safe-sex practices across a wide swath of sexual activities, we won't be able to follow through on our most primary job in their lives: keeping them safe and healthy.

It's impossible to talk about how sex has changed without referencing the massive availability of pornography over the last two decades. The internet has made pornography available to anyone with a device—both kids and adults—transforming people's early and ongoing image of sex. Yes, there has been porn for centuries, evolving with each technological revolution (printing press, photography, film, internet). But free online porn marked an exponential shift in access, a glut of information redefining for a generation they way sex looks, feels, and sounds, even when kids know the sex is staged. Maybe they recognize it as unrealistic (or maybe they're too young to realize), but if they see it enough, porn can begin to seem like a version of the truth.

Porn was once a hushed conversation that might only have come up among the bravest when talking about sex. Today, it is an integral conversation, equally relevant to parenting and sex ed classes, because the vast majority of kids have seen it and many continue to watch repeatedly. Here's the top-line data, all of which has emerged in the past couple of decades as online porn has gone mainstream and found its way to middle schoolers with laptops and smartphones:

- The average age for first porn viewing is 12 years old among boys; girls are not far behind.

- 15 percent of teens say their first exposure to porn happened when they were 10 years old. Most people who work in porn education estimate that by the senior year of high school, 85 to 95 percent of teens have been exposed.

- Reasons why kids view porn include the following: someone showed it to them (they didn't seek it out); curiosity (they sought it out); masturbation aid; means to cope with stress or negative emotions. An accidental Google search with one mistyped letter is unlikely to lead a kid to porn, but intentional Google searches ("naked," "boobs," etc.) and embedded social media links are more common paths to get there.

- More than half of teenagers who have viewed porn say the content included violent or aggressive behavior. Pornography viewing by adolescents is associated with sexual aggression, and so there is concern about the future path of their sexual relationships.

- COVID had far less impact on porn consumption than initially predicted—in fact, porn viewing stayed pretty consistent between 2019 and 2021: somewhere between 5 and 23 percent of adolescents and young adults increased their porn viewing during this period, but the rest either kept their viewing habits steady or watched less.

Some researchers theorize that the rise in access to online porn is driving teenagers' later forays into real-life sex, arguing that porn viewing with masturbation has replaced in-the-flesh sexual experimentation. It's hard to say whether this is true. On the one hand, it makes perfect sense, and when phone sex in the form of swapping nude images and videos is layered on top, cause and effect seem obvious. But again, we don't really know if kids are waiting longer to have sex (in its most expansive definition), so before explaining why this is so, it feels like we ought to go back, ask clearer questions, and document the phenomenon first. *Then* the role of pornography viewing can be added into the mix.

The jury is out on how any or all of this—shifting definitions of sex, hookup culture, sexual fluidity, porn—might affect down-the-road adult relationships and even the very concept of marriage or committed partnerships in our society. We do know, however, that because hookup culture means one person having several sexual partners, it is responsible for increased rates of STIs. Lucky you, that's covered in chapter 17 too!

Ultimately, we all want the kids around us to grow into adults engaged in loving relationships with meaningful connections and, if they choose, consensual, pleasurable sex. To get there, we need to talk to them about sex and relationships in inclusive ways reflecting how times have changed, even if this feels hard and complicated and uncomfortable.

🗣)) HOW TO TALK ABOUT IT

We're going to take a very brass-tacks approach here, a greatest hits of what to cover on the topic of sex, hookups, and porn. Because there's so much territory to cover, we've subdivided this section.

How to talk about sex

Starting with the most important, broadest piece of advice: the sex talk is not The Talk (that's so 1980s) but rather many, *many* small talks over years, using increasingly sophisticated language and ramping up the information as kids get older. For those of you who had hoped it would be one-and-done, sorry.

Before you begin these conversations, make sure to establish that a kid knows the basic anatomy and physiology of all genders. The OG approach limited information to one's own gender—this doesn't fly anymore (and hallelujah to that!).

As you get further into these conversations, you really need to cover the mechanics of sex with different potential partners. Our "four types of sex" approach—vaginal sex, oral sex, anal sex, and masturbation—offers one clear way to wade into these waters, but you do you. How adults and kids talk about sex depends not only on their personalities, temperaments, and communication styles, but also on the setting (are there four other kids within earshot?), and on and on. Our suggestions are just that, suggestions. The trap to avoid is the one in which you assume a kid knows it all—don't let their sophisticated facade fool you. One great way to do this: if they swear they know something, ask them to teach you about it.

Beyond those basics, here are some other general strategies to use while having these conversations. But before you jump in, one last piece of advice: don't worry about screwing this up! (Yes, sex pun intended.) Remember the power of taking a do-over? If there's one place where you are almost guaranteed to need one, it's in the coverage of sex. So feel free to try communicating one way, and if that doesn't resonate, pivot and start again. Once they realize you're not shying away from this topic, they will start talking—or at least listening—more.

Don't sexualize young kids

Our culture holds tight to a surprising hypocrisy: teaching kids about sex is often criticized as happening too early, and yet kids are sexualized at those same—yes, young—ages. Ever heard someone describing a three-year-old's close friendship as a crush? Or a relative asking a nine-year-old if he has any girlfriends? Our hope is to flip that dynamic, normalizing age-appropriate sex education starting early while refraining from projecting sexuality onto kids when they're this young. And while we're at it, let's stop layering on heteronormative assumptions.

Celebrate—rather than minimize—feelings

It's easy to forget that crushes and attractions involve powerful feelings at every age, so don't underestimate the potential for romantic feelings to carry great weight. When a kid comes home excited or heartbroken or confused about a burgeoning or ending relationship, take their big emotions seriously. Dismissive comments like *It's only middle school—get over it!* or *What's the big deal?—it's not like you're old enough to be in love!* undermine future conversations about meaningful, loving relationships. Minimizing a kid's feelings also reduces the chance that they will circle back in the future to talk about social or emotional highs and lows.

Start teaching consent early and often

Start teaching kids about consent before sex is even on their radars. The conversations can be about asking for and granting permission to pretty much anything: taking a bite of a sandwich, sitting on someone's lap, playing with someone else's hair, borrowing someone's clothes. This entrenches thoughtfulness and permission-seeking years before bringing sex into the conversation, building the muscle of noticing other people's feelings and increasing the likelihood that a kid will make respectful choices when engaging with others. Not only does this translate into better communication when they become sexually active, but it also avoids what adolescent psychologist Lisa Damour describes the "offense/defense" approach to sex.

Everyone deserves to know about pleasure

One thing that hasn't evolved much over the past couple of generations is the gendering of conversations about pleasure: boys tend to hear *all* about it, while girls get much less of this messaging. But it doesn't have to be that way and frankly, it shouldn't! So make sure conversations with all kids, regardless of gender, cover the parts of the body that feel good when they're touched. Do your best to present this information shame-free. And don't assume kids are getting this education in their sex ed classes, because many don't teach about the clitoris or masturbation. So include these at some point, though maybe when you're driving or walking side by side, anything to avoid direct eye contact to make talking about self-pleasure just a little less awkward. If you don't know how to start, try this: *Isn't it so cool that there's a part of the body whose only job is to feel good when it's touched?* (P.S.: people with clitorises deserve to know!)

Be inclusive and never assume anyone's sexual orientation, including your kid's

Unless a kid has explicitly defined their sexual orientation, make no assumptions. And while you're at it, check your baseline, heteronormative language. It's hard for some of us to break old habits, but inclusive language removes shame and judgment, dramatically increasing the likelihood that a kid will continue to open up to you. Plus, it's easier than you think! *Is there someone you're attracted to? Do you know what you'd want in a sexual partner? Do you understand the concept of respect when you're inti-mate with someone?*

Anticipate questions about your own sexual history (because they will eventually ask, guaranteed)

We can promise with 100 percent certainty that kids will ask you about your past. Sometimes they keep the questions general, but other times they dive deep into specifics. Anticipate this! Figure out well in advance what you want to keep private (and by the way, you are absolutely al-lowed to keep some things private from your kids). Then figure out how you are going to answer without lying. Because once you tell a lie and they figure that out, the trust is gone. Here's a great way to validate a question without answering it: *I'm so glad you feel comfortable asking me, but that's something I'm actually going to keep private. You can always ask me a question—sometimes I may choose not to answer it.* Other times, you may decide you're comfortable sharing; however, make sure it is age appropri-ate for you to share that information with your kid. The content might ultimately be something you want your kid to know, but the timing may not be right. Finally, make sure to answer what they're asking. If you're not exactly sure, saying, *That's such an interesting question—what makes you ask it?* will help narrow the scope. Pro tip: Avoid oversharing; younger kids almost never want the mass of information you think they're requesting.

How to talk about hookups

It's especially important to leave your judgment at the door during con-versations about hooking up. If you don't, your kids are not going to share even a morsel with you, and forget about being able to offer advice to keep them safe and healthy. Here are some ways to strike a balance between talking about the relationships they're in and painting a picture of the type you're hoping they'll strive for.

Talk about love

Sometimes conversations about sex are mechanical or biological, but we need to include conversations about love and human connection too. It can be intimidating or overwhelming to tell them how sex can be beautiful and loving, but these key concepts must be communicated, particularly as a counterbalance to what they might have seen in porn. One approach: *I know you know about the mechanics of sex, and even the pleasures of it, but sex can be something really special between two people who love each other.*

Teach that it's okay to talk during hookups and sex

Media—from rom-coms to porn—often portray sex as a silent act performed by mind-readers who naturally intuit how to get the other person to orgasm. Disabuse your kid of that notion, stat! Otherwise they're in for some major disappointment. Spoiler alert! Their sexual partner can't read their mind, and they won't automatically orgasm the first time they hook up with someone, even with someone they really like or love. Normalizing communication during sex provides an open channel for ongoing and enthusiastic consent. *Are you good with this? Does this feel okay? Do you want to keep going or do you want to stop?* It also teaches that sex is as much about the journey as it is about the destination—road trips get pretty boring if no one is talking in the car.

Avoid the my-kid-would-never trap

The pace at which kids' bodies, experiences, attitudes, and relationships change is mind-boggling. Were they not just sitting in a high chair smearing pureed food all over their face? It's on us to keep up with their rapid social, emotional, and sexual transformations, while honestly discussing what's actually happening. When it comes to sex in general and hooking up in particular, don't assume they're not escalating through physical and emotional interactions just because they're not sharing. In fact, remember that many kids don't share unless asked—and some still don't unless asked repeatedly, nonjudgmentally, and kindly. Ideally, cover important topics before they've already jumped into those waters, letting go of any worry that introducing the subject of sex encourages them to try it, because the opposite turns out to be true: educating kids about sex actually slows their pace toward it. *I'm not sure if this has come up yet, but I just want to make sure I cover it with you before it does. I'm always here to talk more about it, but this is a quick first pass.* And if you're a little late to the game, start talking now. *I know we haven't really talked about this, but I've been reading about hookups and situationships. I'm not sure I really understand what they are. Can you explain them to me?*

Gauge where things are without interrogating

It's challenging to get a sense of where a kid is on their sexual journey without the conversation turning into an interrogation session. Start by pulling out of the panicked, accusatory you-versus-me dynamic and instead act casual and curious. *I'm reading this book and they mentioned . . . I was listening to a podcast and it brought up something . . . I saw a headline in the news and wondered if you've heard of this . . .* To get more specific information, try: *Have you noticed this issue at school? Do your friends ever talk about this?* (Don't ask which friend!) *Has this come up on your team?* Here's the ticket: if they do choose to share, keep it together and listen, even if you're breaking into a cold sweat. Do not freak out and jump all over them unless you want a guaranteed way to make them clam up immediately.

How to talk about porn

Simply put, the porn industry represents two steps back when it comes to framing sex as loving and respectful. And whether we like it or not, the reality is that today, kids are far more porn-exposed than ever before:

they see it younger, and much of what they're viewing, usually video rather than still images, is violent and aggressive. *Playboy* doesn't hold a candle to this stuff. If the issue hasn't surfaced before age 10, we recommend having a first, basic conversation about porn by then; if younger kids have been exposed, they need these conversations as soon as you learn of the exposure. Even though the idea of talking to a 10-year-old about pornography makes most of us want to throw up in our mouths, it's more nauseating to imagine the porn industry—with its endless stream of misogynistic, violent videos showcasing paid actors with totally unrealistic bodies—sex-educating an entire generation. No matter how awkward, uncomfortable, or utterly mortifying this topic may be, it's become non-negotiable. Here are some suggestions for ways to get into a conversation about pornography.

Define your terms

It's important to define any terms used around tricky topics to avoid causing more confusion. So, for example, if the term *sex* is used in the definition of porn, make sure to also explain what sex is. This turns out to be a tall order for some because explaining sex might consume all of your kid's attention before even getting to porn, so keep the definition brief in order to move to the main event. Or stick with sex in the first conversation and come back to porn in the next. *One of the ways people have sex is by putting their penis or vagina on or in someone else's body.*

Don't assume they already know what porn is

Because many kids have heard the word *porn* or *pornography* on the school bus or at a friend's house, they feel like they're *supposed* to know what it means. Most infer its badness, but that's where their knowledge on the topic ends. Your first conversation introducing porn can begin with a question as simple as *I'm wondering if you've ever heard the word porn or pornography?* If the reply involves a "yes," ask for their definition and then clarify or elaborate. If they say they don't know, start simple: *Pornography means people taking photos or videos of themselves or others having sex.*

Explain why pornography is concerning

It can be hard to put into words why kids shouldn't watch porn without simultaneously blanketing sex with a layer of shame and judgment. If the goal is for kids to eventually have meaningful sexual relationships, they need help differentiating what they might see in porn from real-life intimacy. You can say: *When you're old enough, sex can be a wonderful thing between consenting partners who respect each other's feelings and bodies.* This provides a contrast with violent and misogynistic porn. It's important for kids to understand that porn doesn't represent the entirety of sexual relationships, but rather a very specific corner of that world. We can offer counternarratives to what kids might have seen, but ideally, as kids grow up hopefully they will write their own narratives based upon what they experience, not what someone else posted online.

Porn's effect on body image

Professional porn actors of all genders tend to have hairless, waxed, bleached, tanned bodies, head to toe, including every single orifice. This makes for quite an unrealistic image of nudity that includes everything from breast augmentation to labiaplasty (vulval surgery), exceptional penis size to bleached anuses. Emphasizing body normalcy resets expectations: *Neither your breasts nor your labia are meant to be perfectly symmetrical—it's normal for them to be slightly different sizes and shapes.* Or *Porn actors can be cast based upon the size of their penises, which are not representative of the average penis size.* Believe it or not, it's actually very important to explicitly tell teens that it's natural and normal for someone to have hair on their genitals, because the ones who have seen porn before seeing a real-life sexual partner may find this surprising. That said, be careful about the approach here, because that very same kid may be removing significant amounts of hair from places you don't see, and they might interpret the comments as shaming.

Leave the door open by removing judgment

Many people will have the first conversation about porn (knowingly or unknowingly) *after* their kids have already seen it for the first time. If we go in heavy with *If you watch porn, you're grounded for life!*, it makes it pretty hard for a kid to admit to having already watched. And if they're exposed to it after a conversation with a parent who says, *You are absolutely, positively forbidden to ever see porn,* that kid is highly unlikely to circle back with questions or worries. The trick to talking to kids about porn is sharing your concerns while removing judgment so they know they can come to you. It could be some version of *We've talked about why porn isn't appropriate for you to watch, but having said that, if you see it, you can always, always come to me. I won't freak out.*

Relying on porn for masturbation

Everyone deserves to know certain parts of the body feel good when touched. There is nothing wrong with masturbation—it's a healthy part of sexuality! However, some people become dependent on pornography in order to masturbate. This predominantly affects boys and men (though not always) and can present a variety of sexual and relational problems: erectile dysfunction, inability to orgasm without porn, disconnection from real-life partners, and a need for more and more extreme versions of visual stimulation. When this happens, it's referred to as porn addiction. It's important to discuss this with kids—not as a first-take on a porn conversation, but a down-the-road conversation.

Exhausted yet? This is a long journey. Through it all, don't forget to pace yourself, emphasize respect, and listen more than you speak. This may not be easy, and depending on your own history it might be really tough to go down this road with your kid. But it will get easier over time the more you practice it.

Adults will have these conversations differently, but it's important to *choose* to have these conversations. Putting your head in the sand and pretending it's not an issue causes much more harm than having an uncomfortable conversation. And if it's truly just too hard to address, find someone else in your kid's life—an older sibling, a guidance counselor, an aunt or uncle—to discuss it with them. Porn exposure can be traumatic for kids. We can't always prevent them from seeing it, but if lines of communication are open, we can help them make sense of what they've seen.

FROM PEOPLE JUST OUT THE OTHER SIDE

B.C., he/him, age 16

On porn

When I was young, my family along with all of my cousins went to my grandparents' house over the summer. I have a group of cousins around my age, so we did everything together, such as played sports, went in the pool, and watched a lot of TV. Something to note about the TVs at my grandparents' house is that the remote controls were built around iPhone 4s. (You'll have to take it up with them on why they'd ever think it was a good idea to do that.) We were still young and didn't have phones or iPad time yet, so while we watched TV, we would also play on the phones and search for different celebrities we knew. When on Katy Perry's page, my cousin randomly said, "What if we see her naked?"

At the time, this was one of the funniest things I could ever imagine. The great Katy Perry, naked. Just the thought of it sent a shot of adrenaline through our spines. We immediately put the words into Safari and found what we were looking for: Katy Perry naked. We swiped through hundreds of photoshopped images of Katy Perry (at the time I thought these were totally real): posed on a beach, crouching over a penis, naked with another woman. Name anything and you could probably find a photoshopped picture of Katy Perry doing it. This was a feeling unlike any other I'd ever had. I obviously had a boner because who wouldn't, but had no idea what that was at the time. We were all stunned into silence and just simply couldn't believe what we were seeing.

A few days later I found myself sitting alone searching the phone for any celebrity I could think of naked. The same exhilarating feeling rushed through my body as I surfed the web for close to an hour, when all of a sudden my dad came down to watch TV. I panicked. I turned the phone off and put it in the charging port, but never flicked out of the app, meaning that although I felt like I had just played the situation out superbly, the first thing my dad saw when he opened the phone was Beyoncé. On a beach. Sitting with her legs apart. With her breasts out. He called me back in, asking what I'd been looking at, and me, being the great liar I am, told him it must have been my cousins. My dad obviously knew what I was looking at, and that I was lying to his face, but I guess he didn't want to get into what the inspiration was behind my search for "Beyoncé naked," so he let me go, and I left the scene thinking I'd just gotten away with it.

I didn't know it at the time, but this was my first time ever encountering porn, and I was about 6. One would think the first meeting with porn comes when you're in puberty at the age of 12 or 13, but it's impossible to tell. It's also impossible to parent. No parent could ever sit down and have a serious conversation with their 6-year-old kid about porn because I, like any other 6-year-old kid, found just the thought of a penis *hilarious*.

I think my parents actually did a great job on the topic of porn. They talked to me early enough that I was able to understand what goes into the making of porn, such as the treatment of the actors and how unrealistic it is. They also took the conversation seriously but allowed me to feel uncomfortable and giggle at the funny things. They also made me feel safe about it. They told me that everything I felt was natural and I should embrace the feeling.

C.A., she/her, age 19

Hookup culture

Dating is not what it used to be, plain and simple. The whole trajectory of two people's relationship has changed completely. Imagine what 90s rom-coms might have shown—two people flirting, going on some dates, *maybe* a hookup or two, and then a full blossoming relationship—and mix it up, jumble it around, make it more casual, throw in about 20 more hookups, and new terminology and slang. Confusing, right? It's confusing for us too. In all honesty, the majority of people our age are active participants in the crazy, backward, 2023 method of romance, whereas some people—very few, but some—try their best to stick to the traditional "90s rom-com" notion (still with more sex, however).

What in the past might have qualified as dating—meeting someone, going on a couple of dates, being casual—has now taken a much more serious route and carries a different weight. It refers to two people who are exclusive and are each other's significant others, the be-all and end-all of all relationships. I can tell you this because whenever I would mention a boy to my parents that maybe I liked or maybe I hung out with a few times, my parents would ask, *Are you dating?* and my response would be *insert gasp* *Of course not! Are you crazy?* So let's talk about the new path kids usually take.

What comes first is either "talking" or hooking up. Real dates such as going to the movies or going out to dinner are unusual for teenagers outside of a relationship or at least an agreed exclusivity. The most common occurrence—if you don't meet at a party and hook up within an hour of meeting each other—is "talking" some on social media, maybe texting or FaceTiming, and then hanging out with the person. This hanging out is, more often than not, cuddling, watching a movie, and, you guessed it, hooking up. After a few weeks of this, then the two might become exclusive, *not* dating, but exclusive. This means that the two are not significant others but are not hooking up with or talking to anyone else. Once this goes on for a while, maybe then they will make it official and start to use the now-taboo word *dating*.

Every parent has a different relationship with their child when it comes to talking about difficult and uncomfortable topics. Whatever your relationship may be, it is important to keep a few things in mind. The first is never to invalidate your child's emotions, whether it be sadness, anger, happiness, fear, love, and so on. Just because your child might be naive about sex and relationships, less mature, or their brain might not be fully developed does not mean that they don't understand how they feel. To your child, a first romance could be one of the most important things in their life—don't invalidate your child's feelings.

S.H., he/him, age 19

On sex

In my experience, talking about sex and sexual health can be awkward with my parents. Although they are very accepting with my habits and opinions on it, it will always feel uncomfortable. For example, my parents let me have girls over during my senior year of high school, and I hung out with two different girls. Both of them happened to be petite, and when the second girl walked out to her car, my mom saw her. Later in the evening, my mom asked, *Do you have a thing for petite girls?* This example highlights the uncomfortable nature of my parents commenting on my sexual partners. I realized that I feel more comfortable discussing the health aspect but often feel awkward talking about other aspects of sex with my parents.

I have a brother who is three years younger than I am. He opened up to me about how he is more comfortable discussing sex with me than my parents. I think of myself as an educator for my brother at times because he confides in me about his sexual journey and is not as comfortable talking about sex with my parents. I think parents displaying mixed emotions on their kid's sexual habits can produce a situation where the kid will shut them out. Sometimes this results in kids confiding in siblings or friends instead.

CHAPTER 17

Contraception, STIs, and STDs

One of the biggest misses in sex education across the United States— frankly, in how we talk about sex with kids in almost any setting in this country—is the inbalance between conversations about healthy, normal, pleasurable activity (which doesn't happen enough in most classrooms) and all of its possible pitfalls (which is important, but often talked about too much). For a long time, sex ed has doubled as sexual fearmongering.

This is not without good reason, because the two biggest negative consequences of sex, unwanted pregnancy and sexually transmitted infections (STIs), are both very real and can be life altering. But this approach buries the lede: sex will be an integral, exciting part of adult life. This is precisely why we have made a concerted effort in this book to separate out information about pregnancy prevention and disease transmission from the previous chapter about sex in general.

Many of our favorite sex educators praise the Dutch in particular for how they go about teaching sex, romance, respect, and consent, still getting to the scarier bits and pieces but not hammering them home every single time the conversation is raised. With their far more comprehensive sex ed, compared with that in the United States, the Dutch get this right, and the data proves it: Dutch teens have lower rates of pregnancy and fewer abortions than U.S. teens, and they get fewer STIs (10 percent of the total number of Dutch people with STIs are teens versus 25 percent in the United States). Overall, the Dutch report more satisfaction with sex than their American counterparts.

The Dutch prove that the overarching approach to information about sex makes a big difference when it comes to its biggest consequences. Real-world examples offer proof. The Dutch, by the way, don't avoid the downsides of sex—they just approach the entire topic through a different lens. Their glass is half-full (*Sex is wonderful! But know these few things . . .*), while we, as a country, seem to see ours as half-empty (*Sex can lead to all of these terrifying things!*). When it comes to information related to sex, we think the United States should aspire to be a lot more Dutch.

 ## LET'S START WITH SCIENCE

This chapter will cover two big sex-adjacent topics: contraception and STIs/STDs. More than any other chapter in this book, this one presents the content as a knowledge dump rather than a narrative because there's *so much* important information to share. For contraception, we'll walk through the different types available, how they work, and how effective they are. Then we'll dive into each of the sexually transmitted infections (STIs) and sexually transmitted diseases (STDs): how they're passed from one person to another, what the symptoms look like, which ones are treatable, and what that treatment entails. Our goal here is simple: since knowledge is power, get ready to become very powerful.

Contraception

Every form of contraception described in these pages is designed to prevent pregnancy. Only one of them—the barrier method, which includes condoms made for all genders—also stops the passage of STIs. Because we're big believers in getting the most important information out front, if you are looking to kill two birds with one stone here, the only way to do it is to use a barrier. You could also opt for abstinence—not having sex at all—arguably the surest way to avoid pregnancy and STIs. But the content in this chapter is intended to address people who are having sex or planning to have sex. Abstinence relies on a plan *not* to have sex.

Barrier methods: condoms and dental dams

A "male" condom is made from a piece of latex designed to snugly cover the head and shaft of a penis. (When the word *condom* is used solo, it almost always applies to barriers engineered for penises.) Condoms are packaged individually, rolled into the shape of a pancake that's slightly larger than a quarter with a thick circumferential edge. The head of the penis fits into the center of the circle, then the condom is unrolled, stretching down the shaft of an erect penis.

A "female" condom should arguably be renamed an "internal condom," because it fits inside. This type of condom, designed for vaginal or anal sex, is made from latex too. But it's conically shaped, with a thick enclosed ring on one end—that's the end inserted deep inside—and a thin, open ring on the other. If you're imagining one of those orange traffic cones, then you've got the correct general shape. Now shrink that cone down to seven or eight inches, and picture it made out of thin, rubbery latex. To insert this type of condom, the small, thick ring gets squeezed, compressing it into a longer, straighter shape. The bigger outer ring remains external so that when used vaginally, it fits around the labia majora.

There's a third type of condom designed for oral sex: the dental dam. This version is the simplest of the three. It's just a thin latex rectangle, meant to be placed over the vulva or anus before oral sex in order to protect one person's mouth and the other person's genitals from STI exchange. Given their basic design, dental dams can be fashioned out of a bunch of different materials, including polyurethane or even, according to some websites, plastic wrap. To be super clear here, we don't endorse any non–medically approved materials for STI prevention or contraception, so buy your dental dam from the store instead of fashioning it from the supplies in your kitchen. That said, dental dams can also be made by cutting a standard penile condom into a rectangle (cut lengthwise, starting at the open end) and repurposed for oral sex.

All of these versions of condoms come in a range of colors, textures, shapes, and, yes, flavors. The inventors of flavored condoms were doing everything they could to encourage use during oral sex, so don't mock it if someone's willing to try it! Condoms remain the only reliable form of infection prevention because they physically block the exchange of bodily fluids like blood, semen, vaginal secretions, and saliva—the liquids where many STIs grow and thrive. Anytime a person uses one during sex, they make that sex safer.

But condoms aren't perfect. First, they can tear, so always visually inspect them before using (and resist the urge to try to tear them, because you might just succeed). Second, condoms also age, which is why each packet should be stamped with an expiration date. Follow it! Old latex can break down during sex, so even if the condom was intact at the start, if it's old it might fray during the act. Finally, latex and many of the alternative nonlatex materials become porous when exposed to certain chemicals, especially the active ingredient in spermicide (nonoxynol-9) and oil-based products (like baby oil, cooking oil, Vaseline, and other petroleum-based jellies). If partners choose to lube up before or during sex, make sure it's not with anything oil-based—instead, opt for a product that's advertised as "lube" and sold in the condom aisle.

A comment about using condoms as the sole form of birth control: they fail more than any of us would hope. Penile condoms fail 13 percent of the time; female/internal condoms fail 21 percent of the time. When condoms are used in conjunction with other forms of contraception, though, the pairing takes failure close to zero. It doesn't matter if the combination is condom + intrauterine device, or condom + oral contraceptive pill, or condom + just about any other type of contraceptive:

when a condom is part of a two-pronged approach, there's almost no chance of pregnancy. This is why pediatricians, gynecologists, and sex educators all preach using condoms together with pretty much any other method covered in this chapter.

Last note on what to do with a condom when the sex is done: Remove it carefully and throw it away in the trash. Don't try to sneakily flush a condom down the toilet, because it very well may clog the system, and that's never a subtle move.

Diaphragms, cervical caps, and sponges

Diaphragms, cervical caps, and sponges are all barriers, too, but they gatekeep only at the opening of the cervix. This means that they physically prevent pregnancy by blocking the sperm from reaching the uterus and beyond, but they don't stop the exchange of bodily fluids inside the vagina. Quick refresher for those who need it: the vagina is a long muscular canal; the cervix sits at the top of the canal at its far end, beyond which are the uterus, then the fallopian tubes, and eventually the ovaries. Both diaphragms and cervical caps are inserted into the vagina, all the way back near the cervix—usually made of silicon, diaphragms are shaped like shallow domes; cervical caps look more like oversized thimbles. Both work far better when used in conjunction with a spermicide than when used alone.

Cervical caps aren't very common these days, but diaphragms are still used, despite an estimated 17 percent failure rate. This high number may have something to do with the fact that not only does the diaphragm need to be used with spermicide, but the combination must be left in for at least 6 hours (but not more than 24 hours) after sex. With so many other contraception options on the market, it's easy to see why this one's popularity is dwindling.

Sponges work like diaphragms, but they already contain the spermicide (a nice plus). That said, they have the same timing inconvenience: they must be left in for at least 6 hours but no more than 24 hours after sex. Failure rates here range from 14 to 27 percent, even higher than diaphragms!

After a diaphragm or cervical cap is used, it can be washed and re-used. But sponges are one-and-done, meant to be thrown away after a single use.

Spermicides

As the name implies, these products kill sperm. They come in a variety of formulations: foams, gels, creams, films, suppositories, and tablets. Spermicides are designed to go directly into the vagina, but they must be placed there within the hour before having sex; any longer and they cannot be counted on to work well.

These days, spermicides are generally used in conjunction with another form of birth control—namely, diaphragms or cervical caps. Some formulations work well with condoms, but others can cause the condom to disintegrate. The failure rate for spermicides when used without other forms of contraception averages about 21 percent.

Hormonal contraception: the pill, rings, implantables, and injections

Understanding how hormonal contraceptives work requires basic knowledge about the menstrual cycle. If you've forgotten these somewhat complicated fundamentals, flip back to chapter 5. Here's the gist of what you'll need to remember: Hormonal cycling throughout the month tells the ovaries to ripen an egg, then ovulate that egg. If the egg remains unfertilized, the body disposes of it first and the uterine lining shortly after. Luteinizing hormone (LH), follicle-stimulating hormone (FSH), estrogen, and progesterone play leading roles here. The very simplest explanation for how hormonal contraception works is that it blunts the cycling of these hormones, holding either estrogen or progesterone (or both) relatively steady. This hormonal flatlining interrupts normal signaling to the brain that should trigger surges and drops of LH and FSH;

deprives the ovaries of their signal to ovulate; stops the uterus from thickening or shedding its lining; and even changes the cervical mucus so that it becomes basically impenetrable to sperm. Different hormone combinations and doses affect each of these steps along the path in their own ways, but overall, the menstrual cycle depends entirely upon hormones rising and falling—without these highs and lows, the cycle basically stops. That's the magic of hormonal contraception.

Just to be extremely clear: when someone uses hormonal contraception, they may have spotting or bleeding reminiscent of a period, but they're not having a true period. They're not shedding a robust uterine lining in preparation for ripening and ovulating a new egg. This means that the sign so many count on to prove they're not pregnant—bloodshed—isn't reliable here.

The Pill, aka oral contraception pills (OCPs)

The most commonly used and widely talked about hormonal contraception comes in a pill. As for what's in these pills, well, that varies: some have estrogen in one form or another (estradiol, ethinyl estradiol, or the newest formulation, estetrol, which is not actually a version of the hormone but an estrogenic steroid that modulates estrogen receptors), combined with a progestin (the synthetic version of progesterone). "Mini-pills" contain only progestin. Dozens and dozens of versions of OCPs have been developed over the years because bodies are uniquely sensitive to formulations of hormones and small dosing shifts.

The hormones in OCPs replace the hormones produced by the body, tricking the brain into thinking that the ovaries are churning out a specific amount of estrogen and progesterone. This turns out to be especially important in terms of dose timing: to maximize effectiveness of an OCP, it really should be taken around the same time each day (or night). That way, the hormone circulates at a steadier state, which means that the hormone levels won't drop, the brain won't sense the drop, the innate hormonal cycling that has been turned way down won't resume, and ovulation won't occur. Finally, a big word of caution about blood clots: taking hormones increases the risk of getting them. Smoking increases the risk even more. So for anyone on an OCP, no smoking and no vaping, unless you want a potentially life-threatening blood clot in the legs, lungs, heart, or brain.

Speaking of blood, the bleeding that happens on an OCP is not menstrual bleeding—it doesn't represent the shedding of a robust uterine lining—so it shouldn't be considered reassurance that there's no pregnancy. Instead, bleeding occurs because of either hormone-induced spotting or "withdrawal bleeding," which is essentially a mini-shedding of the very minimal uterine lining that still grows while someone is on the pill. This mini-shed coincides with taking the placebo (sugar) pills that come in packs of OCPs. Because there's no benefit to a faux period, these days most pill packs have two, three, or four days of placebo pills per month, and many have none at all.

OCPs are quite reliable, with a failure rate around 7 percent. But when pills are taken at the same time each day and without any other medications that affect their metabolism (i.e., "perfect use"), that failure rate drops to 0.3 percent. Remember, though, that OCPs do not protect against STIs.

Vaginal rings

Estrogen and progestin can be delivered through a vaginal ring. This flexible circular device is inserted into the vagina and sits inside the canal (deep, so it shouldn't be noticeable or irritating) for three weeks; then the ring is removed and thrown away, and after another week a new one can be inserted. This method has all of the same pros and cons of a combined hormone OCP with one big exception: you don't need to remember to take it every day. It does need to be removed after three weeks, though, which requires some planning, and of course you need to have a new one on hand! A ring's risk profile looks very similar to OCPs, with clots and some irregular bleeding at the top of the list. So the same words of caution apply here: no smoking or vaping. On the pro side: withdrawal-periods can be shorter and lighter (and less crampy), and rings have no association with weight gain, while some pill formulations do. On the con side, the hormones in rings can thin the vaginal walls, making sex painful for some people.

Implantable hormonal contraception

Implantables work using the same concept as the pill, except no swallowing (or remembering) required. With implantable contraceptives, the hormone is preloaded into a small, flexible rod, which is then inserted under the skin of the inner, nondominant upper arm. The hormone—this formulation uses only progestin—is released slowly over time, *really* slowly. Implants usually stay in for three years.

This method has some major upsides starting with the part about not having to remember to take a medicine or insert a device. Because of this, its failure rate is super low, around 0.1 percent. It's also particularly nice for people who cannot take estrogen, since this formulation contains only progestin. On the downside, the implant must be placed by a trained healthcare professional. The implant can occasionally cause irritation or get infected (any foreign object inside the body can). And, of course, because it's not a barrier it does not protect against STIs.

Injectable hormonal contraception

Injectables are almost exactly like implantables, except here the drug is delivered via a shot given every three months. Just like implantables, injectables are made from progestin only. The dosing is not quite as steady as with implantables, so the failure rate is a little bit higher, at 4 percent. But injectables, like implantables, require no remembering (except remembering to go back to the doctor four times per year for a shot) and contain no estrogen, an advantage for those who cannot take that hormone. Plus, they involve no foreign body that could potentially become infected.

Intrauterine devices (IUDs)

These have been around for decades but have recently surged in popularity. Intrauterine devices (IUDs) are small, quarter-sized, T-shaped implants that sit inside the uterus (which itself is about the size of your closed fist). An IUD works in a bunch of different ways simultaneously: (1) it occupies a fair amount of space in the uterus, providing a physical obstruction to the implantation of a fertilized egg; (2) the presence of the IUD causes some local inflammation in the uterus, an inflammatory response that is toxic to sperm and eggs and is nonconducive to implantation; and (3) it affects the nearby fallopian tubes as well, reducing sperm and egg survival there too. IUDs can stay in place for up to 10 years.

IUDs come in two types: copper- and hormone-coated. Copper increases the local inflammatory effect, impairing sperm viability and implantation above and beyond the baseline impact of the device. Hormone coatings (always a type of progestin) thicken the cervical mucus, making it harder for sperm to pass through and therefore harder for them to reach an unfertilized egg.

Unlike those in hormonal contraceptives—OCPs, rings, implantables, and injectables—the hormones in IUDs do *not* reliably affect the menstrual cycle: copper IUDs do not interfere with ovulation at all; the hormone-coated IUDs stop ovulation in some people but not all. This means that most ovaries still ovulate in the presence of an IUD, so their users still have periods—sometimes even heavier periods than they had before, with more cramping and bleeding, and at other times the exact opposite. There are those who consider getting a period a plus, because they like the reassurance of knowing they're not pregnant, but most consider it a minus because they'd love to bypass monthly bleeding, breakouts, and emotional ups and downs.

One major advantage of the IUD is that once it's in, it's in—no pill to remember, no regular doctor visit to schedule. But on the downside, IUDs can cause irregular bleeding (sometimes daily and heavy) for the first several months. There are also lots of reports of increases in acne, mood swings, headaches, and breast swelling or tenderness with IUDs. And, of course, they must be placed by a trained healthcare professional and do not protect against STIs. The failure rates of IUDs are very low: less than 0.5 percent for hormone-coated and around 0.8 percent for copper.

One comment about the IUD's "string." The T-shaped device is inserted upright, with its horizontal extensions at the top inside the uterus, and the long post of the T running down its length. Hanging from the bottom of the T is a thin wire called a string (but it's a wire!) that comes through the cervix. When the device is eventually removed, the healthcare provider pulls this string. Of course, there's a viral TikTok showing someone removing their own IUD accidentally. First, don't try this! It's not safe—IUDs should be removed in a healthcare setting. And second, *No!* this is not a common thing.

Emergency contraception

While it's very important for people to know about the availability of emergency contraception, this is *not* something that should be used on a regular basis as a planned form of birth control. Rather, emergency contraception is meant to be just that: in an emergency—when the condom breaks or the pill wasn't taken or no other form of birth control was used—there's still an option available.

One method is to take a dosing regimen of OCPs that will make implantation nearly impossible and the uterus itself inhospitable. This is the science behind the morning-after pill. Plan B is one of many available brands, which are all designed to be used only within the 72 hours following unprotected intercourse (and the sooner it is taken, the more effective it will be). It works by providing a particularly large surge of levonorgestrel—the hormone used in lots of OCPs—to halt LH, thereby stopping ovulation. One critical sidenote: There's ongoing debate over the dosing of Plan B and other emergency contraceptives for people who weigh more than 70 kilograms (154 pounds). Unfortunately, there's not much data about this yet.

Another method is to have a copper IUD inserted within five days of the intercourse. There are lots of reasons why this is far less accessible and less convenient. Still, it's an option to know about.

Emergency contraception refers to hormones used within a few days of unprotected sex in order to reduce the likelihood of conception and implantation. This is quite different from medical abortion, which uses oral medications to terminate pregnancy through the first and second trimesters. With the overturning of *Roe v. Wade* and reduced access to abortion in many parts of the country, doctors and reproductive rights advocates are actively disseminating dosing information for the most commonly used medical abortion drugs, misoprostil and mifepristone. But to say it again for extra clarity, this is not the same as emergency contraception.

EMERGENCY CONTRACEPTION IS NOT THE SAME AS ABORTION

Emergency contraception prevents fertilization or implantation. When hormones are taken in the hours (and sometimes days) following unprotected sex, the sperm and egg may have trouble fusing, or the fertilized egg may find it impossible to implant in the uterine lining. Both scenarios prevent a successful pregnancy because for pregnancy to occur, the egg must be fertilized *and* find a spacious, nutritionally rich environment where it can grow.

Abortion, on the other hand, generally occurs several weeks after fertilization and implantation. Surgical abortion—also called dilation and curettage (D&C)—involves physically removing the uterine lining. Medical abortion relies upon oral medications that cause the uterus to shed its lining, very similar to a menstrual period. In both cases, if a fertilized egg has implanted itself and begun to grow in that lining (at which point it is called an *embryo* or *fetus*), it will be expelled.

It's important to mention abortion for ectopic pregnancy, which is often lifesaving for the mother. An *ectopic pregnancy* occurs when a fertilized egg has implanted outside of the uterus, in a place that cannot support the pregnancy. Most commonly, this happens in the fallopian tubes, but it can also occur in the cervix, the abdomen, or even the ovary itself. A fallopian tube is about 1 cm (0.39 inches) in diameter, which is about the width of a pea—clearly not spacious enough for a thriving pregnancy. If the fertilized egg is able to implant here, as it grows over time it eventually becomes big enough to rupture the tube, risking major internal bleeding and possibly death. Caught early enough, an ectopic pregnancy can be treated with a medical abortion; but if it has progressed far enough, emergency abdominal surgery may be required.

Permanent contraception or sterilization

Permanent methods of preventing pregnancy are surgeries that interfere with fertilization: tubal ligation for genetic females and vasectomy for genetic males.

Tubal ligation

Often referred to as "tying tubes," tubal ligation involves a small surgery in which the fallopian tubes are cut and sewn. This way, any ovum traveling from one of the ovaries down a fallopian tube cannot physically join with sperm swimming up the vagina, through the uterus, and inside that same-sided fallopian tube, because the tube has been severed. The surgery is very short, almost always done in an outpatient surgical center or in a hospital but without an overnight stay (unless there's something else going on medically). The effect is immediate, but it can take a few days for someone to feel like they're back to their regular active self. Tubal ligation has a failure rate of around 0.5 percent because sometimes those tubes don't completely separate the way the surgeon intended.

Vasectomy

Vasectomy is the penile equivalent to tube tying. Here, an incision is made in the vas deferens, the tube that carries sperm away from the testicles toward the tip of the penis (that's where the name comes from: *vas* + *ectomy*, which means "surgical removal"). Like tubal ligation, this surgery is usually done at an outpatient center or in a hospital with no overnight stay. Sperm counts drop very quickly, but it can take 12 weeks before they reach zero, so doctors ask patients to come in so they can check (yes, by having them ejaculate into a container). There's also a fair amount of swelling down there for some people, slowing their return to sexual activity for a few days. The failure rate here is 0.15 percent.

STIs and STDs

All right, deep exhale here—we're done with the contraception section. Now it's time to move on to STIs and STDs. Compared with conversations about birth control, this topic tends to be a little harder to frame in a positive light. But there's a way to talk about avoiding warts, sores, and green discharge without demonizing or disgustifying sex. We get to that a little later in the chapter. First, the facts.

Let's start broadly, with the difference between an STI and an STD. *S* and *T* stand for the same thing both times: *sexually transmitted. I* is for *infection*, which happens when an organism like a bacterium, virus, or parasite enters the body. *D* is for *disease*: the physical, often symptomatic manifestations of the infection. All STDs start as STIs, but many STIs never progress to STDs.

So let's say two people have sex and one passes a bacterial infection on to the other. Those bacteria enter the body, then begin to grow and multiply. That's an STI. It's highly possible that the newly infected person has no idea the bacteria are in their body because they are asymptomatic, but they still have an STI and are capable of passing it along to someone else. Now let's say that person begins to have symptoms: maybe some funky-colored discharge or sharp lower-abdominal pain or a sore somewhere along the genitals—with symptoms, the STI has progressed to become an STD.

Most STIs enter the body one of two ways: via skin-to-skin contact or via exchange of bodily fluids like saliva, blood, or semen. Lest you think otherwise, this happens *all the time*. It's estimated that globally, a million STIs are passed every single day. Anyone who has unprotected oral, vaginal, or anal sex is at risk, with *unprotected* in this sentence meaning not using a barrier like a condom.

What follows is a list of the most common STIs, with a brief description of the type of infection, how it's passed, typical symptoms when it flips into an STD, and most frequently used treatments. If you are looking for more detailed information—like a comprehensive list of every possible physical manifestation or all of the different ways a particular infection can be treated—there exist many excellent online resources. We recommend sites created by hospitals or medical education centers, almost all of which have websites ending with *.org* or *.edu* rather than *.com*. This is an excellent opportunity to bookmark a couple of reliable websites for general medical information. Not sure you've hit upon a good one? Ask your doctor for some recommendations.

Chlamydia

Chlamydia is the most common STD in the United States. It's caused by the bacterium *Chlamydia trachomatis*. About a quarter of infected females and half of infected males develop symptoms like painful urination, vaginal discharge or atypical bleeding, epididymitis (exquisite pain in one testicle), proctitis (rectal inflammation), pharyngitis (sore throat), and conjunctivitis (infection in the eye). One of the most worrisome complications of chlamydia is pelvic inflammatory disease, which involves infection of the uterus, fallopian tubes, and even ovaries; it causes intense abdominal and pelvic pain and, if left untreated for long enough, can lead to scarring and fertility issues later.

The good news about chlamydia is that it's treatable with antibiotics. The unfortunate part is that people don't always know they have it. This is especially frustrating, because diagnosing this infection is not difficult: a swab of the cervix, vagina, or urethra, or even a urine sample can detect chlamydia. Once it is diagnosed, a doctor will prescribe an antibiotic, most commonly doxycycline or azithromycin, though depending upon the patient and the severity, other antibiotics may be used. Don't be surprised if a doctor checks for chlamydia as part of a routine exam—this test, as simple a checking the urine, increases the likelihood of picking it up before it has a chance to turn symptomatic.

Gonorrhea

Another bacterial source of STIs is *Neisseria gonorrhoeae*, the bacterium that causes the constellation of symptoms known as gonorrhea. It turns out, gonorrhea can exist on its own or show up alongside chlamydia. Yes, you read that right: sometimes people get two STIs for the price of one. The symptoms of gonorrhea can also resemble chlamydia—causing issues like vaginal discharge, rectal inflammation (sometimes with pus-like discharge), vaginal bleeding, pain and swelling of one testicle, and conjunctivitis—making the two tricky to distinguish. (An interesting sidenote: gonorrhea tends to cause symptoms in males more often than in females, not typical for most STDs.) But a swab or urine test can do the diagnostic hard work for healthcare providers, and then the right antibiotic can be prescribed. So again, don't be surprised to find a urine screening part of a routine exam.

Herpes

This is a well-known infection, largely because the sores of herpes are generally noticeable, painful, or both. It's also well-known because so many people have it!

Herpes is caused by the herpes simplex virus (HSV), a member of the herpes virus family. Fun fact: there are lots of non-STIs caused by different types of herpes virus (the varicella-zoster virus causes chicken pox and the Epstein-Barr virus causes mono), but this is the only herpes virus that goes by the name *herpes*. HSV actually comes in two types, conveniently named type 1 and type 2. Both types are passed through sex, as well as skin-to-skin contact, including contact between a birthing baby and its mother—when herpes is contracted by a newborn baby, it is called congenital herpes.

HSV-1 is the most common form of herpes, with well over half (some studies suggest two-thirds) of the world's population infected. Yes, you read that right! It's hard to overstate how widespread this infection really is: recent estimations predict that, globally, 3.7 billion people under the age of 50 carry HSV-1, and another 500 million carry HSV-2. In the olden days (when we were growing up), HSV-1 was known as the form that caused cold sores around the mouth and HSV-2 as the type responsible for genital lesions, but that classification of an above-the-waist herpes and a below-the-belt herpes turns out to be completely wrong: both exist in both places. It also used to be said that the only way for HSV to be passed from one person to another was when a lesion was visible, but now we know that subclinical transmission occurs, which means that even without a sore, a body can shed virus and infect another body. This is yet another reason why barrier method contraception is so important—not just genital barriers but oral too.

Once HSV has entered the body, it often can be entirely asymptomatic, but when it makes itself known, it first appears as a rash that starts out looking like a pimple and then evolves into a blister that crusts over with a scab. *Primary herpes* describes the first outbreak, usually with a large cluster of sores; *reactivated herpes* refers to every outbreak that follows, sometimes with just a solitary sore but other times with a crop. The rashes most often appear either around the mouth or in the genitals, and just before they erupt, searing pain begins. Pain is a classic hallmark of HSV infection because the virus lives along nerves, lying dormant in nerve roots. When the virus reactivates throughout life (especially at times of high stress), it travels along the nerve, triggering pain fibers to fire before a lesion ever appears. Anyone who has ever had a cold sore knows this extremely uncomfortable dance.

While bacteria can be eradicated with antibiotics, most viruses must run their course. Some of them die off over time, but HSV never really goes away: it lives in the nerve roots for the rest of an infected person's life. There are, however, antiviral medications (such as acyclovir, famciclovir, and valacyclovir) that can make HSV reactivations shorter and less painful.

HIV

Human immunodeficiency virus (HIV) first emerged in the 1980s. Because it spreads via semen, vaginal secretions, and blood, it can be passed between sexual partners, from mother to child during birth, and between any two people who share needles. It is no longer passed through blood transfusions now that blood is effectively screened for HIV.

The symptoms of HIV can be extremely vague: fever, headache, muscle aches, joint pains, rashes, sore throat, and swollen glands top the list. Over time, if left untreated, HIV wreaks havoc on the body's immune system, eventually rendering a person incapable of fending off most infections. When the disease reaches this stage, it's called acquired immunodeficiency syndrome (AIDS).

Over the past four decades of its existence, HIV has evolved from a death sentence to an infection people live with, now held at bay by a combination of antiviral drugs. The specific drug cocktail varies based upon a patient's needs. There's also now a preventive drug combination available called pre-exposure prophylaxis (PrEP). Again, exact medications and dosing schedules depend upon the individual.

HPV

Human papillomavirus (HPV) is the most commonly diagnosed STI in the United States (though chlamydia takes the prize for most common STD), with more than 40 different subtypes circulating at any given time. HPV exists worldwide, with the World Health Organization estimating more than 600,000 new infections in 2020 alone.

While some strains remain benign, several have been associated with cancers of the penis, cervix, mouth, and throat (esophagus). Two strains in particular, HPV-16 and HPV-18, are responsible for over half of all HPV-induced cancers. HPV is also one of the only vaccine-preventable STIs, and since HPV can cause cancer, this means that there is a vaccine (actually there are three: Gardasil, Gardasil-9, and Cervarix) that can prevent cancer, a huge scientific feat! The vaccines prevent only certain strains of HPV, but these include the most virulent ones.

HPV is often asymptomatic. However, when it does show itself on the body, it likes to do so in the form of warts: genital warts; warts on the fingers and palms; plantar warts on the soles of the feet; and flat warts on the face or legs. These warts can be treated by topical medicines (like imiquimod or podofilox) or burned off using acids (salicylic acid or tricholoracetic acid). When HPV is found internally by a gynecologist during a Pap smear—a part of the routine vaginal checkup for sexually active people that involves swabbing the vagina and cervix to look for infections like HPV—it can be treated using cryotherapy (freezing), electrocautery (burning), or loop electrosurgical excision procedure (LEEP). All of these procedures involve something called colposcopy, which uses an instrument (colposcope) to magnify and better visualize the inside of the vagina and the cervix in order to take biopsies of any worrisome spots.

Syphilis

This STI is caused by the bacterium *Treponema pallidum*, which is passed either through direct contact with the rash, via shared body fluids during sex, or through blood. It is easily treatable with penicillin if it's picked up early on. The problem is, even healthcare providers can miss the diagnosis of syphilis because it can present in so many different ways, often mimicking other infections—this is what earned syphilis its nickname "the Great Pretender."

Syphilis is remarkably common. Worldwide there are an estimated 20 million cases in people between the ages of 15 and 49. In the United States specifically, the disease has ebbed and flowed, but over the past decade rates have risen steadily, particularly among women.

Syphilis has four stages: primary, secondary, latent, and tertiary. In primary syphilis, small sores (called chancres) appear; even though they last between three and six weeks, they're not always noticeable to the person who has them. The rashes of secondary syphilis tend to be harder-to-miss large, wart-like sores in the mouth and genital region, sometimes accompanied by muscle aches, hair loss, or big, swollen lymph nodes. These symptoms last anywhere from a few weeks to a full year, but they are often nonspecific enough to be misdiagnosed as something else, like a flu or canker sores or strep throat. The latent stage means that the syphilis has reverted to no symptoms at all. Sometimes this is how things play out for the rest of a person's life, with the syphilis going silent and the doctor reassured of their wrong diagnosis when everything "gets better" on its own. But in 15 to 30 percent of untreated people, latent syphilis evolves into tertiary syphilis, causing damage to the brain, nervous system, blood vessels, eyes, heart, liver, bones, or joints. Sometimes tertiary syphilis causes problems in only one of these systems, but there are people who wind up with issues head to toe. Suddenly, a once-treatable infection wreaks permanent havoc on the body.

Trichomoniasis

This is the one STI on the list caused by a parasite. Trichomoniasis is more common in women, and it is more likely to become symptomatic in women too. Across all genders it causes strong-smelling greenish discharge (from penises and vaginas), red and itchy genitals, and pain with both peeing and sex.

Trichomoniasis is treated with an antiparasitic medication usually taken in the form of a pill. While the medicine works well, about 20 percent of all people wind up reinfected within three months. Condoms can prevent transmission when they're used correctly, but the parasite easily attaches itself to the condom, so for this particular infection, in order for a barrier method to work well it must be removed properly!

 ## WHAT'S CHANGED OVER THE PAST 20, 30, 40 YEARS

On the contraception front

There's been a boom in contraception since the birth of most people reading this book. The first hormonal pill received FDA approval in 1957—ostensibly, it was designed not to prevent pregnancy but rather to regulate periods. Still, by 1959, 500,000 women were using it, doubling down on its "side effect" of pregnancy prevention (clever women!). In 1960, the FDA granted approval for the first OCP, and within five years, one out of every four married women in the United States under the age of 45 had tried it; 13 million were taking it globally. Over the past 60 years, pills have been drastically reformulated to minimize side effects and cater to a broader swath of daily users, a number that now far surpasses 100 million. "Change" is an understatement here.

That same time period saw the evolution of several other forms of contraception, every single one described in this chapter besides condoms, which were first documented back in the 1560s but officially patented nearly 300 years later, in 1844. Sponges, diaphragms, rings, and most certainly IUDs have a time line that stretches across the last couple of generations, their impact massive.

So when it comes to contraception, almost everything has changed—which is why many adults feel out of the loop here. It's okay. Hopefully you're more educated now, or at least you've gotten off to a decent start. Keep going, as the world of birth control will not stop evolving anytime soon.

This is especially true given that during the writing of this book, the U.S. Supreme Court overturned *Roe v. Wade*, the 1973 decision guaranteeing the constitutional right to abortion. This, in turn, increases the urgency for today's kids to understand the various forms of contraception discussed in this chapter so that they can thread that fine needle of giving over to sexual urges while preventing pregnancy.

On the STI/STD front

Not much has changed about STIs and STDs themselves over the past several decades—HIV and HPV were the last of the "new" ones. Of course, HIV created shock waves of fear, and rightfully so, through the end of the twentieth century. One downstream consequence appeared inside of schools. Before HIV, sex ed classes—if they were even taught—focused on pregnancy prevention, but in 1986, as the AIDS epidemic surged, the U.S. surgeon general called for comprehensive sex education to include teaching about both heterosexual and homosexual sex as well as specific information about HIV/AIDS. The fear of getting pregnant or getting someone else pregnant became secondary to the fear of acquiring this new STD and then dying from it. Bear in mind, 1986 was a *Roe*-protected time in which pregnancy was reversible but AIDS was not. Today the inverse is true: abortion is no longer constitutionally protected, but HIV is highly manageable as a chronic illness.

After the emergence of HIV, and over the years since, conversations about how to prevent infection have moved out of the shadows and keeping them there became a matter of life and death. Schools stepped up curricula, and states set sex ed standards. Parents and other adults raising kids recognized the importance of this information, with most incorporating it into their family conversations even when they themselves had had little or no modeling of how to do this in their own childhoods. Unfortunately, sex ed is still the short-straw class, much of the time taught by a teacher with no formal training. And state standards exist, but there's little enforcement that their lessons are taught.

Despite waves of fear throughout the 1980s and 1990s, today sex education has settled back into a general rut of apathy or even antipathy thanks to school-based issues like underfunding, lack of time, and general bewilderment, along with the profound social shift of outsourcing all sorts of information to the internet. In addition, growing political divides around gender identity and sexual orientation have given conservative activists an opportunity to attempt shut down (some successfully) *all* sex education in the name of "protecting kids." Worries about killer STDs have abated to the point of a backlash, in which some sex educators say people don't think about HIV (or any other STI, for that matter) nearly enough—or at all. No one would disagree that the revolution in HIV therapies has been miraculous, but it's no walk in the park living with a chronic infection and taking medications daily to hold it at bay. The same may be said for syphilis, HPV, herpes, and all the rest.

Another massively fundamental shift—this one outside the classroom, the home, and even the bedroom—is that scientific innovations in contraception have resulted in a wide variety of new birth control products. Meanwhile, STI prevention has stagnated, still fully reliant upon the traditional condom. As a result, most newly sexually active people need to use two different forms of protection to be truly "safe"—an IUD plus a condom; the pill plus a condom; a sponge plus a condom. While this is fine and doable, it seems surprising that we haven't doubled down on evolving STI prevention with the same fervor, especially given the oft-heard refrain that sex with a condom doesn't feel as good as sex without it. Shouldn't that industry be booming with innovation?

On the bright side, access to STI screening and STD testing has vastly improved over the decades. The biggest game changer here is probably the introduction of urine-based tests to screen for chlamydia and gonorrhea. Other technologies, like the nucleic acid amplification test (NAAT) and the polymerase chain reaction (PCR) test, allow for easier diagnostics across many different STIs, so long as a person has access to healthcare. And the same goes for vaccine prevention of STIs, most notably HPV. The HPV vaccine is geared toward kids between 11 and 14 years old, ideally inoculating them before they ever become sexually active. This chapter didn't cover hepatitis B, but that infection, too, transmits during sex and through blood, can cause a form of cancer of its own (liver cancer), and is also preventable with immunization. The medical innovations that diagnose STIs early or even stop them altogether have been nothing short of miraculous.

Sex itself has changed, something we talk about in great detail in chapter 16. Everything from hookup culture to hair removal affects the way teens are stepping into sexual culture, not to mention the consequences. The mainstreaming of multiple sexual partners outside of committed relationships fuels the spread of STIs/STDs among participants, explaining the CDC's findings in the 2019 *Youth Risk Behavior Study*: chlamydia, gonorrhea, and syphilis were on the rise—newer data is anticipated soon but COVID slowed its collection.

Things have changed, really changed. Repeating the same warning phrases that were recited a generation ago doesn't work because the landscape has shifted so dramatically (even while teenage urges have, for all intents and purposes, remained the same). Our conversations with adolescents about STIs, STDs, and contraception need to evolve along with the times.

HOW TO TALK ABOUT IT

Conversations about contraception, STIs, and STDs are deeply uncomfortable because they require acknowledging that someday a kid will likely have sex with someone, and statistically speaking, it will happen a lot sooner than their wedding day. Or maybe they're already having sex, making the dynamics even more awkward in the attempt to catch up. No matter when you're doing this or how much it makes you cringe, bear in mind that forthright, age-appropriate conversations about sex need to address both pregnancy and disease, giving kids enough information to keep them healthy but not so much as to frighten them. Remember, the ultimate goal is for them to have loving, meaningful sexual relationships with their partners. Scaring the crap out of them on *all* fronts will undermine that goal and will almost certainly stop them from talking to you about any of it. Still, helping them understand what to fear and how to make good decisions is a part of this complicated journey.

Kids really enjoy understanding how their bodies and brains work, so explain the science to them (you've got pages filled with golden nuggets above) in nonjudgmental ways. Adjust descriptions, giving varying levels of detail depending on your audience—not just how old they are, but also their level of sophistication and also their lived experiences. Don't worry, we all screw it up from time to time. But with practice and a lot of feedback from kids, we get better at figuring out who can handle what information and when.

Talking about pregnancy eventually requires talking about sex

Start with pregnancy because that is something kids are used to talking about throughout childhood. Maybe they have younger siblings, or their teacher recently had a baby—this isn't a totally foreign concept, even if they were originally told the baby was *brought by a stork* or *came out of Mommy's belly*. Interestingly, in our puberty workshops, the topic of sex almost always gets pushed aside for the far more fascinating (according to them) information about ovulation and menstruation—*these* are the things tweens especially are into. Eventually, though, all kids need a scientifically accurate version of how babies are made. If they're asking you directly, they're ready. If they're not asking but you think they

need to know, they need to know! Do not lie or make up information, but make sure to be inclusive of types of sex other than heterosexual, penis-in-vagina. Here are some simple starter sentences for this
conversation:

> **For the youngest kids:** *Babies are made when a sperm meets
> an egg and they grow together in a womb.*

> **For the kids who are ready for more detail:** *During some
> forms of sex, a penis goes into a vagina and the sperm that is
> ejaculated from the penis can fertilize an egg, leading to
> pregnancy.*

> **For kids who have mastered—or heard of—the basics:**
> *There are all different kinds of sex—vaginal, anal, oral, and
> masturbation—I will walk you through each one. Just a
> reminder: when you have penile/vaginal sex without a
> condom or other form of birth control, the sperm can fertilize
> the egg and cause pregnancy.*

Only after making sure a kid knows how a sperm can fertilize an egg
during vaginal intercourse can you move on to pregnancy prevention.
For younger kids, the gap in those conversations may last months or
even years! For older kids, the two may be discussed back-to-back in one
talk. Some notes on the contraception conversation:

> **Be extremely specific that "pulling out" is not an
> effective way to prevent pregnancy.** Explain that a small
> amount of semen (some call it pre-cum) often leaks out
> before full ejaculation, and all semen carries sperm. So
> even if a person is able to pull the penis out before
> ejaculating, there may still be semen in the vagina,
> making fertilization possible.

Demonstrate to kids of all genders how to put a condom on a penis even if they tell you they already know. If it's just too awkward, watch an educational video together—we've got links on the resources section of our website.

For a kid using birth control like the pill or an IUD, stay in dialogue about their experience. Don't assume the conversation can end just because they have a prescription in hand (or in their arm or uterus). Topics to revisit include the timing of pill-taking, the risks of blood clots with smoking or vaping, and of course the risks of STIs without barrier protection. Kids who experience side effects with contraception—weight gain, sore breasts, depression—might stop using their birth control, leaving them at risk for pregnancy; or they might silently manage pain, discomfort, and heavy bleeding, all of which can be really tough for people of any age. Encourage them to talk about it all rather than suffer alone.

Make sure to be explicit about current abortion laws

The legal landscape has changed dramatically with the Supreme Court's overturning of *Roe v. Wade,* the decision that federally protected the right to abortion 50 years ago. Now abortion laws are determined by individual states. Some states immediately banned all abortions, including in cases of rape and incest; others guaranteed the right and access; many have pending votes and will shift their positions between our writing of this book and your reading of it. Several states have threatened prosecution of people who order abortion pills from other states; some plan to track data on period apps and across pharmacies looking for evidence of medicine-induced abortion. Teens and young adults must be informed on all of these fronts, especially as they move from state to state to attend college. Regardless of gender, they need help thinking through what they would do if they got pregnant or their sexual partner got pregnant—walking through the possibilities is a caregiver's responsibility, as hard or complicated as that might feel.

Move beyond penis-meets-vagina

We can't emphasize enough how important it is to cover all the different forms of sex in order to help keep kids safe. Some kids don't understand that while oral and anal sex won't result in a baby, they can lead to the exchange of bodily fluids infected with STIs. Broadening the dialogue to include a wide range of experiences demonstrates the removal of judgment from the discussion, which turns out to be the key to keeping dialogue open.

Talking to adolescents about the safest ways to have anal sex is particularly tricky for many adults, especially if it feels taboo—maybe it's something they've never talked about with anyone, ever. Anal sex is more common than many imagine: as we touched on in chapter 16, a 2018 study reported that 11 percent of 15- to 19-year-old respondents (both male and female) had engaged in anal sex. *Not* talking about it can have safety implications. For instance, anal sex often results in microtearing of the anal skin, providing small openings for STIs to enter the body. It's a fact that, once understood, can encourage the wearing of condoms. Some women also report feeling coerced to engage in anal sex—they don't want to do it, but they think they have to. Opening up this line of conversation becomes hugely important in terms of both physical and emotional safety.

And then there's oral sex, which tends to fall into some sort of in-between land: kids who have engaged in oral but not vaginal or anal sex are usually considered virgins, but these virgins can pick up almost every STI on the list if they don't use protection. While dental dams and condoms during oral sex serve as classic punchlines during sex-ed classes, understanding the risk that oral sex carries in transmitting infections can increase the use of barriers and decrease the spread of disease.

Always meet kids where they are, especially during tricky conversations

When Vanessa took her oldest child, who was 12 at the time, to get his first HPV vaccine, he was extremely reluctant to get the shot. (Sidenote: he really *hates* shots.) So Vanessa turned to his pediatrician and asked, "Can you please explain why this shot is so important?"

Without missing a beat, the doctor turned to Vanessa's son and asked, "Do you want warts on your penis?"

"No!" he hollered.

The doctor replied, "Great. This shot helps prevent you from getting warts on your penis," and boom, gave him the shot.

It is important to meet kids where they are cognitively, emotionally, and physically, no matter what the topic. But when it's foreign and scary—STIs are the perfect example here—this approach becomes critical. If the doctor had expounded on how the HPV virus can eventually cause cervical cancer, it might not have resonated with the 12-year-old sitting in his office: he probably didn't know what a cervix was, if he did he would know he didn't have one, and cancer would seem like a very distant possibility. But warts on your penis? *That* spoke to him. Finding ways into really serious (and possibly frightening) topics in relatable ways always works best.

Don't let discomfort get in the way

It can be downright terrifying for adults to think about kids having sex. But whether we're talking about sex or anything else covered in this book, we can't let our fear drive the discussion. Teaching them about STIs, STDs, and birth control is as absolutely necessary as it is petrifying, but leaving them in the dark is downright dangerous.

We've said it many times before, but here it's especially true: covering the consequences of sex should be done in many (many!) small conversations stretched out over a long period of time. One massive talk will almost certainly leave everyone involved equal parts confused and exhausted.

Decide whichever topic feels easier or more urgent: prevention of infection or prevention of pregnancy. Start there. And remember, choose language that makes no assumptions about a kid's sexual orientation while still covering all the bases—you never know when they may decide to experiment sexually or have a partner who is experimenting.

Finally—and this one works extremely well—name your discomfort with the topic when raising it with a kid: *This is hard for me to talk about. I didn't grow up in a house where we talked about sex at all. But I know it's really important for us to discuss this in order to keep you healthy and safe, so here we go!*

The most important part is to stay in conversation

We say it in every chapter of this book, but here our advice to keep the conversation going becomes critically important. Just talking equals success because it opens the door. A kid who fears an adult reaction may make some pretty dumb and dangerous decisions to avoid those reactions. Kids who know that their parents or other caregivers are willing to hear them out will still make some poor choices, but they are far more likely to admit their mistakes and talk things through, often before a situation gets worse. If you've ever asked a kid why they said or did something that made absolutely zero sense, chances are their response was *I thought my parents would get mad at me.* Make sure they know that nothing is more important than their health and safety, and to that end, they can come to us with any problem, even if they think we'll be mad.

Ultimately, talking about contraception and infections brings many adults' greatest fears to the surface. Sometimes that discomfort stems from the simple fact that a kid is having sex in the first place; other times it is the fear of pregnancy or acquiring an STI. We're going to land this chapter where we started, with a reminder that safe, pleasurable sex is the goal. Some kids may delay it, while others have it long before we've got a clue. Either way, it's our job to keep them safe and healthy whenever and however they're doing it.

 ## FROM PEOPLE JUST OUT THE OTHER SIDE

R.E., she/her, age 21

On contraception

When I was a senior in high school, I remember sitting with a friend and hearing an alarm chime on her phone. The alarm was reminding my friend to take her birth control. It felt like everyone around me was on birth control—it was almost like "all the cool kids were doing it." I suddenly felt left out. Years later, I now wonder if I felt left out because my lack of interest in birth control stemmed from the fact that it was not something I would be needing anytime soon, if it was because I just wanted to be part of the alarms and talk of the pill, or if it was a combination of both.

I had a great deal of difficulty talking about anything that had to do with my body, romance, and growing up. I did not want to be seen as a "woman" and all grown up, but now I was eager to be on the pill too. The summer before I went to college, I brought up the idea of going on the pill while at a doctor's appointment. I wanted to be part of the "birth-control-pill club." Because I was a late bloomer and also a ballerina growing up, my doctor actually liked the idea of me being on birth control as I transitioned to college and my activity level changed. I was so excited.

My mom came back into the room and my doctor announced the news: She is going on birth control! My mom looked a bit confused and started asking me more about this decision. I did not want to engage in the conversation and felt uncomfortable talking about it. But if I had been able to talk about it, maybe I would have been a bit more prepared for what happened next.

I started taking the pill. It was fine at first, until I got to college and felt like my skin was no longer my own. My clothes were not fitting right, and I was physically uncomfortable. I gave it three months, and it just kept getting worse. So my doctor put me on a new pill. My body started feeling a little more normal, but I still really did not feel like myself. I was feeling down and upset all the time. My head was a sea of darkness, and my body still felt like it was revolting against me. So I decided to go off of the pill. I no longer wanted to be in the birth-control-pill club.

Flash forward to a year later when it was time to talk about birth control again. I *refused* to go back on the pill. After talking to my doctor and my mom, I decided to get a hormonal IUD. This was the right decision for me, and there was actual thought and conversation that went into making it, unlike my choice two years earlier.

T.A., she/her, age 19

On STIs and STDs

My entire ninth-grade class was required to sit through an assembly about why we should use birth control, which included photographic evidence of genital herpes. That assembly will forever be one of the most memorable in my life. STDs and STIs, once you learn about them and see their effects on the body, immediately become a fear to every person in the room. It's basically a one-and-done conversation, even if your kid's eyes are closed and then they peek at the screen for a split second.

Two years after that horrifying day, a friend of mine and I decided to devote our final biology project to the reproductive system. The assignment was to create an educational board game about a body system of our choice and a corresponding slideshow about a specific topic within that system.

Our game, *Dr. Diagnosis: Planned Parenthood*, was a piece of art, if I do say so myself. Each player used a tampon-shaped game piece to move across the board. Each new block they landed on would ask them to pick up a Patient Card, a small card with a patient's name, age, assigned gender at birth, and symptoms. The player would then diagnose the patient with an STD or STI (or occasionally break it to the patient that they were pregnant), and if they were right, they would continue to move through the game.

Our slideshow, on the other hand, was a work of fact, with many photos that would be considered the opposite of art. We had decided to present on STDs and STIs, reminding our classmates of the presentation given two years prior. With lots of vivid imagery, we effectively retraumatized each student; even with all the time spent researching, I still shudder at the thought of gonorrhea.

Depending on what school your child attends, reproductive health may be a subject they are taught, but assume it's not. Even if you are the second or third person they've heard talk about STDs and STIs, the conversation will hold just as much relevance (and possibly scare them even more, and with the topic at hand, that's a great thing).

Be prepared for awkwardness, but embrace it too—it's essential to everyone (not just your kids) to discuss the differences between curable and incurable STDs, the importance of a barrier method, and why conversations with a partner (and testing) are so valuable. It may remind you of a few things too!

I've grown up with a mom who writes and speaks about puberty and sex for a living, but the STD and STI conversations are still a nerve-racking conversation for us both. That being said, we understand the importance of these talks, and I've used the knowledge from her to talk with my friends too. With these conversations, we are all keeping each other safe and healthy, which is all a parent wants for their kid, right?

CHAPTER 18

Sexual Orientation

Across many cultures (maybe even most) and throughout history, people have debated which attractions are virtuous—even allowable—and which are not. Feelings of attraction, innate to each person, somehow live in the public sphere: there's always been lots of opinions about whom one person can and should like, love, date, fool around with, sleep with, or marry. Over time, these notions get translated into religious edicts, cultural norms, and laws, sometimes supporting free expression, other times punishing it.

 ## LET'S START WITH SCIENCE

Feelings of sexual attraction first emerge during puberty. Sure, there are prepubescent five-year-olds running around saying they have a crush on so-and-so or they're going to marry so-and-so, but these are mostly expressions of emotional closeness, not sexual interest, that nonetheless get further reinforced by the world around them (*Oh it's so cute that those two preschoolers spent their playdate acting out their wedding ceremony!*). The authentic feelings that drive sexual urges are chemical, reliant upon higher baseline levels of testosterone, estrogen, and other hormones that start to rise in puberty.

So kids begin to think about sexual interactions during puberty. The limbic system—home to so many highly motivated, feel-good, risk-breeds-reward behaviors classic to middle and high school—is packed with androgen receptors, which means testosterone and its cousins are capable of amping up this part of the brain, manifesting first as crushes (technically one-way attraction, though the win is when a crush is recip-rocated) and eventually as full-on sexual arousal. From early days, tweens and teens feel desire for others and a wish to be desired in return. How they choose to act on that desire evolves over time.

Concurrent with what's happening in the brain emotionally is what's happening everywhere else physically. Those hallmarks of puberty—like linear growth spurts; increased weight and curviness; newfound hair, es-pecially facial hair; and breast development—often cause one kid to be deemed more attractive than another.

The science of who is attracted to whom and why turns out to be remarkably thin when it comes to tweens and teens. We know a fair amount about the hormonal on and off switches of adult sexual desire, but this is a tricky subject to study in younger kids, particularly kids so young that they can't even articulate the feelings associated with lust. Now try layering on questions about sexual orientation . . . Exactly! That's why there's not much data hanging around.

But there is a growing body of information about older adolescents' sexual orientation, which we dive into in the pages that follow. And while tremendous stigma and discrimination continue to be aimed at nonheterosexual individuals across the world, we are also living in a moment of dramatic cultural shifts that help normalize different sexual orientations, which further increases adolescents' willingness to speak openly.

The first place to start is always with a definition of terms. The words related to sexual orientation can create a fair amount of confusion for people who didn't grow up using them. What's more, the abbreviation dedicated to describing people identifying as sexual minorities—basically everyone other than heterosexuals—is an ever-growing list of letters that includes sexual orientations *and* gender descriptors. As of the writing of this book, the most inclusive oft-used version stands at LGBTQIAA+.

Before jumping into the list letter by letter, we would like to comment about combining sexual orientation and gender identity minority groups under one umbrella. It originally made sense to do this, but the concept feels like it is rapidly outgrowing itself. All of the people represented by this diverse banner of letters have faced decades (more like centuries . . . even millennia!) of social ostracism, from bullying to discrimination to hate crimes to murder. Uniting their causes under one flag—literally, the rainbow flag—meant their numbers swelled, strengthening their social and political capital. From a financial standpoint, fundraising is more efficient when aimed at one large group: donors can give more money or time to a single cause, advocates have a bigger base, and the various constituencies benefit from economies of scale. The problem is that sexual orientation and gender identity are really two separate issues, and rolling them together has created a fair amount of confusion, especially for older generations new to these concepts. Stephanie Brill and Rachel Pepper, authors of *The Transgender Child,* describe the distinction beautifully: "Gender and sexual orientation are two distinct, but related, aspects of self. Gender is personal while sexual orientation is interpersonal. While these are two separate aspects of each person, they are defined by gender, so it can feel confusing! A person's sexual orientation reflects the gender(s) of those they are attracted to."

This is why we split the two topics into distinct chapters in this book—they *are* distinct. The worries, challenges, and needs of people in these two groups can be very different. Still, they share more than they diverge, particularly in their social status, and so at the moment and for very good reason, the language remains intertwined.

WHAT LGBTQIAA+ STANDS FOR

L = Lesbian, a woman who is emotionally, romantically, or sexually attracted to other women. Women and nonbinary people may use this term to describe themselves.

G = Gay, a person who is emotionally, romantically, or sexually attracted to members of the same gender. Men, women, and nonbinary people may use this term to describe themselves.

B = Bisexual, a person emotionally, romantically, or sexually attracted to more than one sex, gender, or gender identity, though not necessarily simultaneously, in the same way, or to the same degree; sometimes used interchangeably with *pansexual*.

T = Transgender, an umbrella term for people whose gender identity and/or expression is different from cultural expectations based on the sex they were assigned at birth. Being transgender does not imply any specific sexual orientation—therefore, transgender people may identify as straight, gay, lesbian, bisexual, et cetera.

T can also = Transsexual, an older term that originated in the medical and psychological communities and is still preferred by some people who have changed—or seek to change—their bodies through medical interventions (including but not limited to hormones and/or surgeries). Unlike *transgender, transsexual* is not an umbrella term, and many transgender people do not identify as transsexual.

Q = Queer, a term people often use to express a spectrum of identities and orientations that are counter to the mainstream, a catchall that can include people who do not identify as exclusively straight and/or have nonbinary or gender-expansive identities. This term was previously used as a slur but has been reclaimed by many parts of the LGBTQ+ movement.

Q can also = Questioning, a term used to describe people who are in the process of exploring their sexual orientation or gender identity.

I = Intersex, people who are born with any of a wide variety of differences in their sex traits and reproductive anatomy, including differences in genitalia, chromosomes, gonads, internal sex organs, hormone production, hormone response, and/or secondary sex traits.

A = Asexual, often called "ace" for short, referring to a complete or partial lack of sexual attraction or lack of interest in sexual activity with others. Asexuality exists on a spectrum, and asexual people may experience no, little, or conditional sexual attraction.

A can also = Ally, a term used to describe someone who is actively supportive of LGBTQ+ people, encompassing straight and cisgender allies as well as those within the LGBTQ+ community who support each other (e.g., a lesbian who is an ally to the bisexual community).

P (usually inferred in the +) = Pansexual, a term for someone who has the potential for emotional, romantic, or sexual attraction to people of any gender though not necessarily simultaneously, in the same way, or to the same degree. Sometimes used interchangeably with bisexual.

Sources: PortlandOregon.gov and Lambda Legal.

How a person defines their sexual orientation relies on three different elements: attraction, identity, and behavior. For instance, a guy might be attracted to other guys but identify as heterosexual and engage sexually only with women. Or a guy might be attracted to other guys but identify as heterosexual while engaging in some limited intimacies with guys but having penetrative sex only with women. Or a guy might be attracted to women but find himself drawn to one particular guy and, whether or not he engages with him sexually, might identify as bi. We could offer up many other versions of this guy's attractions, identity, and behavior. Clearly, the semantics are confusing and even sometimes subjective, but it's key to recognize that attraction is not always the same as identity, and behavior can align with one but doesn't always align with both.

Recent research suggests that, unlike older generations, most adolescents consider attraction—either sexual or romantic—and *not* sexual activity to be the defining principle of sexual orientation. But because stigma often drives teenagers to define themselves in categories where they don't actually belong, they won't necessarily disclose these attractions to researchers or anyone else. It's difficult to collect accurate data if these questions aren't asked in the clearest of ways, and even then it's understandable why answers might not be forthcoming.

Here's another research complication: just because sexual orientation unfolds during adolescence doesn't mean that it will remain stable and enduring for life. Of course not! Who doesn't know someone—either personally or a public figure—whose sexual orientation proved fluid over the course of their life? It seems, though, that today sexual identity is a less stable trait than ever before: teens and twenty-somethings express far more ambiguity than generations past, and they are more likely to redefine their labels over time. A 2019 study done in the southeastern United States found that up to 20 percent of teenagers report some change in self-labeled sexual orientation (with females far outnumbering males here), and even more report shifts in their sexual attraction. Fluidity has become an important aspect of sexual orientation.

If definitions are shifting and changing, with Gen Z in particular eschewing heteronormative and even binary labels, then there's an argument to stop labeling everyone altogether, especially because studies show that sexual minorities experience dramatic health disparities not as a result of their sexual orientation per se but because of societal marginalization. They are discriminated against on the basis of their sexual attractions and behaviors, and as a result, the risks among sexual minorities include all of the following:

- Higher rates of depression, self-harm, suicidal ideation, and suicide attempts.

- Higher prevalence of nicotine, alcohol, and other drug use (up to three times higher).

- Increased likelihood of having an eating disorder, especially bingeing and purging.

- A far greater likelihood of being targeted for physical abuse; sexual abuse and assault, including sexual dating violence by dating partners; and harassment or bullying at school.

One day, hopefully, labels and stigma will disappear. But for now, while they are very much present, identifying the people at greatest risk offers a chance at early intervention and protection.

WHAT'S CHANGED OVER THE PAST 20, 30, 40 YEARS

A few massive shifts have rocked the way people talk—and think—about sexual orientation. The first came in the early 1980s with the emergence of HIV/AIDS, a deadly infection largely affecting gay and bisexual men along with IV drug users and people receiving blood transfusions. Human immunodeficiency virus (HIV) spreads via bodily fluids and blood. The constellation of symptoms associated with acquired immunodeficiency syndrome (AIDS) first appeared in 1981, but the disease wasn't named until 1982, and HIV, the virus responsible for AIDS, didn't get its name until 1986, a sign of how little we understood about this killer virus for such a prolonged time. Once the path from HIV to AIDS was identified, the people most at risk were shunned. Gay men and IV drug users in particular faced vicious discrimination, driving them into the shadows but also galvanizing a new civil rights movement. While no cure for HIV has yet been found, HIV has become treatable: now people live with it rather than die from it. In part because of this progress (and in part because of the other social shifts described below), there is less fear of and for people with HIV/AIDS today, even as sexual minorities continue to face inequities.

The next social earthquake to shift the status of sexual orientation came in the form of marriage equality laws. Through the early 2000s, a handful of states began to legalize same-sex marriage. Following the legal shift, mental health among sexual minorities improved: a study published in 2015 showed a 7 percent reduction in suicide attempts among sexual minorities in these states. In the same year, in a case called *Obergefell v. Hodges,* the U.S. Supreme Court protected marriage between two people of the same gender as a federal legal right under the Equal Protection Clause of the 14th Amendment in the U.S. Constitution. Not only did this ruling level the playing field for *all* married couples, but it redefined the legal definition of marriage as a contract between two people, not a contract between two heterosexual people. The ruling does more than remove stigma—it normalized sexual orientations once considered fringe in the eyes of the law.

The impacts of these medical advances and legal rulings trickle down to schools and communities, where local advocacy organizations have also moved into the mainstream. The last few decades have seen many school communities dramatically increase their support of LGBTQIAA+ students: the CDC reports that nearly 80 percent of schools across 43 states host safe spaces for sexual minorities and over 95 percent have adopted policies prohibiting harassment of these students. Students in schools with support groups like gay-straight alliances report fewer threats of violence, fewer missed days of school on account of feeling unsafe, and fewer suicidal thoughts and attempts compared with students in schools without these support groups.

All of this reshapes the social and sexual experiences of teens and young adults. There are an estimated 2 million lesbian, gay, and bisexual teens between 13 and 17 years old living in the United States. When public figures live openly gay lives and see no impact on their success, the kids who look up to them have no reason to think of sexual orientation as a hurdle in the way of their own achievement. Nearly 25 years ago, a year after Ellen DeGeneres came out as a gay woman, her eponymous sitcom was canceled. These days, news anchors, television and film stars, music icons, and professional athletes are living openly gay lives in the public eye. Celebrity magazines now feature not just same-sex weddings but also families created using sperm donors, adoption, and surrogacy. High-profile people living openly gay lives provide nonheterosexual kids with many public paradigms that didn't exist before, giving power to the saying "If you can see it, you can be it."

HOW TO TALK ABOUT IT

While we have dedicated our careers to talking to tweens and teens of all stripes—including across the sexual orientation spectrum—our own lived experiences are as cisgender heterosexual females. Therefore, in a chapter focused on sexual minorities, it feels important to share advice from people who have walked in those shoes. That said, much of the content of this book is about the lived experience of a generation that's notably different from our own. If there's one through line we hope you'll have picked up on by now, it's that none of us have to share the exact same experiences in order to listen to, support, and love our kids. So here's how to do that, regardless of your own sexual orientation and the amount of overlap you experience with the kids in your life.

Be inclusive

One way to create an environment welcoming to people of all sexual orientations is to use inclusive language. With younger kids, start by emphasizing that people of all sexual orientations can create loving families even if kids are "made" differently: via sperm donors, adoption, surrogacy, or in vitro fertilization (IVF). As kids grow older, let go of any assumptions that they are romantically interested in people of the opposite sex—instead stick with neutral language. For example, if your daughter tells you there's someone she has a crush on, you can say, *That's great. What's their name? What kind of stuff are they interested in?* If you notice your teenager spending a lot of time video chatting with a mystery person, instead of saying, *Oooooh, do you have a girlfriend?* try asking, *I noticed you've been chatting a lot lately. Is it with someone special or just a friend?*

It should go without saying—but we'll say it—that it's critical to adopt a zero-tolerance policy for homophobic slurs. Stop the use of those words right away and explain to their utterers why they are offensive. Many kids will say *I was just joking,* and perhaps they were, but it's never funny or acceptable.

Another way to create an inclusive atmosphere is to talk about *all* kinds of sex, not just heterosexual, vaginal intercourse. We don't know what any given kid's sexual orientation will be (or if it will even be set at all), so the only way to teach them about safe and pleasurable sex is discussion that includes the full range of options. Kids should never be led to feel that there's something wrong, shameful, or secretive about whom they're attracted to or how they express that attraction.

Get over your own discomfort

We get that it's uncomfortable, but naming your discomfort with tweens and teens goes a long way to disarming them and takes the pressure off you to be some kind of ultimate authority. It also injects much-needed humor into tough conversations. *My armpits are sweaty and my heart is pounding, but I'm going to try my best here!*

If a kid asks questions about sex that you don't know how to answer, that's okay. You can always say: *I'm not sure, let me look up the answer,* or *That's a good question, let me ask some other adults and get back to you.* But then, get back to them! Nothing shuts the communication door faster than failing to follow through on a promise to circle back on a topic. As kids get older and have a better sense of their sexual orientation, if it's different from yours, help to foster relationships with mentors, adults who have been down the same path, or community resources and support groups. Knowledge and affirmation around sexual orientation can come from many different places.

Make room for fluidity

Some adults want to label their kids—they don't care if they're heterosexual or homosexual, but they want to be able to name it. The reality is that sexual orientation doesn't always work that way. Some people are bisexual; some are pansexual; some identify as queer/questioning, an even broader category; and some continue to have fluid sexual identities throughout life. This can create confusion for the adults who love them, but a gentle reminder here: The goal for kids is to grow into adults who have loving, respectful, meaningful, sexually pleasurable relationships. The label on any given relationship doesn't change anything about its outcome. Pushing a kid (or anyone of any age, for that matter) to choose or articulate a path when they're not sure yet just adds pressure. Instead, let them lead their own journey, while continuing to check in and making yourself available as a support: *I'm always here for you . . . Looks like it's been quite a week—wondering if there's anything you want to talk about?*

Advocate at school

Research shows that the emotional and physical health of LGBTQIAA+ students is significantly improved in school environments offering support in the form of student organizations; support from faculty, staff, and administrators; safe spaces; inclusive sex education curricula; and an environment that consistently prohibits bullying, harassment, or violence. Self-advocacy can sometimes be overwhelming for kids, particularly if they are feeling physically or emotionally unsafe. Adults can play a role in helping school communities implement and sustain these efforts to ensure the well-being of all students.

If you think your kid might be lesbian, gay, bi, pan . . .

We love this advice from the author of *This Is a Book for Parents of Gay Kids:* "If you think that your child might be gay, the best approach is to create a safe and accepting environment. If your child *is* gay, this will help them work up the courage to talk with you once they better understand their own identity."

Inclusive language, education, and attitudes are important regardless of a kid's sexual identity. Despite how badly you might want to know a particular kid's sexual orientation, experts recommend *not* asking outright. Even if the kid knows, they might not be ready to talk about it. Or perhaps they're not sure yet, and being pushed to answer questions might feel like too much pressure, closing a door you've worked hard to keep open. Besides, when was the last time a cisgender, heterosexual kid faced pressure to disclose that preference to their close friends and family? The imbalance is very real. So let any kid know you're ready to listen when they're ready to talk, and make resources available without pushing any agenda.

If they come out to you

Some parents are shocked when their kid comes out as gay or bisexual; others have been waiting for years for their kid to make it official; a slew of parents live everywhere in between. Regardless of where you fall on this spectrum, the response almost every kid is looking for comes down to a very simple sentiment: *I love you so much and I am proud to be your parent . . . Is there any way I can support you in this journey?*

By the same token, experts working with LGBTQIAA+ kids have some important advice about what *not* to do when a kid comes out:

> **Don't change your dynamic with them:** They still have
> the same sense of humor, interests, taste in food, and all

the rest. Altering the relationship might make them feel rejected, even if that's not the intention.

Don't make it about you: Whether you're mourning your vision of what their lives would be like or celebrating a statement that's been a long time coming, download your reaction with another adult, not your kid. The story of their sexual orientation is *theirs* to write, not yours—give them agency from the first moment they share with you.

Don't ask them if they're going to change their mind: That implies that you don't accept the choice they are making. Even if you're feeling concerned about what it means to have a gay kid, reserve expressing that concern for another adult, not the child who has taken the brave step of coming out.

Don't isolate yourself: Join PFLAG or any organization that supports the families and allies of LGBTQIAA+ kids, or find another support group or community with whom you can comfortably share your thoughts and experiences.

 ## FROM PEOPLE JUST OUT THE OTHER SIDE

T.E., he/him, age 21

Coming out was not just one singular event or moment of clarity. Many think it is just something that you do or say. One action that defines who you are for the rest of your life, as some dramatically like to say. However, it really is not that simple. One of the hardest parts for me was coming to the realization that I was questioning my sexuality. I always sort of knew since my childhood that I thought about love differently, but I always thought I would just end up doing what was the "typical" way of life, love, and marriage.

From the movies, books, and television shows I was exposed to, I had only one model to base the standards of a romantic relationship and marriage. This media would tell me how I was supposed to feel about someone and the life I was supposed to live. Not a lot I was exposed to would show me the many different ways someone could live their life to be happy.

In terms of those around me, the people who knew me the best (or who thought they did) became the most difficult to be around. They had this fixed view of me after knowing me since I was little. The idea of revealing myself as a different person to someone who thinks they know all about me was a scary thought. How were they going to react? Would they be mad? Confused?

Thankfully, another force allowed me to realize the power I had to reevaluate my identity. This external force was when I had to change schools and move to another state in eighth grade. This gave me the opportunity to start fresh in a new community, where nobody had preconceived notions of me. I realized I could re-create myself in a more authentic way and would not have to worry about how people would react. From this experience, I was able to overcome the hardest hurdle, accepting my sexuality *myself*.

Slowly, I started to come out to the new friends I made. Conveniently, many of them had been in the same place, questioning and exploring the idea of their own sexuality. I had people who could support me and give me advice from their own experiences and thoughts. After about a year, I was ready to tell my parents.

I remember sitting on the end of my mom's bed. I wasn't scared that she would react negatively. I knew she was tolerant of whoever people wanted to be or whoever they wanted to love. I just couldn't get over this feeling of embarrassment. However, I quickly got over it, told her I liked guys, and we hugged. Obviously, it was a big moment for me, but I am a firm believer that coming out shouldn't be this huge moment of revelation, especially not for others when it is truly an experience for the self. I hope that teenagers and people in general will get to the point where coming out doesn't start with *Mom, I need to tell you something*. Instead, *coming out* could just be the words *He is cute* when a guy is watching TV with his mom and that is all that needs to happen.

When I think about my own experience of discovering my sexuality, I am so beyond lucky to be in the circumstances I am in. I have a supportive family. I went to an extremely diverse and supportive school that provided me with a safe environment where I could discover myself. I had it incredibly easy, which I can promise is not the same for many. I was lucky that my parents were loving and my friends were there to understand what I was going through.

I have seen much worse situations with some of my friends. One of them told her parents she liked a girl and they told her she couldn't see her anymore. They said to her when we were around 15, "How could you possibly like girls? There's no way you can find out you like girls when T. knew he was gay his entire life." There could be nothing more wrong with that statement. At that time, I was just lucky I could come out earlier and reach a point where it seemed like my whole life I knew who I was and who I loved. In extreme cases, people who come out have been known to get kicked out of their houses and forced to support themselves. Not far from my high school, there was a homeless shelter for LGBTQ+ teens who got kicked out of the home by their parents.

I think it is incredibly important that people, regardless of their sexuality, should get opportunities throughout their childhood to rethink their identity. This could include moving or simply going to camp during the summer or finding some way to be in a new community that doesn't know who you already are. I have found that many people who struggle to come out are those that have gone to a pre-K–12 school and are not given the opportunity to reset and have that "clean slate" of their identity.

Thankfully, for me, I had the support of both my parents and my friends, but it is really important that someone has the foundation of supportive friends if they don't feel like they can rely on their parents. I also had the support of advisers and teachers. I really looked up to my freshman adviser, who is married to a woman, and she was someone who made me realize the realistic and relatable model of love at the start of high school. When I lived with a family in Spain, I became friends with our program leaders, and one of them was a gay guy. He taught me a lot about being comfortable and safe as a gay man, and of course, my friend group was a resource I wouldn't have made it through school without. We would give each other advice on pretty much anything and share books, shows, and movies we thought would help us better understand ourselves.

CHAPTER 19

Gender Identity

Throughout history and across the globe, there has never been one singu-lar concept of gender. Historical and anthropological documents tell us so, as do current-day cultures around the world in which people continue to approach gender in their own ways. Sometimes it feels like there's been a radical shift in the language used by modern Western society, but these constructs have actually been around for millennia. To reassure the uninitiated, gender identity is complex. But it's important to dig in to the language and ideas because gender has become a big part of the conversation around adolescent wellness.

There's no doubt that, like a new car that starts depreciating the minute it's driven off the dealer's lot, at least some of the terminology and guidance we offer here will be antiquated by the time this book is published. But that's okay, because for many of you reading, the confusion around gender identity stems from decades of never talking (or thinking or even knowing) about it. Open conversation on this topic was essentially nonexistent in American society a generation ago—most people weren't even aware it was a thing. Fast-forward to today, when some kids comfortably switch up pronouns, adopt new names to better fit their gender identities, and/or fully transition, much of this barely ranking on their larger social scale. For adults, this gender landscape has changed more than almost anything else covered in these pages, and so it is on all of us to become fluent in the language and educate ourselves about what gender does and doesn't mean.

LET'S START WITH SCIENCE

When a baby is born, their sex is assigned on the basis of the appearance of their external genitalia: a baby with a penis above a testicle-filled scrotum (or sometimes not, if the testicles haven't descended yet) is male, while one with labia majora and labia minora surrounding a vaginal opening is deemed female. Most of the time the organs look almost exactly like the textbook images, making sex assignment fairly straightforward.

Back in the 1990s, when Cara was training in pediatrics, she spent hundreds of hours in delivery rooms, checking newborns seconds after they emerged from the womb. Sometimes it was the obstetrician in the room who would declare gender, but mostly the task fell to the pediatrician who had just taken the baby in a quick handoff. Prenatal ultrasound and amniocentesis were old hat already, so lots of parents knew in advance whether they were having a boy or a girl. Still, genital examination appeared high on the health checklist—just behind breathing, a strong heartbeat, and 10 fingers and 10 toes. After a quick exam, Cara would declare, *He looks great!* or *She's so alert.* It wasn't exactly *It's a boy!* or *It's a girl!* but in hindsight, using the pronoun *he* or *she* in the first moments after birth carried some significant weight. The burden didn't really register back then except in about 1 in every 2,000 births, when a baby emerged with certain features of their genitalia much bigger or smaller than expected, or ambiguous genitalia that appeared neither distinctly male nor obviously female.

The first fundamental tenet necessary to understand the bigger gender conversation is this: a person's assigned sex at birth is distinct from their gender identity. What follows is a list of terms which are pulled from a combination of sources including the book *The Transgender Child* and various Human Rights Commission websites. Gender identity is a person's psychological sense of self: who they know themselves to be on the basis of their alignment (or lack thereof) with physical characteristics of different genders. Said another way, a person's gender identity is their deep internal sense of being female, male, a combination of both, somewhere in between, or neither, resulting from a multifaceted interaction of biological traits, environmental factors, self-understanding, and cultural expectations. The old way of thinking offered two genders— binary options—male and female. But today most people embrace the idea of a nonbinary gender spectrum with a wide range of identifications and expressions, including people who do not feel like they have any gender at all. Sitting along this spectrum are the following:

> **Nonbinary:** people who do not subscribe to the gender binary—some exist between or beyond the man-woman binary; others use the term interchangeably with terms like *genderqueer, genderfluid, gender nonconforming, gender diverse,* or *gender expansive.*

> **Cisgender:** a person who identifies with and expresses the culturally defined norms of the gender assigned to them at birth.

> **Transgender:** a person whose gender identity does not match their sex assigned at birth, a feeling that remains persistent, consistent, and insistent over time.

> **Gender expansive:** a person whose interests, self-expression, and behaviors don't fit within the typical societal expectations of that gender; an umbrella term for people who do not follow gender stereotypes.

Gender diverse: a broad categorical term including transgender, nonbinary, and gender-expansive people.

Gender dysphoria: not a descriptor of a person but rather a clinical term describing the distress caused when a gender-diverse person's assigned gender and their gender identity are out of sync—it can be described as a feeling of incongruence, that something is off in relation to their gender; it can also be used by psychiatrists and psychologists as a diagnosis.

As we define these terms, an important note: a person's gender identity is not the same thing as their sexual orientation. This can be confusing to many, because society often conflates the two. The best way to keep the thread separate in your mind is to remember this simple explanation: Gender has nothing to do with who a person is attracted to, while sexual orientation has everything to do with it. If you want more detail about sexual orientation, flip back to chapter 18.

Unlike sexual attraction, which begins to crystallize during puberty when the sex hormones start to surge, gender questioning can begin at any age. There are three life stages when questioning peaks: early childhood, the onset of puberty, and later in adolescence. Of course, stories abound about older adults who discover their true gender-selves (perhaps the most famous recent example being that of Caitlin Jenner), but younger is far more typical. Just like so many other topics in this book, the age at which kids express their identities shapes how the adults in their lives can best support them. It also dictates many aspects of gender-affirming care—the broad term for how clinicians, therapists, and caretakers can support kids in gender-inclusive ways, everything from psychotherapy to hormone therapy, from medical to surgical to social services.

No one knows the exact number of transgender youth in the United States. In 2017, a CDC study of 10 states and 9 large urban school districts found that, on average, 1.8 percent of teens identify as transgender. A smaller 2022 study out of UCLA puts the number slightly lower, at 1.4 percent. What is clear is that teenagers represent a large share of the transgender population: about one in every five people identifying as trans are between the ages of 13 and 17. From these numbers, we can extrapolate there are around 300,000 transgender teens in the United States, and more when the broader category of gender-expansive kids is added into the mix.

Ultimately, the goal for any kid of any gender is to find the fullest, most joyful expression of themselves. The data that follows largely focuses on negatives: the physical and psychological risks faced by gender-expansive teens. Do not confuse this with catastrophizing. There are studies that clearly show the benefits of inclusive communities and gender-affirming care—we need even more data here. But if our job is to keep kids safe and healthy, it is critical that we also name the risks confronting kids in this category.

CDC data shows significantly higher rates of depression, anxiety, substance abuse, eating disorders, victimization, self-harm, and suicide among transgender kids compared with their cisgender peers. According to a 2019 study published by the Trevor Project, over the prior year one in three transgender youth attempted suicide, almost one-third reported being a victim of sexual violence, and more than half reported a period of depression lasting two weeks or more. There's a fair amount of debate in the research literature questioning the association between gender diversity and mental health challenges, especially depression and suicidality: some people conclude cause and effect (gender dysphoria causes depression, for instance), while others contend that they coexist and are correlated, but there's not yet enough proof to state that gender incongruity is actually *causing* these downstream mental health issues any more than adolescence itself. No doubt, lots more data (and debate) will emerge here.

Mainstream conversations about gender have shifted radically over the past few decades, concepts covered in the "What's Changed" section that follows. So, too, have treatments. But before we dive into the debates around therapies, it's important to understand the basic science behind each one.

Gender-diverse kids, tweens, and teens who seek out ways to align their gender expression with their gender identity proceed along two separate therapeutic paths, one social and the other medical. Social transition aims to solve for social congruence: name changes and new pronouns fall into this category, as do external shifts in appearance like changing hairstyles and clothing. This path often involves psychotherapy along with support from the family, school, and community. The medical approach seeks phenotypic congruence, which means shifting observable physical characteristics using prescribed drugs like puberty blockers and hormones and sometimes gender-affirming surgery to address the feelings of living in the wrong-gendered body. These two pathways of care exist in parallel, with some kids traveling down one, the other, or both paths in tandem; some kids start on their journey and then stop quickly, while others proceed as far as they can go. What follows are the details about all of these approaches.

Social interventions

Pronouns and name changes

Simply using a person's chosen name and pronouns goes a long way toward supporting them. Studies show that when kids are called by the names and pronouns they align with, they are less likely to experience symptoms of depression, report thoughts of suicide, or attempt suicide.

Mental health services

One gigantic cornerstone of supporting trans and gender-questioning youth is mental health care—not just for gender-diverse kids but for their families and caregivers as well. Therapists play massive roles in the lives of gender-questioning and trans kids, from mediating conversations, to offering anticipatory guidance, to identifying urgent mental health issues. Many consider it the standard of care for gender-dysphoric youth to receive mental health support and comprehensive assessment before proceeding on to medical treatment.

Unfortunately, the process of finding trained mental health providers and entering the recommended period of therapeutic care can take months, sometimes years if there are other coexistent issues, and too few mental health experts are trained in this work. Sometimes it is literally impossible for families to find a provider with the necessary skill set and room in their practice, let alone an affordable one. Add to that the required time investment concurrent with a kid's progression through puberty, which is taking them further from the gender by which they identify. The goals are at odds when a gender-expansive child is required to spend months and months in therapy before any medical next step, all the while developing the externalized secondary sexual characteristics of the gender with which they do not identify. That said, no one denies the benefit of having mental health support in place, especially because the biggest risks to gender-nonconforming kids are mental health emergencies manifesting as self-harm.

Environmental support

A child's environment—their family, friends, school, and local community—can affect their experience of gender questioning and expression in profound ways. Transgender students report higher rates of bullying, both in person and online, and violent victimization. According to a 2017 CDC study on transgender identity and victimization, nearly a quarter of transgender students reported being forced to have sexual intercourse, and more than a quarter have experienced dating violence. On the flip side, gender-diverse kids supported by their family have lower rates of depression, suicidality, and self-harm. Gender-affirming school environments and communities are proven to further bolster emotional well-being.

Medical interventions

Puberty blockers

Puberty blockers are medications used to stop the progression of puberty, sometimes to offer a pause for a gender-questioning kid who isn't sure what physical direction they want to go in, other times to halt advancement through their genetically encoded—some people call it natal—puberty. These medications work by sitting in the GnRH receptors situated in the pituitary gland deep inside the brain. At first, they stimulate LH and FSH release from the gland by occupying the receptor. But when the receptors are occupied over a long enough time, they become desensitized and stop stimulating pituitary production of LH and FSH, which ultimately leads to declines in the production of sex steroids (estrogen and progesterone from the ovaries, testosterone from the testicles). Over several weeks or months, the progression of sexual development ceases. So a genetic female experiencing gender dysphoria concurrent with growing breasts can take a GnRH agonist to stop the progression of breast growth—the breasts usually hold steady at their current size, though there are reported cases of regression (shrinkage or even dissapearance) when puberty blockers are started early enough. GnRH acts as the primary on/off switch here, which also means that discontinuation of GnRH agonist medication allows for reactivation of the feedback loop and resumption of pubertal development.

Progestins can also be used as puberty blockers, though they don't work as well as GnRH agonists. Antiandrogenic progestins for male-to-female patients or proandrogenic progestins for female-to-male patients largely affect secondary sex characteristics like hair growth and fat distribution. They also halt ovulation and menstruation. Progestins tend to cost far less than GnRH agonists, driving their popularity. But they don't work as effectively because they don't act on the central feedback loop of puberty (GnRH → LH/FSH → estrogen/progesterone or testosterone).

The onset of puberty for gender-questioning or transgender kids can be deeply traumatic, moving them even further away from their gender identities. That said, making the choice with a healthcare team to begin puberty blockers, rather than going through this alone or with the help of one sole provider, increases the likelihood that the physical and emotional needs of the child will be met.

Puberty blockers can be life altering and lifesaving when a child engages in self-harming behaviors like cutting; develops school phobia, depression, or anxiety; or expresses suicidal thoughts. They can also be important for kids with no underlying mental health issues who are begging the adults in their lives to halt their progression through puberty. But these medications are not recommended *before* puberty begins, even if a particular child has been crystal clear about their transgender status since the toddler years. Medical experts working in the field uniformly agree that puberty blockers can stop puberty once it has started but should not be used in advance of its onset. Moreover, they're a temporary solution, buying a year or two for a family to consider future options for gender-affirming care—some kids take them for longer, but prolonged use is generally not recommended.

One more important note about blocking puberty: GnRH agonists play a central role in adolescent growth spurts. It's actually the downstream hormones (namely, estrogen and testosterone) that have the most direct impact here, but when their production is blocked by GnRH agonists, kids taking GnRH blockers don't head into their pubertal growth spurt. During treatment, this may leave them shorter than their peers precisely at a time in their life when many of them already feel socially marginalized. But as soon as they stop taking puberty blockers, growth should resume. Theoretically, ultimate adult height shouldn't be affected, and if anything they might wind up taller than anticipated. This has been borne out in studies of kids with precocious puberty (abnormally early onset) who take GnRH agonists to slow their progression through puberty—these kids continue to grow slowly but steadily while on the drugs, and then most have a pubertal growth spurt once they are pulled off.

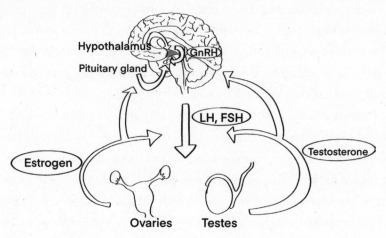

Hormone therapy

One significant step in achieving gender congruence—aligning a person's expressed gender with their gender identity—is to ingest or inject the hormones a body cannot produce on its own. Hormone therapy rebalances a person's naturally occurring hormone ratio by supplementing with hormones that match their gender identity. A trans female with testicles but no ovaries lacks the capacity to produce enough estrogen to grow breasts, and likewise a trans male with ovaries but no testicles cannot naturally manufacture enough testosterone to drop his voice or shift his lean muscle mass composition. Hormone therapy can create these desired changes.

Some studies suggest that when hormone therapy is started in a timely fashion, the risks for more serious mental health problems later in life drop dramatically. One small 2021 study of trans youth between the ages of 13 and 20 looked at gender-affirming care, including puberty blockers and hormones, and found a 60 percent reduction in moderate or severe depression and 73 percent reduction in suicidality.

Gender-affirming surgery

Gender-affirming surgical procedures can help people anatomically transition to their self-identified gender. Some people refer to these as "sex reassignment surgeries." While most medical organizations recommend waiting on surgeries until at least age 18, the age of consent, several advocacy groups have pushed to accelerate this by as much as three years, consistent with the laws and recommendations of many countries across the globe.

Breast removal and chest reconstruction or breast augmentation, aka "top surgery": Transmasculine individuals may opt for mastectomy, the surgical removal of breast tissue. Sometimes a small amount of the tissue is left behind as part of the reconstruction in an effort to create a more masculine-appearing chest. Transfeminine individuals may opt to have breast augmentation surgery using silicone or saline implants, supplementing breast size beyond the growth achieved with hormone therapy.

Genital reconstruction, aka "bottom surgery": Transmasculine people may opt for phalloplasty, which involves reconstruction to create a penis and scrotum in place of the vaginal cavity. The urethra (the tube carrying urine) is extended through the new penis, often along with an inflatable prosthetic penis and testicle implants made from silicon or saline. Prior to phalloplasty, a different surgery called a hysterectomy-salpingo-oophorectory removes the internal female organs (uterus, fallopian tubes, and ovaries respectively). Transfeminine people may opt for orchiectomy (removal of testicles) and vaginoplasty (reconstruction of the genitals to create a vaginal pouch).

 ## WHAT'S CHANGED OVER THE PAST 20, 30, 40 YEARS

Almost all of the topics covered in this chapter have changed over the past 20, 30, 40 years and continue to change. The science around gender has shifted, as have appreciations for the social, emotional, and cultural obstacles faced by gender-diverse people. Perhaps the biggest shift, though, is the aging down of the issue: more kids than ever before are talking about gender-related issues, questioning their own gender, or openly declaring their gender differences.

A generation ago—even five years ago—no one listed their pronouns as a matter of due course. Today, it's the norm. Many opt for *she/her, he/ him,* or *they/them,* but some use a combination of terms (*she/they* or *he/ they*).

Another change, though this one more gradual, has been the acceptance of ungendering or gender-mashing in personal expression. Clothing, hairstyle choices, makeup, jewelry, and more have all become far more gender expansive. Kids who used to stand out—a little boy in a dress or a tomboy-ish girl—generate fewer waves these days thanks to massive celebrities like Harry Styles bringing once-gender-bending style statements into the mainstream.

Partly as a result of these changes and partly in response to them, social opinions about transgender youth have shifted dramatically over the past 15 years. Some gender-diverse kids still find themselves on the receiving end of bullying, fear, or both, but affirmation and acceptance are far more common now. Layers of support have cropped up in communities, within schools, and across social networks, especially social media apps reflecting a newfound sensitivity to many of the coexisting struggles faced by non-cisgender kids—from body image issues to full-blown eating disorder, to depression and anxiety, to being on the receiving end of traumatic bullying and victimization. All of this rolls into a greater overall acceptance of gender-affirming care and a deep commitment by so many to help gender-questioning kids find happiness no matter how they identify.

This is not to say that everyone across the United States rallies behind kids and their families in conversations about gender, not by a long stretch. But even a decade ago, general social receptivity to the topic felt quite different. Today, as more kids self-identify as transgender or gender questioning, there's an ever-shrinking option to deliberately ignore it. One study from 2021 showed that fewer than 3 in 10 people support state laws that prohibit gender-affirming care. Feelings here divide up into rather even thirds: slightly more than one-third think society has gone too far in accepting transgender people; slightly more than one-third think society hasn't gone far enough; and the rest think we're hitting it about right.

That said, even though the culture, in general, has moved toward embracing (or not wholesale rejecting) gender-expansive people, it still harbors elements of furious cultural, political, and legal backlash. The year 2022 alone witnessed swirling controversies around the teaching of gender identity in sex education classes in certain states, efforts by legislators to ban gender-affirming medical interventions, and escalation of a debate around allowing transgender athletes to compete under their expressed gender identity. Advocacy groups are working hard to help guide these conversations, as evidenced by the American Academy of Pediatrics' 2018 policy statement on the importance of gender-affirming care; in 2022, the AAP doubled down in the face of legislative efforts attempting to block the multidisciplinary approach to supporting transgender and gender-diverse kids across a number of states.

If the front-and-center conversations about gender feel very new, especially with respect to kids, there's good reason. The very first pediatric gender clinic in the United States opened at Boston Children's Hospital in 2007, a mere 15 years ago. That's not much time to digest language and notions, let alone medical conventions, which explains sometimes-fierce debates over gender-affirming care strategies like hormone therapy. Some say it shouldn't start until a child is at least 16, while others disagree with a chronological time line and think it should depend upon a particular child's path through their gender identity. As of the writing of this book in 2023, the average age to begin taking hormones is somewhere between 14 and 16 years old, with many (but not all) starting puberty blockers first. By the time these words are printed on a page, the numbers—and opinions—will have undoubtedly shifted again.

Much of the criticism of treatment centers on detransitioners, people who went through the transitioning process to some degree only to reverse course. It's one thing for a child to opt for new pronouns for a few years and then rethink the idea, and another thing entirely to have surgery and do the same. Detransitioning hasn't been very well studied (how could it be, since transitioning at increasingly young ages is so new), but one recent small study of 100 detransitioners found these reasons for going back on the choice:

- Thirty-eight percent believed their gender dysphoria had been caused by a trauma or underlying mental health condition.

- Fifty-five percent felt they didn't receive an adequate evaluation from a doctor or mental health professional before starting transition.

- Twenty-three percent cited experiencing discrimination after transitioning or having difficulty accepting themselves as lesbian, gay, or bisexual.

- Forty-nine percent were concerned about potential medical complications from transitioning.

- Sixty percent simply became more comfortable identifying as their natal sex.

HOW TO TALK ABOUT IT

Addressing any complex topic, especially one that feels out of our depth, is a lot like flying into the Bermuda Triangle: there's a terrifying possibility that we might navigate so poorly, we'll never emerge. Lots of adults acknowledge deep discomfort in talking about gender, worry about every misstep, and are confused by the changing language. *What if I give them the wrong information? What if I accidentally say something hurtful? What if I reveal my own ignorance or bias?* There's no perfect way through any of these conversations (which should sound familiar because that statement has been made in a number of chapters in this book), but it's always best to lead with curiosity, empathy, and humanity. Then don't forget to admit when you've blown it, circle back, and take the do-over, because messing up the navigation of this unfamiliar territory is a given.

Kids can be the teachers

Ask the kids in your life about pronouns and different types of gender identities—you'll learn while opening up the lines of communication. Most young people have a comfort and fluency with the diverse universe of gender, and, frankly, the things that adults see as a big deal just aren't to them. It can be hard to know where to begin without sounding inauthentic or like a complete numbskull, so here are a few suggestions: *I noticed that one of your classmates is going by a different name now—can you tell me more about that?* Or *Your friend's mom told me that they now consider themselves nonbinary—I want to be respectful of their pronouns. Can you tell me which ones to use?*

Let kids lead their own journey

For kids who are gender diverse, transgender, nonbinary, or gender expansive, living in the gray areas is part of their process. Many adults are eager to label a kid's gender or anticipate how they may choose to manifest it. But the kids cannot necessarily answer these questions. While some never waver about their identity from an early age, others don't have clarity until late adolescence, when they're more able to parse the subtleties of gender and sexual orientation. And there are some who never feel the need to label exactly what or who they are at all, comfortable in a genderfluid identity without landing on one particular descriptor or pronoun. Some will continue to express their gender authentically without medical interventions; others may not feel they are their true selves without hormonal treatments and surgeries that allow corporeal gender expression. These are *their* identities, *their* bodies, *their* lives—our desire for clarity or naming cannot drive the process, even when decisions (like medical interventions) require adult participation.

You might try one of the following gentle ways to solicit their thoughts and feelings without inserting yours: *I noticed you've changed your style a bit recently—I'm curious how that feels for you.* Or *I heard someone refer to you with your old name at pickup the other day and was wondering what your reaction was.* Or *We're going to visit Grandma next week, and I wanted to find out if there were any conversations you want me to have with her ahead of time.*

Respect pronouns and chosen names

Research tells us that gender-diverse people benefit tremendously when others use their chosen pronouns and gender-aligned names. The opposite is also true: when pronouns and names are not respected, people often feel negated or rejected, especially when this comes from someone in their close inner circle. We all mess up, and this topic offers no exception—parents, teachers, counselors, relatives, and even friends will accidentally get names and pronouns wrong some of the time. If that happens, just own the mistake and take the do-over: *I'm really sorry I messed up your pronouns. I will work really hard not to do that again.* Or *I apologize for calling you by your old name. Please let me know if I accidentally do it again.*

Find gender-diverse role models

Gender-diverse kids really need role models to look up to, particularly if they live in communities where gender diversity is not welcomed, visible, or celebrated. To some extent, it's our job to find trusted adults for them, helping to identify the people with whom they can talk about small and big issues. Every single kid on earth benefits from a mentor separate from the parent or caregiver raising them. When it comes to finding those go-to adults, identify someone who can help gender-diverse kids with general and specific questions such as the following: *How do you handle it when people get your pronouns wrong? I want to start binding my breasts but I'm not sure how. How can I be intimate with another person when I feel so uncomfortable with my body?*

Be an advocate and ally

The job of every parent, caregiver, and trusted adult is one and the same: keep kids safe and healthy. Regardless of their gender identity, or any other trait they possess, this is our number one task. When it comes to gender-questioning kids, particularly ones needing help with social or medical congruity, here's how to advocate for them:

- Make sure their healthcare providers are knowledgeable about gender-expansive kids and experienced in treating them through adolescence.

- Stand up to discrimination or cruelty whether it comes from adults (including relatives) or other kids.

- Be their safe person when they feel worried, confused, or lonely, providing a supportive environment to safeguard their emotional well-being.

Be realistic

Not everyone will be supportive of a gender-diverse kid. Even within the family, some relatives may not be on board, and their reactions can be unkind, hurtful, or downright cruel. And sometimes, as much as this stings, their reaction is intentional. We can't change the beliefs of all people, but we can help protect kids from harm and maybe even educate a few people along the way.

- Get permission from the kid involved, and then prepare the other people planning to join a family gathering about the kid's new gender identity. Rarely do people behave their best when they are caught off guard; preparation gives them a chance to be supportive.

- If a kid is so inclined, they may opt to lead a conversation, answering questions about their gender, but be prepared to intercede if you see any troubling behavior or unkindness.

- Be patient with generational, cultural, and religious obstacles, which can make it hard for some people to understand gender identity.

- If you need to step in, start by reminding everyone the ultimate goal: for all kids to feel loved and supported by the people around them.

Talk about sex, all kinds of sex

Remember that gender has nothing to do with attraction; sexual orientation has everything to do with it. Yes, it can feel particularly mystifying to address sex with a kid who hasn't cemented their gender. But as we discuss in chapter 16, *all* kids should learn about *all* kinds of sex. Knowledge breeds confidence and agency, even if things are in flux. And all people have the right to meaningful intimate relationships, regardless of their gender identity.

Don't forget about the siblings of gender-diverse kids

When one child in a family takes up a lot of time and energy—for any reason—the other kids in the house can struggle. Some siblings feel obligated to be the "good" one so as not to make home life more complicated; others feel invisible or embarrassed or resentful. Carving out time for other kids provides them with opportunities to have your undivided attention. This gives space for them to air their own issues or private opportunities to express personal concerns. Sometimes they just need to vent. Don't we all?

 FROM PEOPLE JUST OUT THE OTHER SIDE

K.B., he/him, age 17

As a young teen, I had never really felt comfortable with myself. At around the age of 12 and 13, I started wearing boy or gender-neutral clothes. It was also the period when I experienced a sharp decline in my mental health, severe enough that I started to harm myself. I was so out of touch with my mental health and my own psyche that I didn't even know how disconnected I was. My perception of what was happening was just regular old teenage puberty and angst.

A few years pass and I was able to adapt and live with the irregularity.

Now in high school, a period when you're supposed to figure yourself out, I was still the same person I had been before, just a little older. High school was a new experience for me in the sense that I had never been to public school before. There were so many more people than in my old school, and it was much more diverse as well. Before then, my education came from a small charter school that I had been going to for seven years—very isolated and enclosed, and not very many opportunities to expand on general life knowledge. At my new high school, I had the opportunity to experience new people and identities.

But that experience was cut off early by the pandemic. After I'd been alone with my thoughts for months on end, my mental health again went on a downward spiral. At home, I lazed away on my bed doing nothing and talking to no one. With nothing to distract me or occupy my thoughts, I started to reflect internally. Thanks to my experience with queer people in my school, I had a better concept of gender and personal identity. One of my friends who I communicated with online helped me figure out who I really was.

When I first realized that I might actually be a boy, I cried my eyes out. Turns out my whole life up until that point had been wrong. I had been wrong. But now that I knew what was correct, everything that I had gone through made sense. The epiphany of my gender was freeing, and I was able to make the mental changes to align myself with my true identity. I was a boy. Now that the root of my problems had been discovered, I was finally able to move forward and get the help I needed to guide me. Even now, just thinking about my past self, past name, and past gender makes my face scrunch up in distaste. Looking back, I can't believe I ever thought I was a girl. It's as they say: hindsight is 20/20.

CHAPTER 20

Friendships and Peer Influence

It's as complicated as it is developmentally normal for kids' friendships to change during the middle and high school years. Chances are, the best friend since kindergarten won't survive BFF status through adolescence. And it's no wonder given the lead characters here: kids living through simultaneous but not necessarily parallel physical metamorphoses; grappling with massive hormonal swings, partially mature brains, and academic pressures; all while juggling family dynamics playing out in the background. Adults themselves find it hard enough to navigate friendship; for tweens and teens, the net result can amount to full-on social upheaval.

Perspective is everything, though. As kids evolve through puberty, they might try on new identities, start new schools, and discover new interests. These changes drive them to connect more with some people, less with others. So what an adult might see as unstable friend dynamics, a kid might experience as building new bonds. The point of this chapter, above all else, is to reframe the way we understand their friendships and peer influences so that we can be effective at keeping kids safe and healthy. That is, after all, the job. Not to pick their friends, not to hover

over them at a party, not to dictate whom they have a crush on or what they do with those feelings. It's to keep them safe and healthy, which means helping them recognize the importance of friendship and the power of the influence of these friends.

 ## LET'S START WITH SCIENCE

A little brain science before moving to social science: nearly half of the chapters in this book make reference to the incomplete maturation of the tween and teen brain. In case you glossed over them, here's the main point once again: the impulsive, feel-good, pleasure-seeking, risk-taking limbic system in the middle of the brain is fully mature by middle school, which means it sends and receives signals extremely fast; the rational, consequential prefrontal cortex won't be mature for another decade or two, so it gets its input slowly and often cannot react in time to keep up with the middle of the brain. One of the simplest explanations for why tweens and teens tend to be impulsive or take risks boils down to the fact that their limbic systems are in charge. (For more details about brain development, see chapter 11.)

What hasn't been mentioned much until now is the power of the peer group on the midmost brain. It turns out that friends amplify the take-a-chance, make-it-feel-great centers. This is true when friends are in the same room together, hanging out after school, or partying, and it's also true when they are together virtually. In fact, it's not entirely a phenomenon limited to kids: Have you ever found yourself in the midst of an intoxicating conversation—in real life or even via text volley—that clouds your better judgment? Yeah, we have too. Just last week. But our brains can snap out of this rhythm more quickly than our kids' . . . most of the time.

The power of the peer group has been well documented. Friendships improve the quality of adolescent life by positively affecting everything from kids' academic performance to their general sense of well-being. At the same time, bonds with friends reduce the risk for depression. These benefits are thought to last a lifetime, translating into higher psychosocial functioning in adulthood and even adding years to a person's life, two separate phenomena that are certainly also intertwined.

How do friends actually affect the wiring and firing of the neurons in the brain? This question has driven tons of research over the past couple of decades, with scientists looking at different parts of the brain during varying scenarios, measuring friend impact with everything from questionnaires to MRI scanners. One common study design has a group of people engage in a behavior—among teens, the setup often involves playing a video game—with and without friends around. Sometimes those friends are physically present, sometimes they join virtually, and sometimes the researcher simply suggests that friends are watching from nearby when they're really not. In all three scenarios, the actual or assumed presence of friends results in more metabolic activity in the adolescent limbic system, a sign that this part of the brain is consuming fuel (in the form of glucose) to feed firing neurons as the kid decides what to do. In the most classic experiment design, the kid is playing a driving-style video game, and when friends are added into the mix, average speeds increase, as do accident rates and overall risk-taking required to score points to win the game. One pretty interesting sidenote here: Faster speeds resulting in higher crash rates actually slow the virtual car, often resulting in a lower game score. But the limbic system makes choices to do what feels good in the moment—more like the instant—without weighing longer-term consequences like what might happen two or three minutes down the road at the finish line.

The concept of group-think stokes a fair amount of worry among parents and caretakers. After all, they remember well the revelry of a party with kids drinking, smoking, and hooking up (back then called making out) freely. Until the smartphone arrived, this Saturday night setup—complete with a gang chanting *Chug! Chug! Chug!* or some equivalent—held strong as the primary focus of parental worry. But now social media has become an alternate peer-pressure frontier. Maybe kids communicating via screens aren't getting together (then called getting it on), but they might be sending nudes. Or in place of downing beers, they might find themselves following some inanely stupid or even life-threatening dare served up by an algorithm: the sunburn art challenge, the milk crate challenge, the *Bird Box* challenge, the Tide Pod challenge, the outlet challenge—we don't even need to describe these beyond the titles for you to figure out why they're idiotic. And yet many kids jump at doing them.

This type of behavior is often blamed on *peer pressure,* a decidedly negative term that took center stage during Gen X's coming of age. But peer pressure can clearly swing positive as well: study groups resulting in higher grades for all; team workouts and fitness challenges that translate into better baseline health and sports championships; student leaders steering other kids toward service projects. The examples of positive forces are endless, flipping the term *peer pressure* into the sunnier term *peer influence.* The biology works the same way, with bad ideas egged on by friends lighting up the limbic system just as much as good ideas and collaborative projects. Every adult involved in raising a child knows this: if you want to get a kid to do something, the easiest way is to find another kid who is doing that thing (reading, washing the dishes, going to bed at a reasonable time, you name it) to model it. In these instances of positive peer influence, it almost doesn't matter that the prefrontal cortex lags so far behind, because both the short- and long-term implications are good.

We know that friends light up the adolescent limbic system. You know who doesn't light it up? Adults. This translates into the irritating age-old duality of kids caring deeply about the novel things everyone else their age is doing far more than following our dull rules, pitting the primacy of social interactions against responsibilities at home, academics, athletics, community engagement, and hanging out with Grandma. Predictable power struggles ensue over anything and everything—screen time, curfews, school assignments, writing thank-you notes, replying to texts. When their social world wins out, the consequences can be dramatic. Take the example of experimentation with nicotine, alcohol, or any number of drugs: peer influence plays a massive role here, and while many kids will try things and emerge out the other end of adolescence relatively unscathed, some number will slip down the rabbit hole of addiction.

Conversations about decision-making can feel repetitive (because they are!). However, there's good data showing that repeating these talks and particularly role-playing how to manage social scenarios can create a form of muscle memory in the brain. The power of peer influence in the limbic system can be tempered by strategies like waiting before diving into an impulsive decision or planning an answer to a commonplace prompt (*Will you send a nude?* or *Want a hit?*). If a kid doesn't have to rely upon their sluggish prefrontal cortex to generate an answer because you've already practiced one together, the power of negative peer influence diminishes.

Before we move on, let us spend a moment considering how many friends a kid *needs:* one. A single, solid, deep, and meaningful relationship is all it takes to protect against isolation and enjoy the benefits of camaraderie. Given the depiction of adolescent life in film especially, this statement doesn't seem as if it could be true. But it is. All you need is one friend to be okay. The 2008 study "With a Little Help from Your Friends" found that having one supportive and intimate friendship—a single high-quality friendship—is more important for adolescents than the total number of friends they have. It's important to note that having a bigger social network actually increases the likelihood that a person will have individual, strong, one-to-one friendships, but the kids who have only one close friend are protected from the social and mental health impacts of having none.

 ## WHAT'S CHANGED OVER THE PAST 20, 30, 40 YEARS

The construct of friendship hasn't changed much over time. That said, these days, the comparative social landscape can feel unrecognizable.

Smartphones have affected every corner of kids' socializing, but this is not all bad! Technology allows for meaningful social connections among tweens and teens; this became particularly apparent during the dark days of the COVID pandemic when screens extended lifelines between kids (and older generations too). These tools can certainly also exacerbate loneliness, especially among younger users, with some apps allowing kids to see their friends hanging out without them and other apps showing a literal map of everyone together. The negative impacts are not limited to tweens and teens (adults feel them acutely too). Even though developing brains may have difficulty keeping perspective or parsing the reality of it all, these days most parents and professionals working with tweens and teens praise the benefits of devices as much as they curse their very existence.

Social media, however, demands a separate mention. The data is clear that for kids who are struggling socially, social media can make things worse. A 2019 study in *JAMA Psychiatry* showed that three or more hours on social media per day led to increased rates of mental health issues. Meanwhile, the advocacy organization Common Sense Media reported that same year that the average teenager spent between five and seven hours per day on these apps. In other words, there is a vanishingly small group of teenagers who are on social media and not at potential risk.

The social media creators know this. In 2021, the *Wall Street Journal* leaked an internal Facebook study looking at Instagram's impact on adolescents. Here's one example of what the *WSJ* found: "among teens who reported suicidal thoughts, 13 percent of British users and 6 percent of American users traced the desire to kill themselves to Instagram." This is not to say that all social media apps are deadly (they're not) or that the medium doesn't have redeeming qualities (it does). In fact, these days every piece of negative data seems to be matched with an equally compelling positive piece showing the importance of interconnection, support, and kindness that can and does occur online. But different apps create different ripples: Instagram's culture of beauty and likes tends to skew far more toxic for teens, especially girls, while TikTok's short-form visual silliness is playful and fun (of course, until a kid goes down a rabbit hole of negative videos being served up by the algorithm). Social media apps all share the lowest common denominator of airing what everyone else is doing *without them* in excruciating, minute-to-minute detail. Their former best friend? Out with other people on SnapMap. Their teammates? Making a TikTok together. The party they weren't invited to? Playing out on people's private stories. This feature of social media adds a challenge to friendship that wasn't even imaginable when we were growing up—our social turbulence got rehashed on Monday morning in school; today, the slights and shifts occur in real time, from which there's no respite unless kids delete the app.

One other specific downside to life on devices is a shift toward a culture of bullying. Verbal and physical attacks that were once the domain of school hallways, bathrooms, and parking lots now pervade pinging texts on a group chat, spreading humiliation further and faster. Everything from nude photos to cruel jibes reaches across social circles or entire communities with shocking speed. The consequences are devastating, which explains the rise of organizations over the past 15 years especially—coinciding with the launch of the smartphone—dedicated to raising awareness about the dangers of bullying. The stark truth is that while the adults caring for kids on the receiving end of bullying often step into the fray, adults connected with the bullies rarely see or acknowledge the behavior. This is hard when the bullying plays out on screens, and harder still when passwords obstruct an adult's vision or phantom accounts are created. Even if a phone is unlocked and easy to access, following one kid's online behavior can turn into a literal full-time job, and very few of us have the bandwidth to check every text and app every day.

The law has tried desperately to keep pace with technology. In the case of bullying, victims can seek protection and aggressors can face consequences. But certain areas have become extremely murky, like child pornography laws initially intended to protect kids from adult predators—today, these laws are often weaponized against the kids themselves, used to punish, even prosecute, one kid for sending or sharing a nude picture of another kid. Given how slowly the laws creeps along and how quickly technology evolves, the rules in place do not adequately protect kids on all sides of this equation. It has fallen to schools and parents to educate kids about things like taking and sharing nudes. Think back for a moment to your early teenage self: Can you even imagine this back-and-forth with your parents? Can you conceive of having your own phone? Let alone one that wasn't attached to the wall? One that could take pictures (ridiculously high-quality ones) and play your favorite music? Can you imagine the intoxication of a text thread or a request from someone you had a major crush on, and what you might have done on that device? If you're wondering how we got here in a chapter about friendship, *this* is what has changed over the past few decades. The intersection of friendship and screens is messy and muddled, and it has created countless challenges for all of us, kids and adults alike.

HOW TO TALK ABOUT IT

If adults struggle to understand kids' changing friendships, imagine how kids feel! There are many valid reasons why certain kids stop hanging out together during middle and high school, but that doesn't make this shift easy. When they develop on vastly different pubertal time lines— one hitting their growth spurt in every possible way at the same time while another hasn't started to develop at all, or one seeking out romantic or sexual relationships while another isn't remotely interested in any of it yet—they can lose common ground. Tensions within friendships can be sparked by experimentation with vaping or drinking, risk-taking (shoplifting never seems to go out of style), or things as simple as diverging tastes in music, movies, or online content. None of this means that the kids who part ways will *never* be friends again; it just means that for now they're less interesting to each other.

These social upheavals reach beyond tweens and teens, often affecting parents as well. Adults tend to hold on to an ideal of "best friendship" for their kids, and they worry when they see the dynamic shift. And if families have grown close when their young children befriend one another, awkwardness sets in when the relationship between the kids changes. Adults can't let their own agendas drive their kids' friendships— you can try, but it won't work. Here's what does:

Be empathic

Even if a kid is being emotional and vocal in the face of friendship changes, avoid comments like *It's not a big deal . . . Get over it . . . When you're an adult you won't even remember this.* It is a big deal to them, and FYI they will most definitely remember this when they are adults. Better to stick to empathetic murmurs like *I'm so sorry . . . That really sucks . . . I'm here if you want some company.* Then sit in silence and see if they will open up.

Don't interrogate

If you notice that your kid isn't hanging out with their close friend, rather than launching an all-out investigation, lead with curiosity and leave the door open for later conversations. *I noticed you two aren't hanging out as much right now, and I'm wondering if something is going on.* If their response is that everything is fine, remind them: *Well, I'm always here if you want to talk.*

Don't force it

As obvious as the solution to a kid's problem may seem, especially one about friend dynamics, it should not involve swooping in to fix things for them. Trying to force the situation—for example, by planning a family dinner with the former best friend—might make matters worse, not better. Sometimes, being a sounding board rather than an active participant can work. Find out if they're open to suggestions, but if the answer is no, then respect that response.

Help them find other options

When one kid is unceremoniously dumped by another, a cascade of hurt, loneliness, and confusion follows. They may not be willing to open up about it, but a good distraction can help. Without going into manic camp counselor mode, try to plan some things like bowling, a movie night, or a visit to old friends that might pull them out of their funk.

Monitor device usage

Unfortunately, social media allows kids to track moment to moment all of the social events they are *not* part of. This rumination-by-social-media leads nowhere good. Step in, making sure there are consistent rules (and vigilant enforcement) about screen-time limits. Little things like requiring that devices be charged overnight somewhere other than the bedroom helps prevent kids from spending sleepless hours seeing what they're missing.

When you just don't like a kid's friend(s)

Maybe one—or a gaggle of them—are disrespectful, or they're experimenting with drugs or alcohol, or they simply don't behave in loyal or thoughtful ways. Here again, your clarity doesn't necessarily help the situation, and if you blurt out your feelings, chances are your kid will react by going the opposite direction. Remember the person your parents forbid you to date, who instantly became your true love? This is a moment for self-control and measured commentary, which can feel impossible when all you want to yell is *That kid is the biggest jerk and they are a shitty friend to you!* Here are a few tricks when you find yourself on the verge of uttering those very words:

Reflect on your reaction: Think about why you're having such a strong negative response. Good reasons abound: triggers from the past, protective prejudgment, information (usually in the form of rumors). Even when instincts are correct, reflection ups the odds of phrasing responses more constructively.

Different families, different rules: When rules in one house look wildly different from rules in another, it can create conflict. The reality is that no two families will ever make the exact same choices or set the exact same limits. Try not to judge the other family, but unless you're prepared to end the friendship, give over to the fact that when your kids are in someone else's house they may not stick to your family's rules. This is hard! Especially when they come back home and negotiate for a revision on your own family's rules.

Address serious concerns: It's entirely appropriate to raise concerns with a kid when you are worried about one of their friends. If there are flags for things like mental health worries, bullying, or substance use, talk about what you see. Remember, no judgment! Try something like *I'm wondering if so-and-so seems different to you lately? I've noticed they've changed their . . . I'm curious why they haven't hung out at our house much recently.*

If you suspect your kid is being bullied: In this instance, it might be difficult to get information about what's going on. They might be ashamed to tell you, frightened about retribution, or worried about being called a snitch. Instead of lunging into conversation with *I'm going to kill that little asshole who was mean to you,* which will likely just make your kid to zip their mouth shut, try a gentler, nonjudgmental approach—*You don't seem like yourself*— and then wait quietly for an answer. Kids need to know we're on their side, so make sure the lines of communication are open. *I'm always here if you want to talk* takes the pressure off, reassuring them they don't have to spill the beans right that moment. To address increasing worries about bullying, get help from a mental health professional or reach out to their school. Bullying doesn't always blow over—it can have immediate and very long-lasting mental health effects.

How to help them navigate peer influence (aka peer pressure)

There's an old saying: "If everyone was jumping off a bridge, would you?" If they were being completely honest, tweens and teens would most probably answer *Yes.* Here are some strategies kids can use to help themselves make better decisions when peers are pushing them in a questionable direction:

Count to 10 or take 3 slow breaths: This works for everyone involved, adults and kids. It reinforces the importance of pausing and teaches them to take a second before acting, especially when everyone around them is shouting "Do it, do it!" It also gives their prefrontal cortex a fighting chance to help them make a better decision.

Practice language: Have conversations about what words they can use delicately (and age appropriately) to extricate themselves from uncomfortable situations. Anticipate that your first few suggestions will be roundly rejected—which is absolutely fine! You'll get to language that feels authentic to them.

Role-play: Everyone passionately hates this advice but, when it's done, acknowledges its utility. So call it something else instead: How about "practice"? Role playing builds the muscle to demur when it would be easier to join in. Start with a simple prompt: *What would you do if . . . ? How would you handle . . . ? What could you say if . . . ?* filling in the blanks with absolutely any topic du jour (lying, theft, smoking, hooking up, you name it). The very best way to role-play is to fold in the language that you've already settled on so they can try it out and see how it feels.

Use those phones! In a particularly sticky situation, a kid can text a friend (even one who's standing right next to them) or a trusted adult. To maximize this strategy, come up with a code phrase in advance so that the person receiving the text knows to drop whatever they're doing and have the kid's back.

Go to the bathroom: An oldie but goodie, this is one way to physically remove yourself.

Get granular with actual words they can use: Often tweens and teens know the right thing to do, but they're not sure *how* to do it or what language to use without upsetting the social apple cart. Kids often live in fear of the reactions they will get from a friend or romantic interest—this is why they may choose to take a risk (vape, drink, have sex) over upsetting the other person. Our knee-jerk response usually sounds like *If your friend tells you they'll be so mad at you for not doing something really stupid, maybe reconsider the friend, not the decision.* Older teens give the following advice for how younger kids can extricate themselves from peer pressure.

In response to an offer to vape: *Nah, I'm good for now.*

In response to an offer to drink: *I can't—my coach would kill me.*

In response to an offer to have sex: *I just remembered I'm being picked up in five minutes.*

In response to an offer to try drugs: *Sucks, but my parents drug-test me.*

FROM PEOPLE JUST OUT THE OTHER SIDE

B.H., she/her, age 21

People can be some of the best things to happen to you in your life—but also the worst. I have seen both, and I know it's definitely super common to deal with people who were, to put it lightly, not the kindest to you.

Growing up, I was an average kid. I loved to read books (I would boast about reading 20 in a single summer), play video games with my brother, and hang out with my cousins on weekends. I was, however, stuck in between feeling too American to be living in Hong Kong and not American enough to be living in Los Angeles, where I was born. I moved to Hong Kong when I was six and would return to Los Angeles every summer. It was always hard feeling like I never belonged. This was especially apparent in fifth grade.

I was an outsider. My Mandarin wasn't great, and my English was mediocre. I wanted to be friends with the expats and also be friends with the others who were from Hong Kong. I was being tugged in both directions, which was hard for a fifth grader. Luckily, I had my two best friends who were always by my side.

At school, a specific group of girls hated me. I don't know how it started, but I just remember the constant torment of them calling me "fat" (even though I was a very normal weight for a 10-year-old) and a derogatory term for "ghost person" referring to white people or just outsiders in general (even though I am 100 percent Chinese). I was so different from them—I was too American. I also didn't fit in with the non-Chinese kids because I was, in fact, Chinese.

Although I was much too young for a Facebook account, I got one anyway because everybody had one. I remember when the first wave of online comments came in. I was struck with mean comments every day. People were commenting on my weight, my looks, my character, and more. This then turned into comments to my face at school as well as lots of mean glares in the hallways. Some of those words still stick with me today. I learned that not everyone is always on your side, and to trust the right people who will show you time and time again that they are good.

This gave me perspective. I realized that (1) I never want to treat someone the way that I was treated, and (2) I have to value a true friend. I gained a lot of empathy from this traumatizing experience and started to really value the good friendships in my life.

Kids can be mean! I wish I had thicker skin. I also wish that I had told someone earlier. The bullying didn't stop—and sometimes it doesn't even with adult intervention. My aunt friended me on Facebook and saw the mean comments. Then she confronted my cousin (who also went to my school) and asked him what was happening. He told her as much as he knew, and then my aunt told my parents. This was the final straw for my parents; they blamed these kids for my wacky behavior that they didn't understand. They didn't want me growing up in a culture where I felt so out of place, so they moved me to the United States. At first, it was extremely scary because I was still a foreigner: too Chinese for the American kids at school. At the end of the day, I was still happier. I found other Asian American kids who I related to, and found a home in the Asian American community.

I wish my parents had known how bad it was, but it was hard to open up to them because they brushed it off as typical mean-middle-school-kid behavior. If they had seen the extremely racist and sexist comments or heard what they said to me at school, maybe it would've been a different story.

T.E., he/him, age 21

A friendship is a very unique connection, and many underestimate the influence that a friendship will have on someone's life and who they will become. They are unique in that you are not bonded by blood or obligation. You truly cherish each other's company and want to support each other. Throughout life, friendships help form and create our values and interests. That is why it is important to be able to recognize different types of friendships, both good and bad. I believe that once we are able to identify the friendships that bring out the best in us and provide us with a healthy space to be our authentic selves, they will be a lifetime of support.

However, that being said, I have definitely encountered many unhealthy friendships throughout my life, mostly during my childhood. Those relationships are often founded upon negative factors like jealousy, popularity, and insecurity. In my case, they felt good at the moment, and I told myself this was who I wanted to be friends with, not who I should be friends with.

One of those people was a mean girl who seemed to have control over many people around her. It was incredibly formulaic: a typical mean girl whose standoffish behavior is rooted in deep insecurity. But recognizing those types of people was not the hard part. I feel like all the movies at that age were about high school mean girls who always got what they deserved and, in reality, had miserable lives. Why then, despite being given this information, does the allure of a popular high school mean girl still exist in the lives of teenagers today?

Of course, she had that mean-girl persona. Her hair was bleached blond, and she would wear dark eyeliner. She dressed like she was much older than most people of her age. She also was the person in my life who made me feel like one of the most important people in the world. She would tell me secrets about some of the people around me. I had one class with her and she would be 20 minutes late and the first to leave. When she had something to tell you, the teacher seemed to no longer exist. She really did not seem to care about the lives of those around her except her own. She mostly had something negative to say about someone, whether it was the way they talked or dressed or always raised their hand up in class. On a Wednesday morning, she would talk about how she got home at 3 A.M. last night and her parents never even seemed to notice. However, behind all of that bragging came deep insecurity and a lack of familial support.

I would be the first person she would turn to if she had anything negative to say about anyone. Obviously, I felt incredibly important. But I soon realized that when she wasn't there, that same judgmental and negative energy would still follow me around. The way that she thought about others, I began to think as well.

This also included her behavior. She often lied to her parents. She would lie to them when they asked where she was, what she was doing, or who she was with. I began to do the same. It felt fun, like I was playing some fun game. With her, I drank for the first time and started to go to parties when my parents thought I was just at sleepovers.

As many stories go, it took being on the receiving end of her judgment and hatred to make me realize that this friendship was not healthy. Many of the personal things I shared with her were no longer confined to what I thought was a friendship built on loyalty. I realized that the amount of energy I was putting into that specific relationship was not equally being reciprocated. It wasn't surprising to see how the day I confronted her, she was quick to deny everything and quick to turn her back on a friendship that to me had seemed so important.

After that, I began to put my energy into other friendships. I noticed the way I thought began to change again. With these new friendships, I thought less about how I looked or how I acted in a specific social setting. The variety and number of friends I had increased, and I knew that that past friendship was one that limited me in so many ways. I had not allowed myself to meet new people or be my own person. My new friendships brought out the parts of me that were unique rather than trying to conform to what the "cool" way to act was or to blend in with a certain group. I began to experiment with photography and writing.

Thinking about my current best friends, they are people who love me for all of my qualities. They know how I tend to worry about everything, how I fiercely protect those close to me, or how I view the world, and they love all those things about me. They never get upset with me if they want to do something and I express that I do not want to. These are relationships based on factors like respect and loyalty.

Often, I have found it can be difficult to find these relationships. Many times we think we know what we want, but we often have clouded judgment. The allure of popularity will never truly go away, and often it is hard to realize what is best for us in the long term. When making new friends, I think to myself, *How do I feel when I am with this person?* Or, *Do they bring out my best, most positive qualities?*

I realize after this whole situation the only way to understand the true value of a high school mean girl is to face the consequences and betrayal of one firsthand. I feel like a parent's opinion of their child's friends usually has the opposite effect. When my mom told me who not to hang out with, I would just want to hang out with that person more. The whole allure of the high school mean girl is greatly dependent on the adrenaline rush of doing something that feels rebellious and different. However, once they turn on you or you end up in a bad situation you realize that the feeling of rebelling is not as fun as you thought it was.

For me, that was the moment when I was convinced to go to a party and ended up having to call the cops for a friend who was too intoxicated. She had passed out on the ground, and I tried to turn to her for support, who would end up leaving me to handle the situation alone. At that moment, I realized the consequences of lying to my parents and sneaking around would only have a negative impact in the long term once that initial rush disappeared and how in a true time of need I had no one to truly rely on.

I think my parents could have been better about not shaming impulsive behavior or who I was friends with. What parents need to realize is that every teenager is going to want to break the rules. Often, the more a parent tries to control rebelling, the more the child wants to rebel. In my case, if my mom was there to drive me there or talk to me about how much me and my friend were going to drink, maybe I would have eased into the whole experience. Maybe I would not have wanted to go if my mom knew about it because it would not be sneaking out.

After that experience, I gained important skills on how to evaluate friendships through the importance of a friendship circle. I used to believe that everyone I met and wanted to be friends with had to become my best friend. I thought the best friends were the people who made you want to be crazy and step out of your comfort zone. I wanted to be extremely close friends with everyone I liked. However, I realized how hard that would be when maintaining 10-plus relationships. In the end, I realized that it was easier to maintain varying levels (or rings) of friendships, which would include three to four close best friends and many close friends and acquaintances.

Today, my best friends are my innermost circle. These are the people whom I can spend time with in any setting and know I can always rely on. The next circle is good friends, who I really enjoy but maybe I don't always tell my deepest secrets to or call for advice. From this model, I was able to be okay with different kinds of friendships and figure out how to maintain a wide network of friends. The rest of the rings help separate acquaintances you say hi to in passing or collaboration in work or school. When understanding the value of friendship, I found how important it was to establish the expectations you have for each person.

BIBLIOGRAPHY

Below is a list of books, articles, websites, and other resources that proved invaluable to the writing of this book. For some chapters, the list of cited works is thin (or nonexistent). This is because this book is the result of more than print-resource research; it is also the product of 25 years as a pediatrician (for Cara) and decades as writers, speakers, and puberty educators (for both of us). Therefore, many of our insights and guidance are derived from conversations, queries, interviews, *Puberty Podcast* episodes, and workshops on each of these topics. We wish we had kept a running log of every resource that has contributed to our learning and knowledge throughout the years, but we haven't. The resources listed here, however, are ones that we specifically relied upon for this book.

CHAPTER 1: EARLIER PUBERTY

Dick, Danielle M., Richard J. Rose, Lea Pulkkinen, and Jaakko Kaprio. "Measuring Puberty and Understanding Its Impact: A Longitudinal Study of Adolescent Twins." *Journal of Youth and Adolescence* 30, no. 4 (August 2001): 385–400. http://dx.doi.org/10.1023/A:1010471015102.

Greenspan, Louise, and Julianna Deardorff. *The New Puberty: How to Navigate Early Development in Today's Girls.* New York: Rodale, 2014.

Hayward, Chris, Joel D. Killen, Darrell M. Wilson, Lawrence D. Hammer, Iris Litt, H. C. Kraemer, F. Haydel, A. Varady, and C. B. Taylor. "Psychiatric Risk Associated with Early Puberty in Adolescent Girls." *Journal of the American Academy of Child and Adolescent Psychiatry* 36, no. 2 (February 1997): 255–62. http://dx.doi.org/10.1097/00004583-199702000-199700017.

Kaltiala-Heino, Riittakerttu, Matti Rimpelä, Aila Rissanen, and Pivi Rantanen. "Early Puberty and Early Sexual Activity Are Associated with Bulimic-Type Eating Pathology in Middle Adolescence." *Journal of Adolescent Health* 28, no. 4 (May 2001): 346–52. https://doi.org/10.1016/s1054-139x(01)00195-1.

Natterson, Cara. *Decoding Boys: New Science behind the Subtle Art of Raising Sons.* New York: Ballantine, 2020.

Striegel-Moore, Ruth H., and Fary M. Cachelin. "Etiology of Eating Disorders in Women." *The Counseling Psychologist* 29, no. 5 (June 2016): 635–61. https://doi.org/10.1177/0011000001295002.

CHAPTER 3: BREASTS, BOOBS, AND BUDS

Carlson, Lauren, Vanessa Flores Poccia, Bob Z. Sun, Brittany Mosley, Imke Kirste, Annette Rice, Rithi Sridhar, Tairmae Kangarloo, et al. "Early Breast Development in

Overweight Girls: Does Estrogen Made by Adipose Tissue Play a Role?" *International Journal of Obesity* 43, no. 10 (October 2019): 1978–87. https://www.nature.com /articles/s41366-019-0446-5.

Centers for Disease Control and Prevention. "Adult Obesity Facts." Accessed February 11, 2023. https://www.cdc.gov/obesity/data/adult.html.

Centers for Disease Control and Prevention. "Childhood Obesity Facts." Accessed February 11, 2023. https://www.cdc.gov/obesity/data/childhood.html.

CHAPTER 5: PERIODS

Rees, M. "The Age of Menarche." *ORGYN* 4 (1995): 2–4, PMID 12319855. https:// pubmed.ncbi.nlm.nih.gov/12319855/.

CHAPTER 6: HAIR

Auchus, Richard J., and Robert L. Rosenfield. "Physiology and Clinical Manifestations of Normal Adrenarche." *UpToDate*, July 6, 2022. https://www.uptodate.com/contents /physiology-and-clinical-manifestations-of-normal-adrenarche.

Beck, Sheryl, and Robert J. Handa. "Dehydroepiandrosterone (DHEA): A Misunderstood Adrenal Hormone and Spine-Tingling Neurosteroid?" *Endocrinology* 145, no. 3 (March 1, 2004): 1039–41. https://doi.org/10.1210/en.2003-1703.

Liimatta, Jani, Pauliina Utriainen, Raimo Voutilainen, and Jarmo Jääskeläinen. "Girls with a History of Premature Adrenarche Have Advanced Growth and Pubertal Development at the Age of 12 Years." *Frontiers in Endocrinology* 8 (October 31, 2017): 291. http://dx.doi.org/10.3389/fendo.2017.00291.

CHAPTER 7: ACNE, BACKNE, CHESTNE, AND BUTTNE

Centers for Disease Control and Prevention. "Fast Facts: Preventing Adverse Childhood Experiences." Last reviewed April 6, 2022. https://www.cdc.gov/violenceprevention /aces/fastfact.html.

Magruder Hospital. "Community Health Assessment 2020." Accessed April 25, 2023. https://www.co.ottawa.oh.us/DocumentCenter/View/1337/2020-Community -Health-Assessment-PDF

Maninger, Nicole, John P. Capitanio, William A. Mason, John D. Ruys, and Sally P. Mendoza. "Acute and Chronic Stress Increase DHEAS Concentrations in Rhesus Monkeys." *Psychoneuroendocrinology* 35, no. 7 (August 2010): 1055–62. http://dx.doi .org/10.1016/j.psyneuen.2010.01.006.

CHAPTER 8: BODY ODOR

Schwerin, Mac. "The Pungent Legacy of Axe Body Spray." *Vox*, February 19, 2020. https:// www.vox.com/the-highlight/2020/2/12/21122543/axe-body-spray-teenage-boys-ads.

Utriainen, Pauliina, Sally Laakso, Jani Liimatta, Jarmo Jääskeläinen, and Raimo Voutilainen. "Premature Adrenarche—A Common Condition with Variable Presentation." *Hormone Research in Paediatrics* 83, no. 4 (February 2015): 221–31. https://doi.org/10.1159/000369458.

CHAPTER 9: GROWTH SPURTS, WEIGHT GAIN, AND CURVES

Blizzard, R. M., P. M. Martha, J. R. Kerrigan, N. Mauras, and Alan D. Rogol. "Changes in Growth Hormone (GH) Secretion and in Growth during Puberty." *Journal of Endocrinological Investigation* 12, 8 Supplement 3 (February 1989): 65–68, PMID 2809099. https://pubmed.ncbi.nlm.nih.gov/2809099/.

Delemarre-van de Waal, Henriëtte A., S. C. van Coeverden, and J. Rotteveel. "Hormonal

Determinants of Pubertal Growth." *Journal of Pediatric Endocrinology and Metabolism* 14, Supplement 6 (2001): 1521–26, PMID 11837509. https://pubmed.ncbi.nlm.nih. gov/11837509/.

Ritchie, Hannah, and Max Roser. "Obesity." OurWorldInData.org. Accessed February 13, 2023. https://ourworldindata.org/obesity.

Rochira, Vincenzo, Elda Kara, and Cesare Carani. "The Endocrine Role of Estrogens on Human Male Skeleton." In "The Endocrine Role of the Skeleton." Del Fattore, Andrea, Cristina Sobacchi, Martina Rauner, and Amélie Coudert, eds. Special issue, *International Journal of Endocrinology* (March 24, 2015). https://doi.org/10.1155/2015 /165215.

Solorzano, Christine M. Burt, and Christopher R. McCartney. "Obesity and the Pubertal Transition in Girls and Boys." *Reproduction* 140, no. 3 (September 2010): 399–410. https://doi.org/10.1530/REP-10-0119.

CHAPTER 10: SLEEP

Adamska-Patruno, Edyta, Lucyna Ostrowska, Joanna Goscik, Barbara Pietraszewska, Adam Kretowski, and Maria Gorska. "The Relationship between the Leptin/Ghrelin Ratio and Meals with Various Macronutrient Contents in Men with Different Nutritional Status: A Randomized Crossover Study." *Nutrition Journal* 17, no. 118 (December 28, 2018). https://doi.org/10.1186/s12937-018-0427-x.

Shepard, John W., Jr., Daniel Buysse, Andrew L. Chesson, William C. Dement, Rochelle Goldberg, Christian Guilleminault, Cameron D. Harris, et al. "History of the Development of Sleep Medicine in the United States." *Journal of Clinical Sleep Medicine* 1, no. 1 (February 2005): 61–82. http://dx.doi.org/10.5664/jcsm.26298.

Thomas, Liji. "Ghrelin and Sleep." *News-Medical.* Last updated February 26, 2019. https:// www.news-medical.net/health/Ghrelin-and-Sleep.aspx.

Yang, Fan Nils, Weizhen Xie, and Ze Wang. "Effects of Sleep Duration on Neurocognitive Development in Early Adolescents in the USA: A Propensity Score Matched, Longitudinal, Observational Study." *Lancet Child and Adolescent Health* 6, no. 10 (October 2022): 705–12. https://doi.org/10.1016/S2352-4642(22)00188-2.

CHAPTER 11: BRAIN DEVELOPMENT

Hawkins, Jeff, and Subutai Ahmad. "Why Neurons Have Thousands of Synapses, a Theory of Sequence Memory in Neocortex." *Frontiers in Neural Circuits* 10, Article 23 (March 30, 2016). http://dx.doi.org/10.3389/fncir.2016.00023.

Portnow, Leah H., David E. Vaillancourt, and Michael S. Okun. "The History of Cerebral PET Scanning: From Physiology to Cutting-Edge Technology." *Neurology* 80, no. 10 (March 2013): 952–56. http://dx.doi.org/10.1212/WNL.0b013e318285c135. Erratum in *Neurology* 81, no. 14 (October 1, 2013): 1275. https://doi.org/10.1212 /WNL.0b013e3182aa3d3a.

SciShow. "Why Teenagers' Brains Are Wired Differently." YouTube video, 10:06. Accessed February 13, 2023. https://www.youtube.com/watch?v=hiduiTq1ei8.

CHAPTER 12: MOOD SWINGS

Casey, B. J., Aaron S. Heller, Dylan G. Gee, and Alexandra Ochoa Cohen. "Development of the Emotional Brain." *Neuroscience Letters* 693 (February 6, 2019): 29–34. http:// dx.doi.org/10.1016/j.neulet.2017.11.055.

Casey, B. J., Rebecca M. Jones, and Todd A. Hare. "The Adolescent Brain." *The Year in Cognitive Neuroscience 2008* 1124, no. 1 (March 2008): 111–26. https://doi .org/10.1196/annals.1440.010.

CHAPTER 13: MENTAL HEALTH

American Association of Suicidology. "Facts and Statistics 2019." Last updated January 2021. Accessed April 25, 2023. https://suicidology.org/facts-and-statistics/

Centers for Disease Control and Prevention. "YRBSS Results." Last reviewed March 13, 2023. https://www.cdc.gov/healthyyouth/data/yrbs/pdf/YRBS_Data-Summary -Trends_Report2023_508.pdf.

Curtin, Sally C. "State Suicide Rates among Adolescents and Young Adults Aged 10–24: United States, 2000–2018." *National Vital Statistics Reports* 69, no. 11 (September 11, 2020). https://www.cdc.gov/nchs/data/nvsr69/nvsr-69-11-508.pdf.

Kalin, Ned H. "The Critical Relationship between Anxiety and Depression." *American Journal of Psychiatry* 177, no. 5 (May 1, 2020): 365–67. http://dx.doi.org/10.1176/appi .ajp.2020.20030305.

Kelly, Yvonne, Afshin Zilanawala, Cara L. Booker, and Amanda Sacker. "Social Media Use and Adolescent Mental Health: Findings from the UK Millennium Cohort Study." *Lancet* 6 (December 2018): 59–68. https://doi.org/10.1016/j.eclinm.2018.12.005.

Keng, Shian-Ling, Moria J. Smoski, and Clive Robins. "Effects of Mindfulness on Psychological Health: A Review of Empirical Studies." *Clinical Psychology Review* 31, no. 6 (August 2011): 1041–56. http://dx.doi.org/10.1016/j.cpr.2011.04.006.

Linden, David J. "The Truth behind 'Runner's High' and Other Mental Benefits of Running." Accessed February 10, 2023. https://www.hopkinsmedicine.org/health /wellness-and-prevention/the-truth-behind-runners-high-and-other-mental -benefits-of-running.

Mansueto, Charles S. "OCD and Tourette Syndrome: Re-examining the Relationship." International OCD Foundation. Accessed February 10, 2023. https://iocdf.org /expert-opinions/ocd-and-tourette-syndrome/.

Morawski, Jill. "History of Mental Illness." Wesleyan University. Coursera. Last accessed April 25, 2023. https://www.coursera.org/lecture/history-mental-illness/science -mUkRe

National Alliance on Mental Illness. "What You Need to Know About Youth Suicide." Accessed February 10, 2023. https://www.nami.org/Your-Journey/Kids-Teens-and -Young-Adults/What-You-Need-to-Know-About-Youth-Suicide.

National Center for Drug Abuse Statistics. "Drug Use among Youths: Facts and Statistics." Accessed February 10, 2023. https://drugabusestatistics.org/teen-drug-use/.

Nazeer, Ahsan, Finza Latif, Aisha Mondal, Muhammad Waqar Azeem, and Donald E. Greydanus. "Obsessive-Compulsive Disorder in Children and Adolescents: Epidemiology, Diagnosis, and Management." Supplement, *Translational Pediatrics* 9, no. S1 (February 2020): S76–S93. http://dx.doi.org/10.21037/tp.2019.10.02.

Nesi, Jacqueline, Supreet Mann, and Michael B. Robb. *2023 Teens and mental health: How girls really feel about social media.* (San Francisco, CA: Common Sense, 2023). Accessed April 25, 2023. https://www.commonsensemedia.org/sites/default/files/research /report/how-girls-really-feel-about-social-media-researchreport_web_final_2.pdf

Office of Population Affairs, US Department of Health and Human Services. "Mental Health for Adolescents." Accessed February 10, 2023. https://opa.hhs.gov/adolescent -health/mental-health-adolescents.

Usmani, Zafar Ahmad. "Treatment of Anxiety Among Patients with Chronic Obstructive Pumonary Disease." (PhD diss., The University of Adelaide., 2018) https://digital .library.adelaide.edu.au/dspace/bitstream/2440/120259/1/Usmani2018_PhD.pdf

CHAPTER 14: BODY IMAGE

C. S. Mott Children's Hospital, University of Michigan Health. "Parents' Perception of Their Child's Body Image." *Mott Poll Report* 41, no. 5 (September 19, 2022). https://mottpoll.org/sites/default/files/documents/091922_BodyImage.pdf.

Davis, Sarah. "The Pandemic Is Poisoning Body Image—It's Time to Find the Antidote." *Forbes.* Last updated January 26, 2022. https://www.forbes.com/health/body/covid-and-body-image/.

DoSomething.org. "11 Facts About Body Image." Accessed February 10, 2023. https://www.dosomething.org/us/facts/11-facts-about-body-image#fn4.

Johns Hopkins All Children's Hospital. "Eating Disorder Facts." Accessed February 10, 2023. https://www.hopkinsallchildrens.org/Services/Pediatric-and-Adolescent-Medicine/Adolescent-and-Young-Adult-Specialty-Clinic/Eating-Disorders/Eating-Disorder-Facts.

Johns Hopkins Medicine. "Bulimia Nervosa." Accessed February 10, 2023. https://www.hopkinsmedicine.org/health/conditions-and-diseases/eating-disorders/bulimia-nervosa.

National Association of Anorexia Nervosa and Associated Disorders. "Eating Disorder Statistics." Accessed February 10, 2023. https://anad.org/eating-disorders-statistics/.

National Organization for Women. "Get the Facts." Accessed February 10, 2023. https://now.org/now-foundation/love-your-body/love-your-body-whats-it-all-about/get-the-facts/.

CHAPTER 15: YOUTH SPORTS (OVER)SPECIALIZATION

Brenner, Joel S. "Overuse Injuries, Overtraining, and Burnout in Child and Adolescent Athletes." *Pediatrics* 119, no. 6 (July 2007): 1242–45. http://dx.doi.org/10.1542/peds.2007-0887.

Duffek, Jaimie. "A few surprises in the data behind single-sport and multisport athletes." *USA Today High School Sports,* March 28, 2017. https://usatodayhss.com/2017/a-few-surprises-in-the-data-behind-single-sport-and-multisport-athletes

Erickson, Brandon J., Bernard R. Bach Jr., Charles A. Bush-Joseph, Nikhil N. Verma, and Anthony A. Romeo. "Medial Ulnar Collateral Ligament Reconstruction of the Elbow in Major League Baseball Players: Where Do We Stand?" *World Journal of Orthopaedics* 7, no. 6 (June 18, 2016): 355–60. http://dx.doi.org/10.5312/wjo.v7.i6.355.

Gregory, Sean. "How Kids' Sports Became a $15 Billion Industry." *Time,* August 24, 2017. https://time.com/magazine/us/4913681/september-4th-2017-vol-190-no-9-u-s/

Neeru, Jayanthi et al. "Sports Specialization in Young Athletes: Evidence-Based Recommendations," *Sports Health* 5, no. 3 (October 2012): 251–57. https://journals.sagepub.com/doi/10.1177/1941738112464626.

Project Play, the Aspen Institute. *State of Play 2016: Trends and Developments.* Washington, DC: The Aspen Institute, 2016. https://www.aspeninstitute.org/wp-content/uploads/2016/06/State-of-Play-2016-FINAL.pdf.

Project Play, the Aspen Institute. "Youth Sports Facts: Why Play Matters." Accessed February 10, 2023. https://www.aspenprojectplay.org/youth-sports/facts.

Team USA. "State of Play 2020 Report Indicates Trends and Growth in Sport." October 12, 2020. https://www.teamusa.org/USA-Field-Hockey/Features/2020/October/12/State-of-Play-2020-Report-Indicates-Trends-and-Growth-in-Sport.

Tucker Center for Research on Girls and Women in Sport, University of Minnesota. *The 2007 Tucker Center Research Report: Developing Physically Active Girls: An Evidence-Based Multidisciplinary Approach.* Minneapolis: University of Minnesota, 2007. https://www.cehd.umn.edu/tuckercenter/library/docs/research/2007-Tucker-Center-Research-Report.pdf.

Tucker Center for Research on Girls and Women in Sport, University of Minnesota. *The 2018 Tucker Center Research Report: Developing Physically Active Girls: An Evidence-Based Multidisciplinary Approach*. Minneapolis: University of Minnesota, September 2018. https://www.cehd.umn.edu/tuckercenter/research/tcrr2018.html.

CHAPTER 16: SEX, HOOKUP CULTURE, AND PORN

Abma, Joyce C., and Gladys M. Martinez. "Sexual Activity and Contraceptive Use among Teenagers in the United States, 2011–2015." *National Health Statistics Reports*, no. 104. Hyattsville, Md.: National Center for Health Statistics, June 22, 2017. https://www.cdc.gov/nchs/data/nhsr/nhsr104.pdf.

Centers for Disease Control and Prevention. "YRBSS Results." Last reviewed August 20, 2020. https://www.cdc.gov/healthyyouth/data/yrbs/results.htm.

Centers for Disease Control and Prevention. "YRBSS Data Summary 2023." Accessed April 25, 2023. https://www.cdc.gov/healthyyouth/data/yrbs/pdf/yrbs_data-summary -trends_report2023_508.pdf

Habel, Melissa A., Jami Leichliter, Patricia J. Dittus, Ian H. Spicknall, and Sevgi Okten Aral. "Heterosexual Anal and Oral Sex in Adolescents and Adults in the United States, 2011–2015." *Sexually Transmitted Diseases* 45, no. 12 (December 2018): 775–82. http://dx.doi.org/10.1097/OLQ.0000000000000889.

Weiss, Robert. "Porn-Induced Erectile Dysfunction." *Psychology Today*, April 26, 2021. https://www.psychologytoday.com/us/blog/love-and-sex-in-the-digital-age/202104 /porn-induced-erectile-dysfunction.

CHAPTER 17: CONTRACEPTION, STIS, AND STDS

Centers for Disease Control and Prevention. "Contraception." Last reviewed November 1, 2022. https://www.cdc.gov/reproductivehealth/contraception/.

Centers for Disease Control and Prevention. "YRBSS Results." Last reviewed August 20, 2020. https://www.cdc.gov/healthyyouth/data/yrbs/results.htm.

Centers for Disease Control and Prevention. "Genital HPV Infection—Basic Fact Sheet." Last reviewed April 12, 2022. https://www.cdc.gov/std/hpv/stdfact-hpv.htm.

Habel, Melissa A., Jami Leichliter, Patricia J. Dittus, Ian H. Spicknall, and Sevgi Okten Aral. "Heterosexual Anal and Oral Sex in Adolescents and Adults in the United States, 2011–2015." *Sexually Transmitted Diseases* 45, no. 12 (December 2018): 775–82. http://dx.doi.org/10.1097/OLQ.0000000000000889.

Iliades, Chris. "How Do I Know If I Have Herpes or Something Else?" Everyday Health, August 13, 2022. https://www.everydayhealth.com/sexual-health-pictures/is-it-herpes -or-something-else.aspx

Planned Parenthood. "A History of the Fight about Birth Control." Accessed February 10, 2023. https://www.plannedparenthoodaction.org/issues/birth-control/history-fight -about-birth-control.

Rothman, Lily. "How AIDS Changed the History of Sex Education." *Time*, November 12, 2014. https://time.com/3578597/aids-sex-ed-history/.

Rough, Bonnie J. "How the Dutch Do Sex Ed." *The Atlantic*, August 27, 2018. https:// www.theatlantic.com/family/archive/2018/08/the-benefits-of-starting-sex-ed-at-age -4/568225/.

CHAPTER 18: SEXUAL ORIENTATION

Centers for Disease Control and Prevention. "YRBSS Results." Last reviewed August 20, 2020. https://www.cdc.gov/healthyyouth/data/yrbs/results.htm.

The City of Portland, Oregon. "What does LGBTQIP2SAA+ stand for?" Accessed April 25, 2023. https://www.portlandoregon.gov/78738.

Fortenberry, J. Dennis. "Puberty and Adolescent Sexuality." *Hormones and Behavior* 64, no. 2 (July 2013): 280–87. https://doi.org/10.1016/j.yhbeh.2013.03.007.

PFLAG.org. Amicus Brief of the Trevor Project, PFLAG, and Family Equality. Accessed April 25, 2023. https://www.supremecourt.gov/DocketPDF/18/18-107/106964 /20190703120210865_Amicus%20Brief.pdf

Saewyc, Elizabeth M. "Research on Adolescent Sexual Orientation: Development, Health Disparities, Stigma, and Resilience." In "Special Issue: Decade in Review," *Journal of Research on Adolescence* 21, no. 1 (March 2011): 256–72. https://doi. org/10.1111/j.1532-7795.2010.00727.x.

Stewart, J. L., Leigh Spivey-Rita, Laura Widman, Sophia Choukas-Bradley, and Mitchell J. Prinstein. "Developmental Patterns of Sexual Identity, Romantic Attraction, and Sexual Behavior among Adolescents over Three Years." *Journal of Adolescence* 77, no. 1 (December 2019): 90–97. https://doi.org/10.1016/j.adolescence.2019.10.006.

The Trevor Project. *2022 National Survey on LGBTQ Youth Mental Health*. West Hollywood: The Trevor Project, 2022. https://www.thetrevorproject.org/survey-2022 /assets/static/trevor01_2022survey_final.pdf.

CHAPTER 19: GENDER IDENTITY

Boyle, Patrick. "What Is Gender-Affirming Care? Your Questions Answered." Association of American Medical Colleges, April 12, 2022. https://www.aamc.org/news-insights /what-gender-affirming-care-your-questions-answered.

Brill, Stephanie, and Rachel Pepper. *The Transgender Child: A Handbook for Families and Professionals*. San Francisco: Cleis Press, 2008.

Johns, Michelle M., Richard Lowry, Jack Daniel Andrzejewski, Lisa C. Barrios, Zewditu Demissie, Timothy McManus, Catherine N. Rasberry, Leah Robin, and J. Michael Underwood. "Transgender Identity and Experiences of Violence Victimization, Substance Use, Suicide Risk, and Sexual Risk Behaviors among High School Students—19 States and Large Urban School Districts, 2017." *Morbidity and Mortality Weekly Report* 68, no. 3 (January 25, 2019): 67–71. http://dx.doi.org/10 .15585/mmwr.mm6803a3.

Littman, Lisa. "Individuals Treated for Gender Dysphoria with Medical and/or Surgical Transition Who Subsequently Detransitioned: A Survey of 100 Detransitioners." *Archives of Sexual Behavior* 50 (November 2021): 3353–69. https://doi.org/10.1007 /s10508-021-02163-w.

Loffman, Matt. "New poll shows Americans overwhelmingly oppose anti-transgender laws." PBS News Hour, April 16, 2021. https://www.pbs.org/newshour/politics/new -poll-shows-americans-overwhelmingly-oppose-anti-transgender-laws

Mahfouda, Simone et al. "Puberty Suppression in transgender children and adolescents." *The Lancet* 5. no. 10 (October 2017): 816–26. https://doi.org/10.1016/S2213 -8587(17)30099-2.

National Association of Anorexia Nervosa and Associated Disorders. "Eating Disorder Statistics." Accessed February 10, 2023. https://anad.org/eating-disorders-statistics/.

Office of Population Affairs. "Gender-Affirming Care and Young People." Fact sheet. Accessed February 11, 2023. https://opa.hhs.gov/sites/default/files/2022-03/gender -affirming-care-young-people-march-2022.pdf.

Rafferty, Jason. "Ensuring Comprehensive Care and Support for Transgender and Gender-Diverse Children and Adolescents." *Pediatrics* 142, no. 4 (October 1, 2018): e20182162. http://dx.doi.org/10.1542/peds.2018-2162.

Russell, Stephen Thomas, Amanda M. Pollitt, Gu Li, and Arnold H. Grossman. "Chosen Name Use Is Linked to Reduced Depressive Symptoms, Suicidal Ideation, and Suicidal Behavior among Transgender Youth." *Journal of Adolescent Health* 63, no. 4 (October 2018): 503–05. http://dx.doi.org/10.1016/j.jadohealth.2018.02.003.

The Trevor Project. *2022 National Survey on LGBTQ Youth Mental Health.* West Hollywood: The Trevor Project, 2022. https://www.thetrevorproject.org/survey-2022/assets/static/trevor01_2022survey_final.pdf.

Turban, Jack, Dana King, Jason J. Li, and Alex S. Keuroghlian. "Timing of Social Transition for Transgender and Gender Diverse Youth, K-12 Harassment, and Adult Mental Health Outcomes." *Journal of Adolescent Health* 69, no. 6 (December 2021): 991–98. http://dx.doi.org/10.1016/j.jadohealth.2021.06.001.

Van der Grinten, Hedi Claahsen, Chris M. Verhaak, Thomas Steensma, Tim Middelberg, Joep Roeffen, and Daniel Klink. "Gender Incongruence and Gender Dysphoria in Childhood and Adolescence—Current Insights in Diagnostics, Management, and Follow-Up." *European Journal of Pediatrics* 180 (May 2021): 1349–57. https://link.springer.com/article/10.1007/s00431-020-03906-y.

Herman, Jody L., Andrew R. Flores, Kathryn K. O'Neill. Williams Institute at UCLA School of Law. "How many adults and youth identify as Transgender in the United States?" June 2022. Last accessed April 25, 2023. https://williamsinstitute.law.ucla.edu/publications/trans-adults-united-states/

CHAPTER 20: FRIENDSHIPS AND PEER INFLUENCE

Güroğlu, Berna. "The Power of Friendship: The Developmental Significance of Friendships from a Neuroscience Perspective." *Child Development Perspectives* 16, no. 2 (June 2022): 110–17. http://dx.doi.org/10.1111/cdep.12450.

Riehm, Kira, Kenneth A. Feder, Kayla N. Tormohlen, Rosa M. Crum, Andrea S. Young, Kerry M. Green, Lauren R. Pacek, Lareina N. La Flair, and Ramin Mojtabai. "Associations between Time Spent Using Social Media and Internalizing and Externalizing Problems among US Youth." *JAMA Psychiatry* 76, no. 12 (September 11, 2019): 1266–73. http://dx.doi.org/10.1001/jamapsychiatry.2019.2325.

Waldrip, Amy M., Kenya Malcom, and Lauri Jensen-Campbell. "With a Little Help from Your Friends: The Importance of High-Quality Friendships on Early Adolescent Development." *Social Development* 17, no. 4 (November 2008): 832–52. http://dx.doi.org/10.1111/j.1467-9507.2008.00476.x.

Wells, Georgia, Jeff Horwitz, and Deepa Seetharaman. "Facebook Knows Instagram Is Toxic for Teen Girls, Company Documents Show." *Wall Street Journal*, September 14, 2021. https://www.wsj.com/articles/facebook-knows-instagram-is-toxic-for-teen-girls-company-documents-show-11631620739.

ACKNOWLEDGMENTS

It's hard to imagine we have more to say after 100,000 words but . . .
THANK YOU!

Starting with the dynamic duo of agent Heather Jackson and editor Marnie Cochran, two brilliant, huge-hearted badasses in the world of publishing who helped bring this book to life in record time. Remember that day when you both said we could turn it around in 15 months and we said, *If you don't mind, we'll do it in 3*. And then you said, *You're a little nuts, but we're behind you 1000 percent*. You were, from day one, including those 17,000 title iterations. Thank you for your candor, support, faster-than-anyone-in-the-biz feedback, and endless cheerleading. Special thanks to art director Anna Bauer Carr and designer Pete Garceau for designing a cover that beautifully captures this stage of life.

The heart of this book wouldn't have existed without our team of interns, our OOMbassadors, a group who have all contributed to Order of Magnitude's PUBERTY PORTAL and this book. These brave souls raised their hands when we asked if anyone wanted to flip the narrative onto themselves. Their writing is from the heart, honest and true. And now they're published authors! Put that on your resume Kiryan Bailey, Ber Bennett, Samson Bennett, Amanda Bortner, Teddy Cavanaugh, Peggy Helman, Isabella Huang, Ry Natterson, Talia Natterson, Cadence Sommers, and Rebecca Sugerman. And to the inimitable Bebe Landau—who joined after the book was written, but became instantly invaluable to its launch.

To the slew of experts who lent us their time and their brains: Lisa Damour, Louise Greenspan, Nacissé Demeksa, Mary Pat Draddy, Aliza Pressman, Yug Varma, Michele Kofman, and Beth Kawaja. And here's to every guest we've ever hosted on *The Puberty Podcast*, whose advice further informed the words on these pages: Uju Asika, Terri Bacow, Melissa

Berton, Danielle Bezalel, Stacie Billis, Zoe Bisbing, Michele Borba, Betsy Brown Braun, Tina Payne Bryson, Mallika Chopra, Molly Colvin, Jonathan Cristall, Jenn Bowie Curtis, Kelly Fradin, Jill Grimes, Monica Corcoran Harel, Mary Dell Harrington, Lisa Heffernan, Trish Hutchison, Carrie James, Becky Kennedy, Dolly Klock, Amy Lang, Meghan Leahy, Lisa Lewis, Charlotte Markey, Wendy Mogel, Melinda Wenner Moyer, Cynthia Clumeck Muchnick, Ebele Onemya, Brian Platzer, Sophia Rasevic, Eve Rodsky, Valorie Shaefer, Nina Shapiro, Natalie Silverstein, Rachel Simmons, Hina Talib, Emily Weinstein, Jessica Yellin, and Shafia Zaloom. Special thanks to Nick Kroll and Andrew Goldberg, our alternate universe companions on this puberty journey, and to Henry and Zoe Winkler for inspiring us with your deeply loving family.

There are friends whose expertise is simply listening closely and supporting us unconditionally. For Vanessa, the crew includes Amy, Caren, Dana, Elana, Mary Pat, Meg, Nicky, Sophie, and the women with whom I have shared the best and hardest of times—the Wellesley crew and the many (formal and informal) moms' groups over the past 20 years. Then there's the Dynamo crew, all of the DG coaches and especially our health educator extraordinaires: Jen Erdman and Sue Steinberg. For Cara, the crew includes Andrea, Emma, Lindsey, Lisa, Mallika, Michael, Susan, Tracy, Wah, and the Dunster foursome of Allison, Jessica, Kate, and Wicky.

Then there are our work-wives, Ken and Bryan, with whom we ideated this book. We bet you never imagined puberty would have a slot on your weekly work calendar! Thanks for getting past the awkwardness and for always being in our corner.

To our listeners and readers, who share their questions and their truths with us day in and day out: thank you for your honesty and vulnerability—we are all on this wild ride together and whenever you imagine you are the only one, remember you are not alone.

We—Cara and Vanessa—wouldn't have met unless Cara's lifelong friend Amy Schulhof hadn't introduced us. She *thought* she was introducing a couple of people who might enjoy one another over a cup of coffee. Amy, you outdid yourself.

Almost all acknowledgment sections end with gratitude to the people who live with the writer, probably because writers get so . . . let's just call it writerly when they are deep in the hive of researching and authoring books. So here goes our thanks:

Cara would like to thank . . .

Talia and Ry, it doesn't faze you anymore when I write about puberty and sex and all the rest of it. I adore you for that, and about a thousand other things. Paul, with each project you become a bigger and bigger source of support, encouragement, and certainty that the world needs what I am dishing out—this keeps me going in profound ways, especially after 9 P.M. when my body is 100 percent certain I should be asleep. Thank you to Mom, Anthony, Greg, and Seth, who lived through non-modern puberty right alongside me, and to all the Nattersons, who were spared that stage of my life. I couldn't have landed with a better family if I had conjured it.

Vanessa would like to thank . . .

To my Liverpool family, I have the best in-laws in the world, and I am lucky to have married into such a supportive family. To my beloved siblings, Jeremy, Dana, and Nick: your love, laughter, and late-night escapades over the years have nourished and lifted me. To Mom and Dad, you were ahead of your time in so many ways and I am all the better for it. Thank you for always, *always* showing up. To Roger, your bottomless love and unending belief drive me every single day—I'm so grateful to be on this messy, beautiful journey together. And finally, to my kids, Ber, Oz, Samson, and Zion: it is the greatest privilege of my life to be your mom, to learn alongside you, to love you and be loved by you. Thank you for filling my days with meaning and joy.

And to each other. It is no easy feat to write 100,000 words with another person. It takes patience and flexibility (neither are natural traits for either of us!). It also takes respect, admiration, and lots of laughter . . . those we share in spades.

INDEX

ABOUT THE AUTHORS

Cara Natterson, MD, is a pediatrician and the *New York Times* bestselling author of The Care and Keeping of You series, which has more than seven million copies in print, *Guy Stuff,* and *Decoding Boys.* A graduate of Harvard College and Johns Hopkins Medical School, Cara founded Order of Magnitude, a company dedicated to flipping puberty positive. She cohosts *The Puberty Podcast,* coauthors *The Awkward Roller Coaster Newsletter* (both with Vanessa Kroll Bennett), and founded Worry Proof MD. Cara lives in Los Angeles with her husband and their two teenagers.

Vanessa Kroll Bennett is a writer, podcaster, and entrepreneur. She is President of Media at Order of Magnitude, a company dedicated to flipping puberty positive, and cohosts *The Puberty Podcast.* She is the founder of Dynamo Girl, a company focused on building kids' self-esteem through sports and puberty education. She writes for Grown & Flown and Scary Mommy. A graduate of Wellesley College, Vanessa holds an MA from the Jewish Theological Seminary. She lives in New York with her husband and their four teens.

For more information about Cara and Vanessa and for further reading and links to puberty-supportive resources, visit https://myoomla.com/pages/resources-we-love

Also by
CARA NATTERSON, MD

"If you're raising a boy, you need this brilliant book. It is clear, wise, and eye-opening."
—LISA DAMOUR, PH.D., author of *Untangled*

Decoding
BOYS

New Science Behind *the*

Subtle Art *of* Raising Sons

Cara Natterson, M.D.

"Dr. Natterson's practical, wise insight (undergirded by hard science) into young men's development is absolutely essential reading for anyone with a boy in their life!"
—**PEGGY ORENSTEIN, author of** *Boys & Sex*

worryproofmd.com

BALLANTINE
BOOKS

Available wherever books are sold